Our Suffering Brave

OUR SUFFERING BRAVE

WAITSFIELD BOYS AND MEN IN THE CIVIL WAR

ALICE M. EVANS, PH.D.

DISTINCTION PRESS
WAITSFIELD, VERMONT

Our Suffering Brave
Waitsfield Boys and Men in the Civil War

Copyright © 2023 Alice M. Evans, Ph.D.

Distinction Press
Waitsfield, Vermont 05673
distinctionpress.com

Cover image: Winslow Homer "Trooper Meditating beside a Grave" in the public domain

Army Organizational Chart from *Gettysburg: The Souvenir Guide to the National Military Park*, 4th revised edition, presented by James A. Gross and Andre B. Collins, © 1911.

These items not in the public domain are used with permissions as shown.
Figure 1. The Civil War Image Shop, ©2023
Figure 7. Courtesy, Mark Jones Collection (Professionally scanned by *Military Images Magazine*)
Figure 11. Courtesy, Jim Dodds
Figures 13, 23. Courtesy, Gail Blake
Figures 18–20, 24: Library of Congress
Figure 21. CWI, Gettysburg College (2022)
Figure 25. Naval History Heritage Command
Figure 26. Courtesy, Waitsfield Historical Society

Map 1. Courtesy, Earl J. Hess, Ph.D.
Map 2. National Park Service (2021)
Map 3. CWI, Gettysburg College (2022)

Photograph of the author by Kitty Werner (2023)

Back Cover: Shield of the United States of America circa 1862, found during a recent renovation of a building on Main Street, Waitsfield, Vermont long used by the Masonic Lodge

ISBN 978-1-937667-33-7

Library of Congress Control Number: 2023913220

Praise for *Our Suffering Brave*

A richly detailed account of a single Vermont town's contribution to the Civil War. Alice Evans skillfully captures the variegated experiences of the 'boys' of Waitsfield in the war. Her thorough study reveals not only the wartime victories of these Waitsfield soldiers but also the suffering that they incurred along the way.

— Steven E. Sodergren, Ph.D., Dana Professor of History, Norwich University

Well written and researched with an extensive bibliography. Section notes contain interesting nuggets of information and a useful index makes this book worthy of use in a classroom setting. The author has written a book that is a model for anyone interested in creating their own tribute to their town's boys who fought and died, or anyone interested in learning how various towns in Vermont contributed to this monumental event known as the American Civil War.

—Joe Davison, Chairperson, B.F.A. History Department, St. Albans, VT (retired)

Waitsfield historian Dr. Alice Evans has written a thorough, detailed and empathetic volume documenting the participation of and losses of Waitsfield Civil War soldiers and sailors and their families. Her book illustrates the collective losses for Vermont and its towns, but also the shared experiences of local soldiers as they battled for national unity and to end slavery.

Meticulous research over many years allows Evans to dive into details found by cross referencing multiple materials and sources and the result is a fuller, more three-dimensional understanding of the impact of this war on one small town in Vermont.

— Lisa Loomis, Editor, *The Valley Reporter*, Waitsfield, Vermont

Uniquely presented, rich in detail, exhibiting thorough research and meticulous annotation, *Our Suffering Brave* is an engrossing account by Alice Evans, a transplant to Vermont who dedicated herself to the story of her adopted town's men and boys in the War of the Rebellion.

— Jack Anderson, Civil War historian and professor, former Director, Woodstock, Vermont Historical Society

In loving memory of my mother, and

In gratitude for the lives of my children.

I am the man, I suffer'd, I was there.

> Walt Whitman
> *from* "The Song of Myself" (1892)

Table of Contents

Illustrations	xi
Maps	xii
Introduction	xiii
Defining "Waitsfield" service members	xiv
Organization of material in this volume	xv
Accounting for when a man was present for duty	xv
Extensive use of personal narratives	xvi
Why do the sections vary so much in length?	xvi
Different ways to read this book	xvi
Prologue	1
1st Vermont Volunteer Infantry Regiment	3
The Union accepts war	3
The First Vermont Volunteer Infantry Regiment	3
Fighting on two fronts	6
2nd Vermont Volunteer Infantry Regiment	11
Organization of the Second Vermont Volunteer Infantry Regiment and its first battle (Bull Run/Manassas)	11
The Second Vermont Regiment in the Peninsula Campaign	14
Attrition among the remaining Waitsfield men	16
Horace Stoddard's experiences after Gettysburg, inferred from accounts by a Williamstown comrade	17
Spring 1864 campaigning under General U.S. Grant	20
3rd Vermont Volunteer Infantry Regiment	27
A word about army desertions	29
Rude introduction to the horrors of war	29
Military history of the Third Vermont Volunteer Infantry Regiment	30
The Third Vermont Volunteers at Lee's Mill, Virginia	31
Third Vermont action in the Peninsula Campaign after Lee's Mill	33
Camp life just prior to the Battle of Fredericksburg	35
Events in the Third Regiment after Fredericksburg, through June 1865	35
4th Vermont Volunteer Infantry Regiment	41
Impact of disease on the Fourth Vermont Infantry Regiment	42
Significant early actions in which the Fourth Vermont was engaged while one or more Waitsfield men were present	42
A long period when no men from Waitsfield were present in the 4th Regiment	43
Waitsfield soldiers' participation in Fourth Regiment actions at war's end	44

5th Vermont Volunteer Infantry Regiment   47
  Organization of the Fifth Vermont Volunteer Infantry Regiment   47
  Major campaigns involving the Fifth Vermont Regiment   48
  Breakthrough at Petersburg   50
  End of the war for Waitsfield's men in the 5th Volunteer Infantry   51

6th Vermont Volunteer Infantry Regiment   53
  Service records of the Waitsfield men in Company G   55
  Service records of the Waitsfield men in Company H   58
  The Sixth Regiment's march to Gettysburg   60
  Diversion of the Sixth Regiment to New York City   60
  The Overland Campaign   61
  The Sixth Regiment in the Shenandoah Valley; its return to
     Petersburg and the war's end   62
  Casualty rates among Waitsfield soldiers in the Sixth Vermont Regiment   62

7th Vermont Volunteer Infantry Regiment   67
  Service history of the Seventh Vermont Volunteer Infantry Regiment   68
  Tropical diseases rendered huge losses among the
     Seventh Regiment and its brigade   70
  The Mobile Campaign and the last actions of the Seventh Regiment   72

8th Vermont Volunteer Infantry Regiment   77
  Organization of the Eighth Regiment; service in Louisiana   77
  Re-enlistees receive furloughs   79
  The Eighth moves to the Shenandoah Valley of Virginia   79
  The regiment's final assignment   81

9th Vermont Volunteer Infantry Regiment   83
  Waiting for an exchange   85
  Details from the service records of the other Co. I members appear below   87
  Ninth Regiment Waitsfield men in combat, April 1863–June 1865   88
  The Ninth's service draws to a close   90

10th Vermont Volunteer Infantry Regiment   93
  General Meade's Mine Run Campaign   94
  Fighting in 1864 and 1865   94

11th Vermont Volunteer Infantry Regiment   103
  Disaster strikes the regiment; many perish in Southern prisons   105
  Murders of Vermont prisoners at Andersonville   106
  Effects of imprisonment in POW camps on soldiers' religious beliefs   106
  Southern civilians' awareness of conditions in prisoner of war camps   107
  Late-war enlistees from Waitsfield   107
  "Scorched Earth" policy in the Shenandoah Valley; Confederate reprisals
     involving the Eleventh Regiment   108
  Closing out the war   109

12th Vermont Volunteer Infantry Regiment   113
  Officers and early service of the Twelfth Regiment   113

Service in a supporting role at the Battle of Gettysburg	114
Information from the Waitsfield men's service records	115

13th Vermont Volunteer Infantry Regiment — 119
Histories of the Thirteenth Regiment	119
13th Vermont Volunteer Infantry Regiment, Company B	120
The regiment's early months in military service	123
The regiment in the months before Gettysburg	124
The "first battle" of Gettysburg	125
The 13th Regiment's march to Gettysburg and participation in the battle there	125
Casualties among Waitsfield men of Company B	130
Thirteenth Vermont Regiment memorials on the Gettysburg battlefield	131
Re-enlistments by three Waitsfield men	131

14th Vermont Volunteer Infantry Regiment — 137
Exposure to the elements takes its toll	139
The 14th Vermont marches to Gettysburg	139
After the Battle of Gettysburg	142
Subsequent service by one of the Waitsfield soldiers	142

15th Vermont Volunteer Infantry Regiment — 147
Early actions, including frequent moves, by the Fifteenth Vermont Volunteer Infantry Regiment	147
Role of the 15th Regiment in the Gettysburg Campaign	149

17th Vermont Volunteer Infantry Regiment — 153
Overview of wartime service by the Seventeenth Infantry Regiment	153
The 17th Regiment at the Wilderness and Spotsylvania Court House	156
Battlefield attrition among the Waitsfield men in the Seventeenth Regiment	158

1st Vermont Cavalry Regiment — 161
Companies in which Waitsfield men served within the First Vermont Cavalry Regiment	161
Organizational placements of the First Vermont Cavalry Regiment	162
Important engagements in 1862	162
A rest and recovery period for the First Vermont Cavalry	164
The Vermont Cavalry heads to Gettysburg	165
In the aftermath of the Battle of Gettysburg	166
The First Vermont Cavalry after the Gettysburg Campaign	167
Five Waitsfield men enter the First Vermont Cavalry Regiment	167
General Kilpatrick's raids around Richmond; the Dahlgren affair	168
The First Vermont Cavalry during the Overland Campaign	170
First Vermont Cavalry with Sheridan in the Shenandoah Valley	171
Battlefield casualties among Waitsfield men in the First Vermont Cavalry Regiment	175

2nd Vermont Battery, Light Artillery	181
Service by the Second Vermont Battery, Light Artillery prior to the arrival of anyone from Waitsfield	181
Waitsfield enlistees' service in the Second Vermont Battery, Light Artillery	182
3rd Vermont Battery, Light Artillery	185
Waitsfield connections of these men	185
Instruction period of the Vermont Third Battery, Light Artillery; its first assignments	186
Role of the Third Vermont Battery, Light Artillery in bringing about fall of Petersburg	188
Disbanding of the Third Vermont Battery, Light Artillery	188
1st Vermont Company, Heavy Artillery	191
History of the 1st Vermont Company, H.A.	191
Light vs. Heavy Artillery units	192
Contemporary Port Hudson battlefield	193
Waitsfield Men Who Served in Other States' Units	195
12th United States Infantry Regiment	199
Military service of the Twelfth U.S. Infantry Regiment before Julius Ainsworth joined that regiment	199
Action Julius Ainsworth would have seen with the 12th U.S. Regulars	200
17th United States Infantry Regiment	203
George B. Hall's six months in the 17th United States Infantry Regiment	203
2nd Regiment, U.S. Sharpshooters	205
Company H actions with Waitsfield soldiers present	206
Casualties among Waitsfield men in Company H of the Second United States Sharpshooters	209
13th Regiment, U.S. Colored Heavy Artillery	213
Political and military history of United States Colored Troops	213
Camp Nelson now a National Monument	214
United States Army Signal Corps	217
United States Christian Commission	219
Beyond counseling and coffee: the Christian Commission commences a cultural revolution	219
Christian Commission Women's Auxiliary in Waitsfield	221
United States Navy	223
Richardson becomes a Confederate prisoner	225
Epilogue	227
Acknowledgments	229
About the Author	231
Bibliography	232
Index	239

Illustrations

Army Organizational Chart		2
Fig. 1.	Soldier's Identification badge	10
Fig. 2.	Union division field hospital, Savage's Station, Virginia, 1862	15
Fig. 3.	2nd VT Volunteer Infantry's Regimental Standard	25
Fig. 4.	2nd VT Volunteer Infantry's Federal Standard	25
Fig. 5.	Marker in Battery Park, Burlington, Vermont	26
Fig. 6.	Erastus Fairbanks	26
Fig. 7.	3rd Vermont Volunteer Infantry Band	27
Fig. 8.	Major General William F. "Baldy" Smith	30
Fig. 9.	Button, Vermont volunteers' jackets	40
Fig. 10.	"Vermont Brigade" jacket pin	54
Fig. 11.	6th Vermont Veteran's memorial poster	56
Fig. 12.	August 1863 burning and sacking the Colored Orphan Asylum	61
Fig. 13.	Vermont Brigade monument in the Wilderness	97
Fig. 14.	Ford's Old Mill at Wolf Run Shoals, Virginia	118
Fig. 15.	13th VT Infantry Regiment campground, Wolf Run Shoals, VA	118
Fig. 16.	Portraits of 27 Waitsfield soldiers in Co. B.	120
Fig. 17.	The Old Mill near Camp Carusi at Occoquan, VA	124
Fig. 18.	Union breastworks in the Wilderness, 1864	157
Fig. 19.	CSA General Jubal Early	175
Fig. 20.	Heavy artillery, Fort Ward, Alexandria, VA.	192
Fig. 21.	Sharpshooters' rifle and bayonet	206
Fig. 22.	Edwin C. Lewis	212
Fig. 23.	Contemporary Civil War re-enactor	215
Fig. 24.	USCC coffee wagon	220
Fig. 25.	USS *Harriet Lane* destroyed, January 1, 1863	224
Fig. 26.	Mules pulling the Civil War memorial monument	230

Maps

1. De Soto Point opposite Confederate defenses around Vicksburg — 71
2. 10th VT position, Cold Harbor, Virginia battlefield — 99
3. Pickett's Charge, July 3, 1863 — 141

Introduction

I'm often asked by friends who know how long I've labored over this book (and how many miles I've driven to visit sites where Waitsfield men served during the American Civil War), "How did you become so interested in this subject, Alice?" My reply usually begins with Vermont secondary school teachers with whom I was privileged to work more than 20 years ago. We were tasked with developing an assessment framework for an expected statewide history examination. The teachers, all selected by their superintendents as among the best in their districts, were the content experts, of course; as a psychometrician, my role was to guide that committee work such that a valid and reliable test would result. What made that collaboration so rewarding for me was the enthusiasm of those teachers for their areas of specialization. One particular topic stood out: the American Civil War. In our time working together, I began to understand and share their enthusiasm for that period (and the forty or so years of attempted compromises that preceded it) as the crucible that tested the nation's vision of itself.

I commenced reading extensively about that era. I joined a Civil War Round Table (one of many in the U.S., and even some abroad). Round Tables sponsor speakers, films, and travel as ways for adults to educate themselves among like-minded persons.

Naturally, as a transplant to the area, I researched Waitsfield and Vermont Civil War histories. When I first entertained a thought of writing about local men in the war, I intended only an essay that would reconcile discrepancies I was discovering between information in the few primary sources available through local libraries.

Those sources were Jones' *History of the Town of Waitsfield* ((1909) and Peck's *Revised Roster of Vermont Volunteers* (1892). When those accounts differed with respect to a Waitsfield soldier's record, I followed Peck's version as more directly constructed from War Department records. Also, with respect to a soldier's wounds or disability, the *Revised Roster* often offered more details than appeared in Jones' history. An excerpt from a third accounting, Dascomb's *The Memorial Record of Waitsfield, Vermont* (1867), published in *The Valley Reporter* of November 10, 2011, added information for a small number of Waitsfield soldiers.

While almost all the local boys and men who went to war served in army units, two men from the Town served in the U.S. Navy; another, in the U.S. Christian Commission. Abby Maria Hemenway's *The History of Washington County* (1882) provided some information about those outliers.

When that earlier work was well along, I discovered the remarkable website *Vermont in the Civil War, Lest We Forget* (© 2020): https://www.vermontinthecivilwar.org). Maintained and continually expanded by Tom Ledoux and Associates, this resource brings together Vermont service members' personal data from Civil War enlistment records with information about their post-war lives, dates and places of death, and burial sites gathered from pension and cemetery records, obituary notices, and published biographies. Photographs made by website associates and shared from various collections also appear on this website. (Note site restrictions re copyrighted materials.)

It was time to abandon my original writing goal and create a more comprehensive narrative. The project became one of locating other "Waitsfield" service members and then telling all the men's stories in the context of the various military units in which each had served.

Defining "Waitsfield" service members

Jones' history cited service records for those credited to town quotas as determined by the War Department, to which he added limited information about some other men "who were either residents of the town at the time or who had been born and brought up within its limits [who] enlisted from other places."[1]

The Ledoux & Associates website employs somewhat different criteria than did Jones' history.[2] The consequence of following the Ledoux & Associates practice was that I added many names men to Jones' lists. Most were persons whose place of death was established as Waitsfield despite there being no record of their place of birth. (In the Town during the early 1840's, home births were common and often went unrecorded save, perhaps, in a family Bible.)[3]

In 2021 and 2022 I visited local cemeteries, seeking additional names of men who might have served in the war. Those names were compared to the Ledoux & Associates website, with many being confirmed by Town Hall records. All told, this volume includes 163 Waitsfield service members.

Men's names are given here as they appear on the Ledoux & Associates website. Because some readers of this work may be interested in genealogy, I include significant variants of men's names which appear in other sources.

(See footnotes that accompany the first citation of men's names in the text.)

This work seldom cites information about men's promotions or demotions in rank: Interested readers can find that information in the primary sources. Almost all the Waitsfield men who served in army units, like the preponderance of volunteers across all states, were Privates at their mustering-in and remained so throughout their service. Some few were selected for non-commissioned rank when mustered in, and that is noted. At least in the earliest years of the War, Union Captains were elected by the men of their companies. Officers of higher rank held commissions signed by the President. They were free to resign and go home if they chose, unlike enlisted men.

The principal aim of this work, and the reason for its novel organization, is to illuminate the individual and shared experiences of Waitsfield men who served in the American Civil War. Citations of men's illnesses, wounds, deaths, and captures are essential to my theme, the profound suffering of those men.

Organization of material in this volume

This volume is unique in that it is organized by company within regiment for each infantry regiment, artillery battery, *et al.* in which one or more Waitsfield men served during the Civil War.[4] That choice allows readers to know for a given soldier the other "boys" who served in his relatively small group of companions *at the same time*, with whom he would have shared camp and field experiences ranging from weather conditions to food shortages, marches and battles.

Accounting for when a man was present for duty

What most sets the present work apart from prior military records is my effort to describe major events each individual Waitsfield man experienced, based on the dates that man was present with his unit. This work is not at all a complete history of the Civil War, even those parts of it characterized as the Eastern theater. It has been my intent to offer just enough information about important actions in which given Waitsfield men participated, for readers to empathize with them. I do not believe it necessary that a reader be a present-day descendant of a Waitsfield Civil War service member to find his story compelling.

Extensive use of personal narratives

This work makes extensive use of personal narratives. Although there is little source material available from Waitsfield men themselves, much can be inferred from accounts by others who served in the same military unit during a period when Waitsfield men were present. My priority for including content, after giving preference to the words of Waitsfield soldiers whenever such could be found, has been:

1. Material drawn from letters, diaries and memoirs of Vermonters in the same company;
2. Material from Vermonters in the same regiment although not in the same company, especially when it references a company in which Waitsfield men were serving.

Why do the sections vary so much in length?

The number of Waitsfield men enrolled in a discrete military unit (an infantry regiment, artillery battery, *et al.*) varied from one to over thirty, so relating their personal stories necessarily made for sections of varying lengths. Also, sections vary because some include extensive quotations from previously-published accounts; availability of such material differed greatly across sections.

Different ways to read this book

A reader interested only in the experiences of a given soldier or sailor can quickly locate his story *via* the Index. This work also can be read as a repeating history of local men's experiences in the war, beginning with initial enthusiasm for the Union cause and high levels of community and family support, through years of discouragement and despair. Long before the official cessation of hostilities, many Waitsfield families endured terrible losses.

Notes

1. Jones cited 105 men by name, in two rosters. The Town's population in the 1860 Census was 1005.

2. In the website's introduction (*Who We Are*), Tom Ledoux states: "For the purposes of this project, anyone who was born or died in Vermont, regardless of where they served, and anyone who served in a Vermont unit, regardless of where they were born, we consider a Vermonter." I employed Ledoux's criteria, substituting "Waitsfield" for "Vermont" in the first part of that statement such that the men named in this work include those known to have been born or to have died in Waitsfield, regardless of where they enlisted or served. (Obviously, the second of Ledoux's criteria doesn't apply here, as there were no "Waitsfield" units.)

3. The Ledoux & Associates website includes two lists of local men: One is titled "born in Waitsfield"; the other, "credited to Waitsfield." Using both lists, and then adding names I found in local cemetery walks (names that I confirmed from town records and then verified through the L&A website and the *Revised Roster*), yielded many names that did not appear in earlier local histories.

4. Waitsfield men who served in out-of-state regiments or federal units are listed by regiment, given that their assignment to a company was not often found.

Prologue

In what historian David Herbert Donald has termed a "remarkably impersonal address," the re-elected President of the United States, Abraham Lincoln, made scant reference to his first term of office in his brief Second Inaugural Address (March 4, 1865). Neither did he cite the recent Union victories that presaged the war's end, as the enormous inaugural crowd certainly expected he would. Instead, Lincoln used the occasion to address the origins and significance of the ongoing Civil War. Remembering the war's beginning, Lincoln said, "All dreaded it—all sought to avert it." But of the two parties to the conflict, he declared, "One would make war rather than let the nation survive; and the other would accept war rather than let it perish. And the war came."[1]

This small history explores the part played by Waitsfield men in the American Civil War that came in the spring of 1861. Over the next five years, Waitsfield furnished soldiers for all but one of the 17 volunteer infantry regiments raised by the State. Others served in cavalry and artillery units. Waitsfield men also served in units raised by a number of other states and in several federal units, including the U.S. Navy.

The narrative begins with Vermont's First Volunteer Infantry Regiment. While its contribution was small, it seems useful nevertheless to begin with that unit, the first raised in the very earliest days of Vermont's involvement in the war.

---

1. Donald (1995), 566. Donald notes that Lincoln's account did not assign blame; in fact, he avoided referencing the Confederacy or the Southern states.

Army Organizational Chart

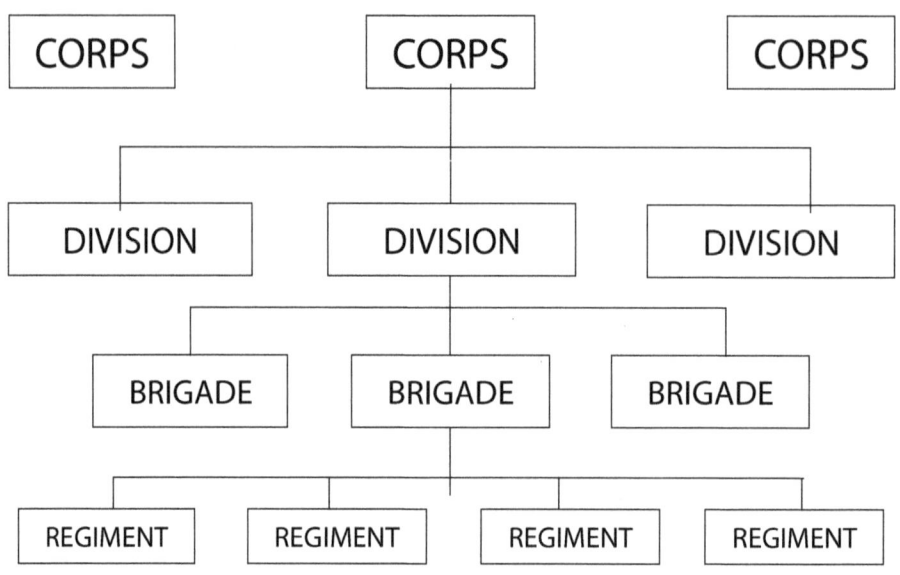

RANK CHART
General
Lieutenant General
Major General
Brigidier General
Colonel
Lieutenant Colonel
Major
Captain
First Lieutenant
Second Lieutenant
Sergeant
Corporal
Private

Army Organizational Chart from *Gettysburg: The Souvenir Guide to the National Military Park*, 4th revised edition, by James A. Gross and Andre B. Collins, © 1911.

1st Vermont Volunteer Infantry Regiment

Even before the election of a Republican Party president in 1860, most citizens in southern states were convinced that northern politicians would pursue an inflexible abolitionist stance that would soon deprive them of their property in slaves, an unacceptable economic loss. Delegates from seven states gathered in opposition in the months before Lincoln was inaugurated, while one-by-one their states voted to secede from the constitutional union.[1]

The Union accepts war

After Fort Sumter fell to a Confederate artillery barrage, President Abraham Lincoln called for Congress, then in recess, to convene in three months. In the interim, with no army at hand, he ran the military response by himself, calling upon Governors of all the non-seceded states to send to the nation's capital regiments made up of men selected from their militia units.[2]

There existed, of course, a regular United States army at the time; however, it consisted of only some 16,000 officers and men. Much of that army was stationed on the Plains, engaged in years-long campaigns of removal and extermination of Native Americans. It would have been impossible to recall those men to the D.C./upper Virginia area where fighting was expected to begin in any reasonably short time frame. In mobilizing states' militias, the President and the Secretary of War were making do with a tool at hand. They, like almost all Americans North and South, expected the earliest battles would be small in scale, not especially deadly, and decisive: Surely the war would not last long before the political issues that prompted it would be resolved.

The First Vermont Volunteer Infantry Regiment

One of the earliest volunteer regiments from any state to arrive in

Washington City in response to the President's call was the First Vermont Volunteer Infantry Regiment, composed of existing town militias the Governor deemed the best prepared. Waitsfield's Floodwoods militia was not among those selected.[3]

Nevertheless, one "Waitsfield" man did serve in the First Vermont Infantry. It would make an interesting story should we learn how Edwin C. Lewis came to join that regiment. Lewis was born in Northfield and was credited to that town upon his enlistment in May 1861, at age 19.[4] Although Northfield was one of the ten Vermont towns whose militia were selected to comprise the First Vermont Volunteer Infantry, Lewis was not mustered in with Northfield's militia. Perhaps Lewis was not a member of his town's militia?[5]

The officers and men of the new regiment would be serving under John W. Phelps from Brattleboro, appointed its Colonel by Governor Erastus Fairbanks. Phelps was an 1836 graduate of the U.S. Military Academy (West Point) and a Captain in the U.S. Army with 23 years' service on the Plains and in Mexico.

The First Vermont Volunteer Infantry Regiment rendezvoused on May second at Camp Fairbanks, established at the State Fairgrounds in Rutland. Three days after the regiment assembled (in what must have been the shortest "basic training" of any unit), Colonel Phelps reported his men were equipped and ready to march. They were only waiting for the arrival of a federal officer designated to inspect the regiment and administer the oath of allegiance that would constitute the regiment's formal muster into service. That designee, Gabriel J. Rains, a Lieutenant-Colonel in the 5th U.S. Infantry, was a native North Carolinian. That fact, plus suspicions of Rains' secessionist inclinations expressed to Governor Fairbanks by various Vermont officeholders, moved the Governor to request Washington to send another officer, forcing a delay.[6]

Despite that early kerfuffle, Vermont's enlistees were mustered into federal service by officer Rains on May 8th in a ceremony that included receiving regimental standards (flags). Those first Vermont inductees were clothed, interestingly enough, in gray uniforms, sewn by women in the ten towns where the companies of the regiment were raised.

The regiment left Rutland by train the following day, traveling via Troy, New York to New York City. There the men, each sporting an evergreen sprig in his cap emblematic of the Green Hills of Vermont, marched down Broadway to City Hall Park where they were quartered in Revolutionary-era barracks while their officers were entertained at the Astor House.[7]

Two days later (May 11) the regiment departed by the steamer *Alabama*, arriving at Fortress Monroe, Virginia on May 13. The nation's General in Chief, Winfield Scott, planned to use three-months' men recruited from states' militias (including Vermont's First Infantry Regiment) to defend the nation's capital. They would garrison Fortress Monroe, thereby freeing up regular Army troops stationed in and near that place, and protect the Potomac River and railroad lines coming into Washington, D.C. from the north and west.

Vermont recorded its first death in the service when Private Benjamin Underwood from Bradford, age 22, died of measles complications at Fortress Monroe on May 20. Soon after, two companies of the First Regiment established the second permanent Union occupation on Virginia soil (after Alexandria), at Newport News.

Company F

Private Edwin C. Lewis, age 19, Waitsfield's only "boy" to serve with the 1st Vermont Infantry, was assigned to Company F. His personal period of service was May 9 to August 15, 1861. Presumably Lewis was mustered-in individually as he missed the regiment's mustering-in ceremony by one day. It's unclear if Lewis was with the regiment when it left on the morning of May 9 for Fortress Monroe, Virginia or if he caught up soon after.

A history of the 1st Vermont written by Roswell Farnham for inclusion in Peck's (1892) *Revised Roster of Vermont Volunteers* states that the biggest event of the First Regiment's term of service was its encounter with an enemy force at Big Bethel, Virginia. Five Vermont companies, including the Northfield company, had been ordered to march at midnight of June 10th with five Massachusetts companies and three New York companies to capture a Confederate outpost at Little Bethel, some six miles from the First Regiment's Newport News camp. The detail took along a mule-drawn 12-pound brass cannon and a 6-pound piece pulled by men from the New York unit. "Friendly fire" among the various forces as they were moving before sunrise toward Little Bethel disrupted the intended plan, and a new plan was substituted. Arriving about 9 A.M. at Big Bethel, two of the Vermont companies were sent out as skirmishers while the other three (including Co. F, Lewis' Northfield group), supplemented by New York Zouaves and the men from Massachusetts, were arrayed in front of a rebel battery of four guns. There were some casualties among those men before a retreat was sounded. Confederate artillery poured on them in their retreat. "The march back to Newport News," writes Farnham, "was hot, dusty and tedious." Soon after sunset the Vermonters filed back into camp, "if not with much glory, yet with a good deal of experience and with the consciousness that [they] had done their duty."[8]

On August 4th the First Vermont embarked on the *Ben de Ford* and the *S.R. Spaulding*, two steamers that took them to New Haven, Connecticut from where they took railroad cars to Brattleboro, Vermont, arriving there late at night on the seventh. Eight days later they collected their pay and started for home.

Five-sixths of the men remaining in the First Vermont Regiment enlisted to serve in other units for three years or the duration of the war.[9]

Edwin Lewis himself subsequently joined the Sixth Vermont Volunteer Infantry. Following that service, he officered a U.S. artillery battery of Black enlistees.[10]

Fighting on two fronts

In the weeks before Congress convened, Lincoln continued to act. He authorized the enlistment of 40,000 three-year volunteers as well as an increase in the size of regular U.S. forces (by 20,000 men in the army and 18,000 in the navy).[11]

Advised by General Winfield Scott, the most revered living military leader in the United States, Lincoln ordered a blockade of southern seaports. Furthermore, Lincoln announced that the U.S. government would invade rebellious states as necessary to repossess Federal properties that had been seized, an announcement that aligned with a pledge he had made in his Inaugural Address.[12]

In a fervor of patriotism Northern states were rushing their earliest regiments to Washington. By the beginning of July, a largely volunteer army had been created and was assigned to Union Brigadier General Irvin McDowell. "This was a completely untrained army," historian Bruce Catton notes. While companies had drilled as militia units back home, they'd never done so as regiments, much less as the larger organizational units of brigades, divisions and corps.[13]

McDowell's orders were to take Richmond, Virginia, which had become the capital of the Confederacy after a brief organizational period spent in Montgomery, Alabama. McDowell led his new Army of Northeastern Virginia towards an opposing force under Confederate Brigadier General P. G. T. Beauregard. Beauregard's command, the Confederate States Army of the Potomac (soon to be reinforced by Brigadier General Joseph E. Johnston's Army of the Shenandoah), was encamped near Manassas, Virginia. The Union and Confederate armies clashed in the Battle of Bull Run.[14]

Edwin Lewis and the others of the First Vermont Volunteer Infantry did not fight at [First] Bull Run, being retained at the Newport News garrison.[15]

There had been Federal/Confederate military encounters before Bull Run (*aka* Manassas), but of far smaller size. While most Union regiments were stationed in or near Washington, D.C. (especially just across the Potomac, in parts of northern Virginia), a second front had been opened in present-day West Virginia.[16]

Confederate and Union forces fought at Philippi, Virginia on June 3, 1861 in an engagement generally considered the first land battle of the Civil War. Weeks earlier a civilian, Thornsbury Bailey Brown, had been killed by a sentinel under Confederate command, becoming the first known civilian war casualty in Virginia.[17]

Numerous small engagements occurred in that mountainous region between May and December 1861, until the Union finally achieved both military and political control of the Trans-Appalachian area. In a late stage of that struggle, Virginia militia were led by Robert E. Lee, whose performance was generally deemed a failure.[18]

Notes

1. In October 1861 South Carolinian radical secessionists had drafted a constitution for a separate nation and had circulated it to counterparts in other slave states. By the time of Lincoln's inauguration, seven states had declared for secession: South Carolina, Mississippi, Florida, Alabama, Georgia, Louisiana and Texas (in that order). Virginia, Arkansas, Tennessee and North Carolina followed later.

2. Lincoln's call was for forces to suppress "...combinations too powerful to be suppressed by the ordinary course of judicial proceedings, or by the powers vested in the marshals by law...." (cited in Basso, 1933, 85). No state of war was declared: Lincoln consistently spoke instead of a rebellion. He recognized that existing law limited a President's use of states' militia to 75,000 men and for only 90 days' service. (Congressional approval would be required to exceed those limits.) Vermont's Governor Erastus Fairbanks received Lincoln's request by telegraph on April 16, 1861, just two days after federal forces vacated Fort Sumter, South Carolina. The War Department assigned Vermont a quota of 780 men within the overall call-up, which the state not only met but exceeded.

3. The *Floodwoods* militia had been activated during the War of 1812, but apparently had declined in efficiency over the intervening years. The name persists as a farm and a road in town to this day.

4. Because Lewis is buried in Waitsfield's Common Cemetery, he meets one of the author's criteria for inclusion here.

5. By age, Lewis ought to have been enrolled in Northfield's militia. However, militia members unwilling or unable to leave home were exempt from the call to service, *per Peck*, I, 4. Perhaps that applied to Lewis.

6. As it happened, Rains did resign his U.S. commission and went with the South early in the war.

7. Benedict (1886), I, 34-35.

8. Farnham, in Peck (1892), I, 9.

9. Benedict, *op. cit.*, 61.

10. Follow Lewis' career in later sections of this work on the 6th Vermont Infantry and the 13th U.S. Colored Heavy Artillery.

11. In this and all subsequent presidential calls to arms, the State of Vermont received quotas, all of which were filled. The first Vermont regiments raised under a call for "three-year" men, the Second and Third Vermont Volunteer Infantry Regiments, will be discussed in the next sections. The focus there and in all subsequent sections will be upon those members of the regiments, batteries, *etc.* who are considered *Waitsfield* men.

12. Catton (1981), 77.

13. *Ibid.*

14. While the Union Army of Northeastern Virginia eventually became the Army of the Potomac, it did not bear the latter designation at the Battle of Bull Run/Manassas (fought on July 21, 1861), the Civil War's largest land battle up to that time. The Confederate Army of the Potomac eventually became the Army of Northern Virginia, the best-known of all Confederate armies. Readers not familiar with the Civil War are alerted to watch for changing names among the many armies of both sides, especially in the first year of the war.

15. Dyer (1959), III, 1649.

16. The political unit now known as West Virginia seceded from Virginia on April 27, 1861, although it was not admitted (as the 35th state) into the United States until June 20, 1863, during the third year of the war.

17. Moore (1963), 52. Although Bailey Brown is often cited as the first Union *battle* casualty, Moore's account tells a different story: On May 22, 1861 Brown was one of two Unionist-inclined civilians who encountered and fired upon a Confederate sentinel guarding a bridge, and Brown was slain by the sentinel in retaliation.

18. Lee then was sent to South Carolina to superintend coastal defenses, an assignment he filled admirably. Subsequently Lee served as an aide to Confederate President Jefferson Davis until Davis elevated him to command of the Army of Northern Virginia after General Joseph E. Johnston was disabled on May 31, 1862, the first day of fighting at the Battle of Seven Pines (*aka* Fair Oaks) on the Virginia Peninsula.

Fig. 1. Identification badge commissioned by Henry C. Jones, a member of the Second Vermont Volunteer Infantry Regiment. (The federal government did not issue ID tags.) Jones' badge is made of solid silver and hangs from a blue silk ribbon. Owned recently by John Gibson, this badge appeared on the consignment website of The Civil War Image Shop © 2023.

2nd Vermont Volunteer Infantry Regiment

Waitsfield "boys" began to enlist in response to Lincoln's earliest call for three-year volunteers. Men from the town served in every Vermont Volunteer Infantry Regiment save one, beginning with the First through the Seventeenth state infantry regiments. Only the Sixteenth Vermont Infantry had no Waitsfield men.

Six Waitsfield men served in the Second Infantry Regiment, five who signed up quite early in the war and one other who joined that fall. Their stories will be told via excerpts from a variety of sources.[1]

The Second Vermont Volunteers served longer in the field than all but one other Vermont regiment. It was engaged in battle from July 21, 1861 (First Battle of Bull Run) through April 6, 1865 (Sailor's Creek, just days before the surrender of the Army of Northern Virginia at Appomattox Court House).[2]

Benedict (1886) describes the role of the Second Vermont Regiment throughout the war. He gives details of the inclusion of the regiment in the First Vermont Brigade and notes controversies within the regiment related to changes of officers. Benedict names all the major campaigns in which the Second Vermont participated. At least one man from Waitsfield was present for all those campaigns until the last townsman was killed in action at the opening of the 1864 Overland Campaign.

Organization of the Second Vermont Volunteer Infantry Regiment and its first battle (Bull Run/Manassas)

George Julius Ainsworth, Charles M. Benedict, Lucius D. Savage, Albert Hezekiah Selleck and **Harlan Page Stoddard** enlisted together in May 1861; in June they were mustered in as privates to the Second Vermont Volunteer Infantry Regiment, assigned to **Company F.**

The Second Vermont, commanded by Colonel Henry Whiting (West Point 1841) previously with the Fifth United States Infantry, rendezvoused in Burlington on June sixth. It would spend the next three weeks in training at the newly-created Camp Underwood (named for Vermont's then-Lieutenant Governor) on fairgrounds north of the city. Colonel Whiting, who was appointed by Governor Fairbanks, was described by the *Vermont Phoenix* newspaper as "an officer of experience, having served in the Florida war with distinction."[3] The regiment's Lieutenant Colonel was Vermonter George J. Stannard.

On June 12th officers and men took the oath of allegiance.[4] A week later arms were distributed: 1842 Springfield smooth-bore muskets, not the rifled muskets the men had anticipated.[5]

It appears that the five early Waitsfield recruits, arriving somewhat late, caught up with the regiment while it still was in the Underwood training camp.

The editor of the *Vermont Phoenix* informed his readers that the men's knapsacks, belts, cartridge boxes, canteens and haversacks all had arrived at Camp Underwood by mid-June, and stated: "It is reported, with how much truth we do not know, that the regiment is to be armed with the Minnie rifle muskets with sabre bayonet," an allusion to muskets that would fire the cylindrical Minié bullet.[6]

During the regiment's time at Camp Underwood, Vermont historian Benedict reports, "Excursion trains brought visitors by the thousands... Women of various towns provided the men with havelocks and towels, and supplied the entire outfit of linen, lint and bandages for the regimental hospital." The Vermont Bible Society distributed testaments, and St. Paul's Church, Burlington, offered prayer books.[7]

Men in the Second Vermont Infantry Regiment wore dark gray, but unlike the uniforms of men in the First Vermont Regiment which were sewn by women from the towns sending those first companies to the field, uniforms for the Second Regiment were manufactured at state expense. Merrill & Co. of Reading, Vermont was paid to provide each man a frock coat, pantaloons, and a cap of gray doeskin with blue cording. [8]

When the regiment—868 officers and men, including a 24-member brass band—departed by train for the nation's capital on June 24, each man's cap bore a sprig of hemlock, an emblem long associated with the Green Mountain Boys of the American Revolution. Five men were left behind, hospitalized.[9]

Two engines and 24 railroad cars were needed to transport the regiment. Traveling by way of Troy, New York, the regiment was feted there by the newly-formed "Sons of Vermont" (Troy residents formerly from Vermont who wished to honor units from their home state). The "Sons" provided a hearty meal at the depot for the men, while their officers were entertained in private homes.¹⁰

The St. Albans Daily Messenger of June 26, 1861 reproduced an account provided by the *Troy Daily Union* that suggested the mood of the Second Regiment men on their way to war:

> About half-past 6 o'clock last evening, Col. Whiting's Vermont Volunteers arrived at the Union depot. They came by the Troy & Boston R.R. train, having left Burlington at 9 o'clock in the morning. They at once disembarked, and under the leadership of their captains, the different companies repaired to the reception rooms of the Railroad offices, where an ample repast had been prepared for the hungered and weary soldier, consisting of cold ham, cold chicken, smoked beef, crackers and cheese, bread, biscuit, cakes of all kinds, pickles, and other substantials for the inner man. During the time occupied in the collation, Doring's Band discoursed sweet and patriotic music to the crowd of citizens, of which there could not have been less than 5,000 present…At 20 minutes past 8 o'clock, the entire force having embarked on board the Hudson River train, took their departure amidst the cheers and affectionate adieus of the many thousands of anxious hearts, who perhaps viewed their pleasant and patriotic faces for the last time.¹¹

In New York City the next morning, the regiment received a regimental standard from the "Sons of Vermont in New York [City]". (Its U.S. standard had been presented earlier by Governor Fairbanks.) Speeches were tendered by an ex-Governor and a sitting U.S. Senator, among others.¹²

Although in the city only some eight hours, the Second Regiment troops were quartered in the City Hall Park barracks as the men of the First Vermont Volunteer Infantry had been. That afternoon the men marched to the Jersey City Ferry *en route* to the Hudson River Railroad depot, cheered by multitudes along their route. Commenting on the appearance of the new arrivals, a reporter for the *New York Herald* marveled: "The men are nearly all six footers."¹³

Passing through Philadelphia at midnight on the way to Baltimore, the Vermont men again were treated to accolades and refreshments. They detrained in Baltimore (site of a deadly encounter between civilians and a Massachusetts regiment on April 19, 1861) and marched across that city with loaded muskets; there they boarded a train traveling on tracks of another gauge that was able to finally deliver them to Washington City on the morning of June 26.

They made camp three-quarters of a mile to the east of the Capitol where 14 regiments from other states already were camped. All units drilled daily on Capitol Hill as General Winfield Scott, the Union's senior general, made preparations for a campaign to assault a Confederate army massing near Manassas, Virginia, not far from the nation's capital. Both Alexandria and Arlington already were in Union hands.[14]

The Second Vermont Volunteer Infantry Regiment took the field for the first major land battle of the Civil War, the [First] Battle of Bull Run/Manassas on July 21, 1861.[15] The Second Vermont was brigaded that day with three regiments from Maine, under the leadership of Maine's Colonel Oliver O. Howard. The first Waitsfield man of the regiment to become a battle casualty was **Albert H. Selleck**, wounded at Bull Run after just one month's military service. Selleck was discharged "for disability" on March 21, 1863, long before his term of service would have expired, which suggests he may have been hospitalized during that entire time.

Manassas was celebrated by the Confederates as a Union rout when federal troops withdrew to their camps around Washington, D.C. It was clear that the war would not be the quick and nearly bloodless affair that many in both the South and the North were predicting, and that troops on both sides needed more training and better leadership.

The Second Vermont Regiment in the Peninsula Campaign

No other major engagements involving the Second Vermont Regiment occurred prior to Major General George B. McClellan's Peninsula Campaign the next spring, when two Waitsfield soldiers, **Lucius D. Savage** and **Harlan Page Stoddard**, were severely wounded in battle at Savage's Station on the York River Railroad east of Richmond, Virginia.

Two corps of Confederate General Robert E. Lee's Army of Northern Virginia, under Generals James Longstreet and A. P. Hill, had crossed the Chickahominy River in pursuit of Union General George B. McClellan's Army of the Potomac that was retreating down the peninsula between the James and York Rivers, after having been just six miles from Richmond. McClellan's escape route would necessitate crossing White Oak Swamp, described as a vast bog on the fringes of the river.[16]

Lee's plan was to follow the river southward and fall upon McClellan's retreating force near the Swamp.

Before abandoning the army's forward supply base at Savage's Station, Union soldiers were ordered to burn vast amounts of forage and food supplies. Railroad cars full of ammunition were sent down the tracks toward a previously destroyed bridge across the Chickahominy River so they would detonate when the cars derailed. Moreover, a Union army hospital at Savage's Station was abandoned. At least 2,000 and perhaps 3,000 patients were left behind, to be captured by the pursuing Confederates.[17]

Knowing that Longstreet's and Hill's forces were only some three to five miles from him, CSA General Jeb Magruder proceeded to attack the federal rear guard at Savage's Station. But Magruder's attack achieved little: McClellan's retreat continued. Disappointed in Magruder's perceived lack of aggressiveness, Lee pulled him back while ordering Longstreet and Hill to advance on parallel routes toward McClellan. Lee intended to next strike the federals south of White Oak Swamp in an area known as Glendale (*aka* Frayser's Farm; also, Riddell's Shop). As the Confederates approached the recently-routed Savage's Station battlefield, they gathered up as prisoners numerous Union stragglers as well as the Union sick and wounded who had been left behind.[18]

Fig. 2. Union division field hospital, Savage's Station, Virginia, 1862

The Second Vermont had been part of the rear guard when its division moved out at 10 P.M. on the night of June 29, 1862, retreating to the south. According to historian Timothy B. Mudgett, the men of the division did "what they most hated to do: leave their badly wounded comrades behind for the Confederates."[19]

One of those wounded men was Lucius Savage. Mudgett describes Private Savage's using "gruesome but effective backwoods medicine" on a leg wound he suffered in that combat.[20]

Savage himself later wrote of lying on the battlefield for hours before being found and taken to the Union field hospital by VI Corps comrades when his regiment retreated after dark with the rest of the Vermont Brigade on the night of June 29/30, after fighting that cost the Vermont Brigade 358 casualties. Savage described his self-administered first aid during those hours. "In spite of all my precautions my wound became maggoty, and there is no describing the misery I was in. I obtained some turpentine…letting it pass entirely through the wound, clearing out the wound and the maggots also."[21]

Savage and Harlan Page Stoddard, who had been wounded in the pelvis, along with all the others captured in the field hospital, were cared for by Confederate surgeons until paroled in a Union/Confederate prisoner exchange a month after the battle. Even then, it seems, they remained hospitalized [in Union care] until their respective early discharges. Lucius Savage was discharged on November 29 of that year, and Harlan Stoddard long after that, on July 30, 1863.[22]

Attrition among the remaining Waitsfield men

Charles Benedict served 14 months before deserting in August 1862. Presumably Benedict took part in all the regiment's marches and battles up until then.

George Julius Ainsworth, just 19 when he enlisted in May 1861, served with Company F until he was wounded in fighting at Marye's Heights in Fredericksburg, Virginia (part of the Chancellorsville Campaign) on May 3, 1863. In late November he was transferred to the Veterans Reserve Corps (VRC), which suggests he was hospitalized and then convalescing throughout that six-months interim.[23]

Ainsworth was discharged from the VRC in June 1864 at the conclusion of his three-year term of enlistment. A month later he joined a regular U.S. Army unit, the Twelfth United States Infantry Regiment. His service record continues in that section.

When **Horace B. Stoddard** joined the original Waitsfield enlistees in September 1861 it is likely that Albert Selleck was absent from the company, still hospitalized because of his Bull Run wound. Horace Stoddard would have participated in the Peninsula Campaign alongside Ainsworth and Benedict, the other Waitsfield men who remained in Company F after Albert Selleck, Lucius Savage and Harlan Stoddard all had become casualties. After Benedict departed, Horace Stoddard would have fought with Ainsworth through the Antietam, Fredericksburg and Chancellorsville Campaigns until Ainsworth also became a casualty. As the last townsman remaining in the regiment, Horace Stoddard carried on through the Gettysburg campaign and beyond.

Horace Stoddard's experiences after Gettysburg, inferred from accounts by a Williamstown comrade

I have found little primary source material written by the Waitsfield men who served in the Second Vermont Volunteer Infantry Regiment. However, much can be inferred from accounts by another Vermonter who served in Company F during a period when Horace Stoddard was present.

A collection of letters titled *Voices from the Attic: The Williamstown Boys in the Civil War* (Young, ed., 2015) contains many letters sent and received by Francis Martin, the older of two brothers in the army.[24]

Francis ("Frank") Martin's correspondence documents Second Regiment movements after his own appearance in the regiment's camp in the Culpeper, Virginia area early in October 1863.[25]

Frank mailed this from Chantilly, Virginia:

> For nearly a week I have had no opportunity to write even if I had felt disposed. We have been marching & counter marching regulating our movements by those of the enemy. Our rests have not been long enough & I have been too tired to write…. [Last Saturday] we were ordered to strike our tents, pack knapsacks, & be ready to move at any moment. At 9 o clock PM we left our encampment and retreated towards Culpepper. The night was very dark. For the first few miles our march was through woods & fields across ditches & small streams. Then the march was easier over traveled roads & smoother fields until we reached Culpepper. Marched through the city & some distance beyond when we recd orders to halt, face about & move in another direction, probably because we had lost our way. After moving about four miles through the fields we spread our blankets on the ground at 1 o clock A.M. & slept until 4. [The regiment then pushed on, stopping at broad daylight, in Frank's words, for a breakfast of meat and coffee. Resuming their march, the men camped that night in woods near Rappahannock Station. Hearing cannonading the next morning, they marched several miles with occasional halts at some breastworks until they drew up in line of battle in some woods that afternoon.] But just before dark we recd orders to encamp & build small fires. At 12 AM. we were ordered to march again, recrossed the Rappahanock & soon heard our men blowing up the bridges. We then marched until dark, making about 25 miles.[26]

Several crossings of the Rappahannock had occurred as the regiment made its way to Chantilly, Virginia. As editor Young explains, "By moving so quickly, the Army of the Potomac gained control of the lands around Centreville. Lee recognized that he could not plan a major offensive at this time. Meade's army began to establish winter camps, with the Vermont Brigade camped at Warrenton."[27]

Skirmishing frequently broke out in the area, and cavalry were kept busy attempting to defend brigade supply lines as Mosby's independent rangers (a Confederate guerrilla force) made repeated raids on the brigade's wagon trains of quartermaster supplies. Fodder for horses and mules, as well as rations for the men, was running short.

On the sixth of November 1863 the Vermont Brigade was issued six days' rations, signifying that Commanding General George Meade had decided to launch an attack. The men would not be staying in their winter camp. They moved out the next day. Meade ordered his VI Corps under John Sedgwick to cross the Rappahannock River at Rappahannock Station and the III Corps to cross at Kelly's Ford five miles below. The two corps then would proceed to Brandy Station. However, when the VI Corps met determined resistance from Confederate General Jubal Early's forces defending Rappahannock Station, that plan stalled. After hours of artillery dueling, Sedgwick launched a sudden infantry attack that led to a Union victory even though retreating Confederates managed to destroy a pontoon bridge they had constructed to link their forces north and south of the Rappahannock. Consequently, Lee ordered his forces south of the Rapidan River.[28]

On November 10 Frank wrote another letter home.

> When I last wrote, I think it was from Warrenton [Virginia]. Remained there two weeks. Many of the boys loged up the sides of their tents and built fire places inside although none of them expected to remain there any length of time. A tent can be made very comfortable in this way and it pays for the labor even if not occupied more than a week.

Frank went on to write that he had not "logged up," and why. In retrospect, he judged almost providential the complications that had prevented him from constructing a more permanent lodging, as his unit had departed within days and his labor would have been wasted. The men packed up, marched about eight miles, formed into line of battle, and advanced.

> Soon we heard cannonading in front and occasionaly saw a cloud of smoke in the air occasioned by the bursting of a shell. We were halted in a sort of hollow & presently a shot passed over our heads causing many of the men to bow to the ground....Shell after shell passed over our heads quickly following the reports of the guns, a few bursting in the air...One man, in the

4th VT which lay to our left lost a leg but I have heard of no other casualties....Our forces were victorious driving the enemy from their fortifications & capturing 1200 prisoners & 6 pieces of artillery.

Thus, Frank Martin summarized the results of that November 7, 1863 battle in which it's likely that Horace B. Stoddard took part.

In the same letter, Martin alluded to a particular contribution that Company F men had made to the Bristoe Campaign shortly after the fighting he had just described:

> On Sunday we (Co. F) were sent scouting and then marched across the Rappahannock & on to Brandy Station where we lay yesterday [November 9th] until five O'clock and then marched two miles & encamped in the woods near the quarters just occupied by the rebels where we are now. It was very cold last night.... There is some thing peculiar penetrating about the air in Virginia when it is cold. Our winter clothing has not got along. [29]

Carleton Young comments, "The Battles of the Bristoe Campaign...had come to an end. Feeling content that it had established a strong position for a spring offensive that could conclude the war, the Army of the Potomac settled into its anticipated winter quarters near Brandy Station."[30]

The rest period expected by this apparent settling into winter quarters was interrupted, however, by General Meade's foray known as the Mine Run Campaign. The VI Corps left its camp on November 26 to meet up with the III Corps (as it had planned to do on November sixth, note) but a failure by the III Corps to receive orders to coordinate with the VI Corps, and then a shortage of pontoon boats they needed for the river crossing, delayed the intended surprise attack. Within days Meade scuttled his plan, and the Second Vermont Regiment, along with the rest of the Vermont Brigade, retreated to the Brandy Station winter camp.

As a war correspondent for a Montpelier newspaper, Frank Martin recounted the Second Vermont Regiment's participation in the Mine Run Campaign. Here, he specifically cites Company F.[31]

> On the 24th of November, before light, we received orders to pack up all but our tents and hold ourselves in readiness to move at day break. Morning dawned upon us, ushering in the day with a drizzling rain, our knapsacks were packed, the mules harnessed and hitched to the supply wagons, and the army in readiness to move, but at 10 A.M., the order was countermanded and not repeated until Thursday the 26th. Then we were roused at 4 A.M. and at 8 o'clock A.M., turned our backs upon our camp, bidding it, as we supposed, a final farewell, and moved further onward toward the heart of rebeldom...At

3:30 A.M. [November 27th] we were awakened by the reveille, and had hardly time to kindle our fires and cook our breakfast before we received orders to advance. Our march, like that of the day before, was slow, with frequent rests....Cannonading and musket firing on our right front were heard during the entire day. Late in the afternoon, it became heavier and more incessant, eliciting the remark from a comrade that "death and glory were busy." Long lines of infantry, and now and then a battery, passed us on their way to the front, but our turn did not come until about 4 o'clock, P.M....

Here the new men began to see for the first time some of the realities of war.[32] Shells were constantly traversing the air, some bursting in front, some in the rear, and some overhead. The burning fuse told us when they were coming, and this was followed in a few seconds by the explosion. Wounded men, borne on stretchers, or, if not too severely injured, assisted by one or two of their comrades, or making the best of their way alone, were constantly passing to the rear. The firing, both of cannon and musketry, was terrific. Three times we heard the cheers of our men as they charged upon the rebels posted behind a stone wall, as we afterwards learned. Three times they were repulsed, when our batteries opened, speedily demolishing the rebel works, which were then easily carried....Once, when a lot of pioneers, musicians and stragglers came double quick to the rear, we feared that our forces were being repulsed; but as the sound of the battle constantly grew more distant, we concluded that the enemy were being driven....[The fight continued into the wee hours of the following day.] As we neared the pine woods from which the sound of firing proceeded we formed in line of battle, and then advanced into the woods, where we halted, stacked arms and remained exposed to a drizzling rain until dark, when Co. F was ordered on to the picket line. We lay with the reserve through the night and until 2 o'clock P.M. the next day....[33]

The winter camp at Brandy Station was interrupted yet again when the VI Corps was ordered out in support of an attempted raid by Union General Judson Kilpatrick's cavalry division.[34]

Usually considered a fiasco because the raid failed to accomplish its objectives and brought calumny upon its planners, that action in late February 1864 did not appear notorious to Francis Martin: *The object of the expedition so far as the 6th Corps was concerned was accomplished*, he wrote.[35]

The men were back in camp in less than a week.

Spring 1864 campaigning under General U. S. Grant

Throughout the late winter of 1863/64 soldiers of the Vermont Brigade were expecting almost day to day that they would be summoned to a new offensive, this time under newly-promoted Lieutenant General Ulysses S. Grant who would be traveling with George Meade's Army of the Potomac. On May third the Brigade finally received its marching orders. Two days later Horace B. Stoddard, the last of Waitsfield's volunteers remaining in the Second Vermont Volunteer Infantry Regiment, took a minié ball to the head, dying on the first day of fighting in the Wilderness. His body never was recovered.

Notes

1. Benedict, G. G. (1886), *Vermont in the Civil War, a history of the part taken by the Vermont soldiers and sailors in the war for the Union, 1861-5*, 1, 62-125; Dyer, Frederick H. (1959), *A Compendium of the War of the Rebellion* (three vols.); Jones, M. B. (1909), *History of the Town of Waitsfield Vermont, 1782-1908, with Family Genealogies*, 84-94; Peck, T. S. (1892), *Revised Roster of Vermont Volunteers in the War of the Rebellion* (field edition, two vols.), 50-96, 125-296, 307-393, 418-487, 581-686, 759-764; Young, C. (2015), *Voices from the Attic: The Williamstown Boys in the Civil War*.

2. Benedict (1886), 124, lists 28 officially recorded battles and engagements in which the Second Vermont Infantry took part. Detailed information about those battles can be found at the *Vermont in the Civil War* website. For readers looking for an ancestor's record of service, it may be useful to note a shorter list of Army of the Potomac infantry actions in which the Second Vermont was *not* engaged. Specifically, during the retreat from Richmond (Seven Days Campaign) the regiment was not at Gaines' Mill, Glendale or Mechanicsville. While it was present for some actions of the Chancellorsville Campaign, including the Battle of Marye's Heights in Fredericksburg (May 3), it was not at the Battle of Chancellorsville. Neither was the regiment involved in the maneuvers of the Bristoe Campaign (October 9-22, 1863). It was engaged with some of the battles around Cold Harbor (June 1-12, 1864) but not at Bethesda Church or Bermuda Hundred. [It also can be noted that the Second Vermont Infantry was not present at Second Bull Run/Second Manassas, an 1862 battle fought by the Army of Virginia, not the Army of the Potomac.]

3. *Vermont Phoenix* of June 20, 1861, cited in *The Camp Griffin Gazette* (XIX, 6), June 2011, 5.

4. Here is an instance of a discrepancy among primary sources. I have chosen to use Benedict's date of June 12, 1861 for the administration of the oath rather than the date of June 20 given by both Peck and Jones.

5. The old muskets soon were exchanged for rifles. Benedict, 65-66.

6. *Vermont Phoenix* cited in *The Camp Griffin Gazette*, 5.

7. Benedict, 66.

8. *Op. cit.*, 67.

9. *Op. cit.*, 66-67.

10. *Op. cit.*, 67.

11. *The Camp Griffin Gazette* (XIX, 6), June 2011, 5-6, cited this June 26, 1861 *St. Albans Daily Messenger* reprint of a *Troy Daily Union* account of the dinner

supplied by Troy citizens. The florid language of the Victorian era conveys a bonhomie shared by the young soldiers and their civilian hosts. Surely the men had not a clue what awaited them less than a month in their future.

12. Benedict, 66.

13. *New York Herald* (June 26, 1861), cited by Benedict, 68.

14. Benedict, *ibid*. When federal troops moved across the Potomac to occupy Arlington Heights, an elevation that would have given the Confederates an advantageous artillery position from which to bombard Washington City, they seized General Robert E. Lee's home. Lee was in Richmond and his wife, Mary Anna Custis Lee, and their daughters already had vacated the property (Mary Lee's ancestral home) for temporary quarters in what became the first of several changes of residence. The Lees never returned to Arlington House (*aka* the Custis-Lee Mansion), which can be visited today within the grounds of Arlington National Cemetery.

15. Bull Run was the name Union leaders gave this encounter, while Confederates called it Manassas. There was a general pattern among the former of naming battles for some nearby geographic feature, while the latter tended to use the name of the town closest to a battle site. Union names of battles are employed throughout this work.

16. Davis (1954), 230.

17. Wert, 110.

18. *Ibid*.

19. Mudgett, 11.

20. *Ibid*.

21. Mudgett, 11, cites Savage's own words as quoted by Benedict, 302.

22. I have observed a knife attributed to "Lucius D. Savage, Waitsfield" on display in a whittling case in the museum at Gettysburg National Military Park—a strange place to see it because Private Savage was not at the Battle of Gettysburg.

23. From the beginning of the war the Union's hospitalized wounded were discharged and sent home when they were judged able to be moved. But in April 1863 the VRC (originally called the Invalid Corps) was created as a system whereby convalescing sick and wounded men could be retained in the service, performing limited duties.

24. *Voices from the Attic* also includes correspondence of the younger brother, Henry, who served in the Fourth Vermont Infantry Regiment. The author of *Voices* sequences the Martin brothers' letters with accounts of Vermont Brigade troop movements, battles and camp life, along with crucial political events affecting the conduct of the war.

25. Frank Martin volunteered when a new federal draft commenced mid-war. He substituted for a drafted Randolph resident, receiving a one-time $300 substitute payment to complement his army pay and Williamstown bounties.

26. Francis Martin to parents Chester and Betsey Martin, October 16, 1863 in Young, 217–218.

27. Young, *op. cit.*, 219.

28. Young, *op. cit.*, 228.

29. Francis Martin to parents, November 10, 1863, in Young, *op. cit.*, 231-233.

30. Young, *op. cit.*, 233.

31. Readers are reminded that Martin's accounts are of interest because Waitsfield soldier Horace B. Stoddard is believed to have shared Martin's experiences in the Second Regiment.

32. By "the new men," it appears Francis Martin was referring to recent inductees, particularly draftees, who had been directed into the regiments of the Vermont Brigade to fill places left vacant by previous casualties.

33. Francis Martin writing as Conscript, his *nom de plume* as a war correspondent, December 21, 1863 (published in *Vermont Watchman and State Journal,* January 1, 1864), cited in Young, 263–264.

34. There were Waitsfield men in Kilpatrick's cavalry unit at the time. The section of this work on the First Vermont Cavalry includes an account of the Kilpatrick-Dahlgren Raid.

35. Francis Martin to parents, March 1864, in Young, 280. (Note: no day appears for this letter.)

Fig. 3. Regimental Standard presented to the Second Vermont Volunteer Infantry Regiment in June 1861.

Fig. 4. Federal Standard [the US flag] of the Second Vermont Volunteer Infantry Regiment as it appeared when that regiment was mustered out of service.

Fig. 5. Marker in Battery Park, Burlington, Vermont that indicates the 1861 rendezvous site of the Second Vermont Volunteer Infantry Regiment.

Fig. 6. Portrait of Erastus Fairbanks, Vermont's Governor when Lincoln asked for militia from the non-seceding states.

3rd Vermont Volunteer Infantry Regiment

Six Waitsfield men served at some time in the Third Vermont Volunteer Infantry Regiment, across five different companies. Third Vermont Regiment recruits trained at Camp Baxter, St. Johnsbury, Vermont.[1]

Company B

Vespucius Daley, whose volunteer service commenced in Company F of the regiment (see below), spent the final 11 months of his military service in Company B.

Fig. 7. Band of the 3rd Vermont Volunteer Infantry Regiment at Camp Baxter. Courtesy of the Mark Jones collection. Professionally scanned by *Military Images Magazine*.

Company C

William Henry Orne served in **Company C** of the Third Vermont Volunteers. Orne enlisted from St. Johnsbury at age 18, but because Orne was born in Waitsfield, he qualifies as a Waitsfield soldier for our purposes.[2] Orne mustered in as a corporal on July 16, 1861, the same date that two Dana men (cited below) entered as privates. Orne was discharged "for disability" on February 18, 1862. His service period encompassed the regiment's early defense of the nation's capital, including excursions into northern Virginia. On December 17, 1863, Orne enlisted in Boston under the name "Augustus Seaton" and was assigned to Co. A of The 56th MA Infantry. He was mustered in as a Private nine days later. The L&A website records Orne's wounding in May 1864 with the notation, "where?" It adds that he was mustered out on May 22, 1865 "while absent wounded, as Corpl." Assuming that date is correct, Orne's wound must have been quite severe. It's likely he was hospitalized throughout that entire interval.

Company E

William F. Wilder joined **Company E** on June 1, 1861 and was discharged "for disability" on the final day of 1862.

Company F

Vespucius Daley began his military service at age 21, in **Company F** of the Third Vermont Infantry Regiment. Daley, like William Orne, had been born in Waitsfield but enlisted elsewhere, Daley from Topsham, Vermont. He was mustered in on September 22, 1862; therefore, he was not present during the Union campaigns of 1861 and most of 1862 (First Bull Run, the Peninsula, and Antietam) although he likely was present in Virginia at the Battle of Fredericksburg (December 13, 1862) and during the "Mud March" of January 1863. He was wounded May 3, 1863 during the Chancellorsville Campaign at the Battle of Marye's Heights (Fredericksburg). He was transferred from Co. F to Co. B of the regiment on July 25, 1864.

Company H

The first of three "boys" from Waitsfield to serve in Co. H, **Bertrand Delos Campbell** was mustered in as a private to Company H on June 3, 1861, at age 19. However, he soon was discharged; no reason is offered in the primary sources I consulted. Campbell parted from the company in August after briefly crossing paths with two others from the Town, **Henry Francis Dana** and **Stillman Foster Dana**.[3] Just a month after his discharge Campbell mustered in as a corporal to Co. G of the Sixth Vermont Volunteer Infantry Regiment. His story continues in the Sixth Volunteers section.

Stillman Dana and Henry Francis Dana were mustered in on July 16, 1861 alongside Corporal Orne. Stillman Dana was wounded the following spring at the Battle of Lee's Mill (April 16, 1862) and two years later at Spotsylvania.[4]

Henry Francis ("Harry") Dana deserted the company on December 29, 1862 after having participated in all the regiment's fighting until then, it seems, including the horrific Battle of Fredericksburg two weeks earlier. He returned to his company on March 26, 1863. Henry Dana was wounded at Spotsylvania on May 18, 1864.

A word about army desertions

When Union survivors of the Fredericksburg disaster returned to their camps across the Rappahannock River at Falmouth, Virginia, it was determined that some 1,800 soldiers had slipped away. One in four members of the Army of the Potomac was AWOL after Fredericksburg.[5] Over the period of the war 1,587 Vermonters deserted the Union army at one time or another, according to a Congressional report.[6]

In a volume described as "the only full account of desertion on both sides of the conflict," 20th century historian Ella Lonn uses records compiled by the War Department to estimate that 200,000 Union soldiers (one in every seven) and somewhat more than 100,000 Confederates (one in every nine) deserted the ranks at some time. Despite the higher rate among Union forces, Lonn argues that desertion harmed the Confederacy to a greater extent because it was far less able to replace its missing men.[7]

Rude introduction to the horrors of war

It is reasonable to assume that Waitsfield's early enlistees in the Third Vermont Volunteers knew about a repulse of Union forces at Big Bethel, Virginia that had occurred June 10, 1861 in which the First Vermont Infantry Regiment had incurred six casualties, including two men killed in action. Their own personal exposure to war-time deaths came while they were still in their Vermont training camp.

Harmon Olds, a Third Regiment company clerk, recorded the first violent death in the regiment, a bizarre shooting that occurred at its rendezvous point in St. Johnsbury. Sgt. John T. Terrill was killed by a fellow soldier in a dispute about guarding a certain sutler's establishment, Pike's Refreshment Saloon, against depredations by soldiers angry over that sutler's prices. (Specifically, the sutler was demanding three cents for a glass of lemonade!)[8]

Shortly after that, while the Third Regiment was traveling by train to Washington, D. C., the Waitsfield recruits learned of another rout of Union forces down in Virginia. Their southbound train passed another traveling north, carrying men who had just experienced the Battle of Bull Run (Battle of Manassas) and were headed home as their 90-day tour of duty had expired. Olds noted there were many wounded among those veterans. Also, many of them seemed to bear nothing save the clothes they were wearing, having either lost or discarded their coats, hats, even their guns. "Ragged and dirty, they did not give us a very good opinion of the pleasures of War," Olds commented.

Just two days later Olds recorded a second violent death in the Third Regiment: A soldier slit his own throat. Olds suggested homesickness could have been the cause.

Military history of the Third Vermont Volunteer Infantry Regiment

The Third Vermont Volunteer Infantry Regiment was headed by Colonel William Farrar Smith, a West Point graduate from St. Albans, Vermont. The Third Vermont Regiment had entered the service somewhat behind the Second Regiment but it fought in some of the same early actions as the Second Regiment, as both belonged for a time to the same brigade (along with units from other states) until the Vermont Brigade was created.

Fig. 8. Major General William F. "Baldy" Smith

Among changes to the Army of the Potomac's organizational structure which were deemed necessary after the Bull Run debacle in July, the Third Vermont Regiment's Colonel, W. F. Smith, advocated for a brigade that would be comprised of four to six Vermont regiments. The Vermont Brigade was created in the fall of 1861, consisting of the Second, Third, Fourth, Fifth and Sixth Vermont Volunteer Infantry Regiments.[9]

With the creation of the Vermont Brigade, "Baldy" Smith was promoted to brigade command, while leadership of the Third Regiment fell to Breed Hyde.

The Third Regiment's earliest assignments were in protection of the nation's capital, first guarding the Chain Bridge into Virginia, then the reservoir that supplied water to the capital. Early in September the Third Regiment participated with two companies from the Second Regiment in a two-day reconnaissance to Lewinsville, Virginia, with a skirmish occurring on the second day. Two weeks later the Third made another reconnaissance to Lewinsville. Subsequently, the regiment established a camp there (Camp Griffin).[10]

In September Olds' company records reported the scheduled execution of a member of the Third Vermont Infantry. The regiment was drawn up in an open square to observe Private William Scott's punishment for having fallen asleep while on guard duty.[11]

The five Waitsfield soldiers[12] would have been among those required to observe Scott's execution. Presumably Scott's four brothers, all serving in the Third Regiment, also were required to be witnesses.

At the last possible moment, so the story goes, a messenger raced up bearing a pardon signed by President Abraham Lincoln. "The man [Scott] was so overcome that he had to be carried back to his quarters," Olds wrote. "I think he suffered more than he would have had he been shot."[13]

In March 1862 the regiment moved to Alexandria, Virginia in anticipation of General George B. McClellan's Peninsula Campaign.

The Army of the Potomac, over 100,000 strong, was transferred that month by ships from Alexandria to the environs of Fortress Monroe at the base of the Virginia Peninsula (between the York and James Rivers) where, when fully assembled by early April, it commenced a long trek towards Richmond. In that context, the early Vermont infantry regiments began fighting *as a brigade* with the Battle of Lee's Mill.

The Third Vermont Volunteers at Lee's Mill, Virginia

An account of the Lee's Mill battle ("…the first serious fighting during McClellan's Peninsular Campaign of 1862," according to historian John Rickard) can be found at the *History of War* website. Also, the *Vermont in the Civil War* website contains an exhaustive account of the battle.[14]

On April 16, 1862 four companies of infantry were ordered by now-Brigadier General W. F. Smith leading a division, to cross the Warwick River, a stream some 20–30 yards wide, at a mill site where Confederates were building a fort. General McClellan's orders to Smith were to "force the enemy to discontinue work" on their entrenchments.[15]

Smith ordered the Vermont Brigade (under Colonel Brooks) and a pair of field batteries to open fire from across the creek. Confederates in rifle pits on the other bank were driven away in about an hour. Smith then sent men, including two companies of the Third Vermont (**D** and **F**), across the water to take and hold the rifle pits. Two other companies (**E** and **K**) were supposed to follow in support.

McClellan then changed his earlier order to Smith: Move up the two other brigades of his division and, if circumstances permitted, attempt to take and hold the dam. Meanwhile, those soldiers of the CS Army of the

Peninsula previously in rifle pits (pickets from the 15th North Carolina Regiment) were being reinforced by the rest of their regiment, hustling there at the double quick. Other CS soldiers from nearby units arrived, not under orders but just running toward the sound of gunfire. Soon the men of Companies D and F, never properly supported, were facing two thousand antagonists. Confederate artillery shelled the Union men. Confederate musket fire roiled the river; many Union men drowned.

The morning after the Battle of Lee's Mill a corporal in the Third Regiment wrote to his wife:

> Thank God I am alive yet & considering the circumstance comparativly well. We went yesterday morn up to within less than 1/4 mile of the enemys works where they had 3 or 4,000 & 2 large Guns mounted & between us & them a creek some 8 to 10 rods wide, from knee to waist deep. Our Reg.t were posted in the woods directly in front of their works & so near that occasionaly a ball from their Rifle pits aimed at our skirmishers would come up quite to us. Our Batterys commenced shelling them about 9 a.m. & continued to do so thru the day & except silencing one of their Guns, appeared not to have much effect. as soon as we got there all but 4 company.s of our Reg.t D, E F & K, were sent off as skirmishers, and continued so thro. the day. these 4 companys & the Color Guard remained perfectly quiet till about 3 p.m. when Col. Hyde came along & told Capt. Harrington of Co. D & Pingrey [Pingree] of Co. F that they must take their 2 Cos. & cross the creek and take the Battery with only Co.s E & K to support them & he said the Colors must go too. It looked wicked, but all we had to do was to go ahead, so we threw off our Blankets & all but our Equipments & started went about 4 rods & come to the water, which we entered & found it about knee deep for the first 4 or 5 rods then we went into our waists & where some crossed they went in up to their necks. I got in about 6 inches above my waist belt. The bullets began to meet us when we first entered the water but when we got in waist deep & within 5 or 6 rods of their Rifle pits they began to shower the balls into us like hail & our poor fellows began to fall. just as I got in up to my waist & directly behind Heath with the Flag a ball struck me on the left side of my head & partly knocked me down but I put one hand down & happened to hit a stump & kept from falling. it cut the cloth & paste board of my cap rim but didnt go thro. the inside leather. It sort of confused me for 2 or 3 hours & that side of my head is some numb yet but thank God that it didn't come ½ inch nearer. about half of us got into their works & drove the Rebels out but couldn't hold it & when Harrington saw how they were cutting us up & that we must all be killed or taken prisoners he ordered us to retreat which we did under a perfect shower of Balls and out of these 4 com.

ys there is 22 killed 56 wounded & 5 missing. I crawled back to Camp & Jim built up a good fire & made me some coffee & after drying myself as well as I could I laid down about 10 oclock, & slept some tho. I ached all night & this morn am so lame I can scarcely go, but I am alive & again I thank God. Our boys all safe. Will write again soon
    Aff. yours H E Dunbar[16]

Historian J. Rickard evaluates the Lee's Mill battle as follows:

> The action at Lee's Mill was a minor skirmish in the context of the Peninsular [Campaign], but in at least one regard it was typical of what was to come. The mid-afternoon attack had been approved by McClellan in person, but with a warning not to continue against heavy resistance. A more determined attack in force would have had a good chance of forcing its way across the river at what [Confederate Major General John B.] Magruder considered the weakest part of his line. Success at Lee's Mills would have made the Confederate position at Yorktown untenable. Instead, the siege was to go on for another three weeks.[17]

Captain Samuel Pingree of Company F, Third Vermont, received the Congressional Medal of Honor for heroism that day. Perhaps even better known in Vermont is Julian Scott, who received the Medal for valor in the same action. Scott, only 16 years old, was serving as Co. E's drummer. During this action at Lee's Mill Scott laid aside his drum and began carrying wounded soldiers back across the Warwick River to Union lines.[18]

Third Vermont action in the Peninsula Campaign after Lee's Mill

It has been noted that at the Battle of Lee's Mill, the Third Vermont Volunteer Infantry Regiment was headed by Breed Hyde. In the next round of promotions Hyde was succeeded as Colonel by Wheelock G. Veazey who led the regiment throughout the rest of the Peninsula Campaign. Portraits of many of these Civil War leaders can be seen in the Vermont State House.[19]

The Third Vermont played a supporting role at the Battle of Williamsburg (May 5, 1862). **William Wilder** and **Henry Dana** would have been present and perhaps **Stillman Foster Dana**, as well. (It's not known how long Stillman Dana's injury at Lee's Mill kept him away from his company.) The Third Vermont went on to participate in later Peninsular actions characterized by Frederick H. Dyer as "the battles of the seven days' retreat from before Richmond," extending from June 25 to July 1 and culminating with rearguard actions by the Vermont Brigade when McClellan ordered the whole Army of the Potomac to retreat to Harrison's Landing on the James River.[20]

Before that retreat, the Third Vermont Regiment had fought in the Battle of Fair Oaks (also known as Seven Pines) on May 31–June 1, 1862, a Union victory that brought Robert E. Lee onto the field as McClellan's opponent.

The Third Regiment participated in fighting at Golding's Farm on June 27 and perhaps also at Garnett's Farm the following day. At Gaines' Mill the Vermont Brigade built some 65 miles of corduroy roads for use by supply trains, siege trains and mortar carriages. The Third Regiment in particular built bridges, constructed heavy earthworks for artillery emplacements, and performed picket duty. It helped build the 1,080 foot-long McClellan Bridge (*aka* the Alexandria bridge) over the Chickahominy River.

On June 29 and 30, the Third Regiment fought in the battles of Savage's Station and White Oak Swamp, respectively. It was at Savage's Station that the Third Regiment took its "first serious battle losses since Lee's Mill," according to historian Robert G. Poirer.[21]

On July first the regiment fought at the Battle of Malvern Hill, the final battle of the Peninsula Campaign.

The Third then was tasked with protecting the VI Corps' retreat to Harrison's Landing. The regiment guarded the bridge across the Chickahominy for 24 hours under heavy fire.[22]

Historian Timothy B. Mudgett quotes Colonel Veazey on the condition of his Third Regiment during that retreat:

> It simply beggared description. Stragglers sick and dying…mud so deep that no bottom could be reached…and then add the sickening feeling of defeat and retreat…only to find a bivouac in water and mud, without fire or rations.[23]

Summarizing, Mudgett writes of the division that included the Third Regiment:

> Every march Baldy Smith's division made during the Seven Days campaign had been at night, so it is hardly surprising the men were worn out morally and physically, a condition not helped by rain and muddy roads on the march, or the lack of supplies once they reached Harrison's.[24]

The regiment remained at Harrison's Landing until August 16 before removing to Fortress Monroe and later returning to Alexandria, Virginia. (Alexandria had been in Union hands since May of 1861.)

No other major action involving the Third Vermont Infantry occurred until that fall, when the regiment participated in movements that terminated at the Battle of Antietam (*aka* Sharpsburg) in Maryland. Before the year was out the Third Regiment would fight at Fredericksburg, Virginia. **Private Vespucius Daley** joined the regiment between those two battles.

Camp life just prior to the Battle of Fredericksburg

The writer of the following letter served in the Third Vermont Volunteer Infantry Regiment although in a different company from any of the Waitsfield soldiers. Nevertheless, it is likely that those men shared the hardships which this Lyndonville soldier describes.

> Dear brother,
> I seat my self to let you know of my health which is very good at present and I hope that these few lines will find you the same....
>
> We are in Virginia about fifty miles from Washington. We have moved into a piece of pine woods and we expect to stay here this winter. We have since the first of this month marched 130 miles. We have had a hard time since we started. The load I have to lug ways sixty pounds....
>
> Good many of the boys is sick and some of them are dying off. We had ten crackers a day and a mess of beans. Once or twice a week some fresh meat and pork and some salt meat. Sugar and coffee and once in a while a mess of black tea. One of the recruits that came out when I did shot his fingers all off on his right hand....
>
> We haven't had any snow since I wrote last. We have had some rain. It is some signs of rain today. The boys is building them some log houses. We are within twelve miles of a large force of rebels....[25]

Events in the Third Regiment after Fredericksburg, through June 1865

As noted earlier, **William Wilder** was discharged "for disability" on the last day of 1862.

The next year the Third Regiment fought in the 1863 Union campaigns from Chancellorsville through Gettysburg to Mine Run. Shortly before the Mine Run Campaign in November, disgrace visited the regiment:

> Captain Beattie of the 3rd VT is being court marshaled for shooting an officer of his Regt. They were gambling & at last there was some misunderstanding arose (they were well soaked with Comisary Whiskey) between them & words were not enough when one drew his revolver & shot the other twice wounding slightly. Both will immediately be cashiered [expelled] from the service.[26]

Dascomb's town history shows **Stillman Dana** as having been wounded at the Battle of Spotsylvania, part of the Union's Overland Campaign in the spring of 1864. (Our other primary sources do not record that.) Henry Dana also was wounded at Spotsylvania. Both Henry Dana and Stillman Foster Dana completed their three-year enlistments and were mustered out July 27, 1864.

Vespucius Daley, who had been transferred to Company B in July 1864, served almost a year there until he was mustered out of service June 19, 1865.

Notes

1. *Vermont Phoenix* (June 20, 1861), cited in *The Camp Griffin Gazette*) published by the Green Mountain Civil War Roundtable, June 11, 5.

2. As explained in another section, I include as "Waitsfield" men all those who meet one or more of the criteria first applied by Tom Ledoux in determining a "Vermont" soldier. (Those criteria are posted at https://www.vermontinthecivilwar.org, the Ledoux & Associates website.) Thus, many men whose names do not appear in Jones' 1909 town history are included in the present work. Here, that applies to Daley, Orne and Wilder.

3. Stillman Foster Dana is cited in Jones' history as Foster Stillman Dana and in Peck's roster, as Foster S. Dana.

4. Dascomb's *Memorial Record of the Town of Waitsfield* (1867) is the only one of our primary sources that reports Stillman Dana as being wounded at Spotsylvania.

5. Egan (2016), 243.

6. House Ex. Doc., 39th Cong., 1st sess., No. 1: IV, pt. 1, cited in Lonn (1998). See Lonn's Table IV: Desertions from the Union Army by States, 234-235.

7. William Blair (1998) in his Introduction to Lonn's *Desertion During the Civil War*, vi.

8. Enraged soldiers battered down Pike's place of business at night and stole some property, which led the Colonel to post a guard. But when some men returned the next night threatening further damage, the guard shot into the crowd, killing Terrill. (Source: Steve Waterford, in a talk delivered at the St. Johnsbury, Vermont History & Heritage Center on October 9, 2019.) Old's account is cited in an online essay by local journalist Matt Bushnell, at https://www.vtdigger.org/2019/08/04/then-again-vermont-diarist-was-a-keen-observer-of-the-civil-war (retrieved February 20, 2020). John T. Terrill from Canaan, Vermont, was killed on only his fourth day in the service.

9. For a time, the 26th New Jersey Infantry was included in the Vermont Brigade. (It was assigned there from its organization in September 1862 until June 1863 when its nine months men were mustered out.) The Vermont Brigade was part of Major General Erasmus Keyes' Second Division of the IV Corps, Army of the Potomac.

10. The Third Vermont Regiment would spend the winter months of 1861/62 at Camp Griffin. Sickness was rampant throughout that winter.

11. William Scott's offense had occurred in April but his court martial did

not take place until September. Scott's death warrant was signed by then-Colonel Hyde, and his execution was scheduled for five days later.

12. "Five" because Private Daley had not yet joined the regiment.

13. William Scott died seven months later. Scott, age 23, was one of five brothers who served in the Third Regiment. At Lee's Mill he was carrying a wounded soldier back across the Warwick River when his body was riddled by five or six bullets. He died the next morning. See Marilyn Hatch-Ruiters "The Story of Groton's Historical Sleeping Sentinel": https://grotonvt.com/the-story-of-grotons-historical-sleeping-sentinel/ (retrieved February 23, 2020).

14. Rickard, J. (5 July 2006), http://www.historyofwar.org/articles/battles_lees_mills.html. Readers will note that this battle is called variously Lee's Mill or Mills (used interchangeably even by the same author at times, as Rickard does). Lee's Mill also is known as the battle of Dam No. 1, the battle of Burnt Chimneys (for three burnt chimneys on that spot) and, less often, as Garrow's Chimneys. Another confusion of nomenclature involves an earlier skirmish at Lee's Mill (April 5, 1862) when Keyes' IV Corps, which included Smith's infantry division and the First Vermont Cavalry, had been stymied when that Corps encountered strongly-entrenched Confederates at the dam and a road crossing there. See http://www.vermontcivilwar.org/battles.

15. Source: Brochure titled "…fitting and proper…", distributed at the 1999 dedication of a granite monument to the Third Vermont Volunteer Infantry Regiment at the site of Dam No.1, Newport News Park, Newport News, Virginia.

16. Henry E. Dunbar to wife Mary (April 17, 1862), cited in Jeffrey Marshall, ed. (1999), 74–75. Dunbar describes his involvement in one of two attempted crossings that day. Apparently, Private William Wilder of Co. E was the only Waitsfield soldier among those who made the crossing Dunbar describes in this letter. Dunbar, a Corporal in Co. C, was discharged for disability a month after the Lee's Mill battle.

17. Rickard, *op. cit.*

18. Julian Scott later became a renowned artist. His monumental (10' x 20') postwar painting *Battle of Cedar Creek* (commissioned by the Vermont legislature and generally thought to be his master work), hangs in the Cedar Creek Room of the Vermont State House.

19. Hyde had succeeded W. F. ("Baldy") Smith as head of the Third Regiment when Smith became commander of the Vermont Brigade. When a second Vermont brigade was organized in October 1862, the earlier brigade was denoted the First Vermont Brigade. (It also was referred to as the Old Vermont Brigade and on occasion, as the Original Vermont Brigade.) In May 1864 the 11th Vermont Infantry was added to the First Vermont Brigade to round up its depleted ranks.

20. Dyer, II, 902–904.

21. Poirer (2005), 53.

22. *Op. cit.*, 54.

23. Veazey, cited by Mudgett (1997), 53.

24. Mudgett, *op. cit.,* 12.

25. James T. Simpson to brother Edward (November 30, 1862). This letter was shared by descendant Dick Simpson at a meeting of the Green Mountain Civil War Round Table in White River Junction, Vermont.

26. Henry Martin to parents, October 30, 1863, in Young, *op. cit.,* 225–226.

Fig. 9. Button used on the jacket of Vermont volunteers

4th Vermont Volunteer Infantry Regiment

Five local "boys" served at various times in the Fourth Vermont Volunteer Infantry Regiment. Their stories follow, organized as usual by their companies within that regiment.

Company E

Edward M. Savage, 18 years old, was a Rochester resident when he enlisted, although he had been born and brought up in Waitsfield. He was mustered into **Company E** when the new Fourth Volunteer Infantry Regiment was being organized at Brattleboro in September 1861. Savage remained with the company until discharged for disabilities on November 27, 1862, two months after the Battle of Antietam (*aka* Sharpsburg) terminated Lee's first invasion of northern states. It's likely that Edward Savage had participated in all the Fourth Regiment's actions until that time.

Company H

As part of unit consolidations late in the war, an entire company from the Second U.S. Sharpshooters Regiment was transferred into **Company H** of the Fourth Vermont Infantry on February 25, 1865. Among those transferees were three Waitsfield men: **Leonard C. Berry**[1], **Eugene Edwin Joslyn** and **John N. Richardson**.[2] Joslyn, who entered the company as a Corporal, was promoted to Sergeant four months after the transfer.

Company K

Charles S. Roulston[3] had joined **Company K** early in the war (September 21, 1861), at age 22. He was discharged for disability on June 6, 1862 and died that same day.

Impact of disease on the Fourth Vermont Infantry Regiment

Discharges for disability, if not designated as due to a wound, can safely be assumed to have been caused by illness. The experience of the Fourth Vermont may be considered typical of Union regiments with respect to the devastation wrought by disease. An historian writing in 1991, Ted Tunnell, analyzed the impact of illness on the Fourth Regiment during their first winter of the war:

> At the start of October [1861] thirty-one men were down sick, but day after day the figure climbed. By November it was 150, and the first week in December it soared to 342. It dropped off after Christmas and hovered around two hundred for the rest of the winter. In the beginning, measles and other childhood diseases were the chief maladies, but then typhoid fever swept the regiment. The probable cause was contaminated water. For two months prior to the regiment's arrival on Smoot's Hill, [4] a thousand cavalry horses had occupied the slope above the stream from which the 4th took its drinking water. By the first of the year, 28 men had died, mostly from typhoid. (In only one of the 4th's battles in the war would that figure be exceeded.) Many of those who survived never returned to duty. In a little over three months, without so much as a skirmish, the regiment's strength dropped from over a thousand men to only 660.[5]

Noting that the Fourth Regiment was not unique within the [Old] Vermont Brigade with respect to the effects of disease, Tunnell adds:

> The other Vermont regiments were also hard hit. Two weeks before Christmas, out of nearly five thousand men in the Vermont Brigade, over one thousand were down sick with measles, pneumonia, bronchitis, typhoid, dysentery, diarrhea, and other afflictions. All the Union forces suffered appallingly that winter, but the Vermonters had the highest ratio of sick men in the army.[6]

Significant early actions in which the Fourth Vermont was engaged while one or more Waitsfield men were present

Charles Roulston may have been present at the April 16, 1862 engagement at Lee's Mills (part of the Siege of Yorktown, Virginia) and even at the Battle of Williamsburg (May 5, 1862), depending on when he developed the illness that took his life in June 1862.

As noted above, it is likely that **Edward Savage** took part in all the movements and actions of the Fourth Vermont Volunteer Infantry Regiment during his time with the regiment. Those included Lee's Mills and Williamsburg, on the Virginia Peninsula; and also, actions at Garnett's and Golding's Farms on June 27 and 28, the Battle of Savage's Station on June 29, an engagement at White Oak Swamp Bridge on June 30 and the Battle of Malvern Hill, July first (all part of the Seven Days' retreat from just south of Richmond). Later that year, in Maryland, Savage fought with the Fourth Infantry Regiment at the Battle at Crampton's Gap on South Mountain (September 14); and at Antietam (September 16–17).

We have this account of the Crampton's Gap action. General William Farrar Smith's division had been ordered to push the Confederates off South Mountain. Timothy B. Mudgett's history of Smith's Second Division of the VI Corps (which included the Vermont Brigade under W. T. H. Brooks) describes the Fourth Vermont Regiment's fighting there.

> The Vermonters attacked at 3 p.m. There wasn't room enough between the road and a stand of woods to its south to deploy two regiments abreast, so Brigadier General Brooks formed the 4th and 2nd Vermont in column, respectively. The 4th moved forward rapidly across open ground under sporadic shellfire while the 2nd followed close behind. At the base of the mountain, Confederates manning one of the many stone fences opened a brisk fire. The 4th Vermonters charged with the bayonet, capturing the Rebel position and twenty prisoners. Now with room to spare, the 2nd Vermont came up on the 4th's right, and the two Green Mountain regiments went up the mountain together against little resistance. At the summit, the 4th Vermont split left to capture 5 officers and 115 men of the 6th Virginia and drive off the offending Rebel battery…. Franklin's VI Corps now had an open road to Harpers Ferry, which cost the 4th Vermont 1 dead and 14 wounded….[7]

Eleven months after he was discharged from the Fourth Regiment for disability, **Edward Savage** re-enlisted, this time with the Third Battery, Vermont Light Artillery. His record of service continues in that unit's section later in this work.

A long period when no men from Waitsfield were present in the Fourth Regiment

Between November 27, 1862 and February 25, 1865 there were no Waitsfield men present with the Fourth Vermont Infantry Regiment. Therefore, Waitsfield men did not participate in the regiment's battles of Fredericksburg, Chancellorsville or Gettysburg or in the 1864 Overland Campaign; nor with the regiment's deployment to the Shenandoah Valley, much less at Cedar Creek.

Waitsfield soldiers' participation in Fourth Regiment actions at war's end

In the final months of the war, the three local men who had been transferred into the Fourth Regiment from a sharpshooter unit, as noted above, saw these actions: March 25, 1865 at Fort Fisher, North Carolina (part of the siege of Petersburg, Virginia); and the battles of Sailor's Creek and Appomattox Court House (April 6 and April 9, respectively). Thereafter, the Fourth Regiment moved within Virginia to Farmville, then Burkesville Junction, then Danville, where it remained until May 18 when it entrained for Washington, D.C. It did not participate in the Grand Review there but did join a later VI Corps review.

Leonard C. Berry, Eugene Edwin Joslyn and **John N. Richardson** mustered out with the Fourth Regiment veterans on July 13, 1865.

Notes

1. Prior to that transfer, Private Berry had been wounded in the arm on June 16, 1864 and had spent three months in a Washington, D.C. hospital.

2. The author has chosen to follow the Ledoux & Associates website (based on army records) that confirms the earlier service of a fourth Waitsfield man, Thomas Theodore Prentis (53), in the same sharpshooters company until his discharge for disability on September 8, 1864. Thus, the author ignores the Jones (1909) entry for Prentis that includes him in the later transfer. Both cannot be correct.

3. Surname spelled "Roulsten" on a marker in Elmwood Cemetery, Northfield, VT.

4. Smoot's Hill outside Lewinsville, Virginia, was the site of Camp Griffin where the Fourth Vermont Infantry spent five months in the winter of 1861–62.

5. Tunnell, *Vermont History*, 59, 2 (Spring 1991), 79. In a footnote, Tunnell attributes his numbers to 4th Vermont Regimental Papers, RG 94, National Archives and to Benedict's *Vermont in the Civil War*, I: 160-161.

6. Tunnell, *loc. cit.* A different footnote in Tunnell's article cites Benedict, I: 237–238 as his source for this comment.

7. Mudgett (1997), 30–31. Unhappily, that attack involving two Vermont regiments failed to preserve the Union garrison at Harpers Ferry, which surrendered the next day, September 15th. Most members of Vermont's Ninth Infantry Regiment were captured there and were sent off to a POW camp. [See the 9th Vermont section later in this work.]

5th Vermont Volunteer Infantry Regiment

Edward L. Allen, Charles L. Hadley, Henry Charles Shaw, M.D. and George W. Steinberg of Waitsfield served in the Fifth Vermont Volunteer Infantry Regiment.

Dr. Henry Shaw's first service had been as Assistant Surgeon of the Second New Hampshire Regiment, a 90-day unit formed at the very beginning of the war. Directly following the mustering-out of that NH regiment, and while Vermont's Fifth Volunteer Infantry Regiment was being organized, Dr. Shaw moved into the position of Assistant Surgeon with that new regiment.[1]

Dr. Shaw's service from the beginning of the war ceased with his death from disease in Alexandria, Virginia on September 7, 1862. Prior to his death, Dr. Shaw would have known, and likely treated personally, all the men of the Fifth Regiment who were hospitalized for diseases or wounds. After Dr. Shaw's death, **George W. Steinberg** was the only Waitsfield soldier in the Fifth Regiment until **Edward L. Allen** and **Charles L. Hadley** joined the regiment toward the end of the war. Their stories appear farther down in this section.

Organization of the Fifth Vermont Volunteer Infantry Regiment

The Fifth Vermont regiment became part of General W. F. ("Baldy") Smith's brigade in the Second Division, IV Army Corps. The regiment commenced service at a disadvantage the earlier regiments had not known. A St. Albans newspaper wrote critically: "This regiment was hurried off to the war only partially equipped; they have had no overcoats until the last few days, and the same men who left St. Albans on the 23rd of September [1861], are now in the Advance Guard of the Army of the Potomac, in the same condition, surrounded by rebels thirsting for their blood....To put our noble and brave sons into camp at this season of the year without overcoats, is cruel and inhuman, but to place them in the face of the enemy without arms, is atrocious."[2]

The writer's outrage was evoked by a letter from local enlistees who informed the home front, "We have nothing to fight with but our hands, and the rebels are all around us." (That situation prevailed in three companies of the regiment, the letter writers attested.) Apparently, those companies had been led to believe that their overcoats and guns were awaiting them in Washington and would be distributed as soon as they arrived there. However, the men went without overcoats for three weeks after they arrived and were still without guns when they wrote their letter on the twelfth of October.

The Fifth Vermont spent most of the 1861–62 winter season at Camp Griffin in Langley, Virginia before moving to Fortress Monroe to participate in the Peninsula Campaign. At Savage's Station (June 29, 1862) the Fifth suffered the greatest loss, in killed and wounded, of any Vermont regiment in any one engagement of the war.[3]

Major campaigns involving the Fifth Vermont Regiment

As a part of the [First] Vermont Brigade, the Fifth Regiment participated in the various battles of the Peninsula Campaign and the Maryland Campaign (1862), as well as the Chancellorsville and Gettysburg Campaigns of 1863. After a brief stay in camp after the Gettysburg Campaign closed, the Fifth Vermont was sent in August to New York City to help quell violent draft riots there. Upon rejoining the Army of the Potomac, the regiment took part in the fall 1863 Mine Run Campaign before going into winter camp near Brandy Station, Virginia.

While at Brandy Station, the Fifth became the first Vermont regiment asked to re-enlist. Because those choosing re-enlistment were relatively few, the regiment was reconstituted as a battalion until new recruits and transfers could build it up once more.[4]

Those who did elect to reenlist were granted a $400 bounty and a thirty-day "veterans" furlough.[5]

The Overland Campaign commencing in May 1864 saw the Fifth Vermont fighting from the Rapidan River through the Wilderness and on to Spotsylvania, with all the horrors of that spring and summer. In one month, the regiment lost 349 officers and men.[6]

In July, the regiment assisted in driving Confederate General Jubal Early's men from the Washington D.C. environs, which entailed the Battle of Monocacy. The regiment pursued the Confederates into the Valley of the Shenandoah.

This brief narrative of the actions of the Fifth Vermont Volunteer Infantry Regiment is carried forward in three soldiers' individual stories.

Company D

George W. Steinberg enlisted August 17, 1861 at age 29 and was credited to Eden. He mustered in to Company D on September 16 that year and re-enlisted in the regiment December 15, 1863 while still serving his three-year term of enlistment. Private Steinerg was promoted to Corporal, then Sergeant, and to 1st Sergeant (October 17, 1864). He had been wounded at the Wilderness May 5, 1864 and he was wounded a second time at Petersburg, April 2, 1865. He was commissioned 2nd Lieutenant June 4, 1865 but was mustered out as a 1st Sergeant. Steinberg was granted a Vermont pension in 1884. He survived until 1906 and was buried in the Waitsfield Village Cemetery.

Charles L. Hadley, who was been born in Waitsfield, enlisted September 2, 1864 at age 19 from Morristown, Vermont for one year's service. Private Hadley's military record indicates he joined the Fifth Regiment during its detachment from the Army of the Potomac as the newly-created Army of the Shenandoah, commanded by Major General Philip Sheridan.[7] Sheridan was ordered by Lt. General Ulysses Grant to Virginia's Shenandoah Valley (the so-called "breadbasket" of the Confederate Army of Northern Virginia) with a mission to destroy crops and granaries in order to deprive the ANV of essential resources and thus hasten the end of the war in the East. I think it likely that Hadley participated in much of Sheridan's Valley Campaign (waged from August 7–November 28, 1864), including Cedar Creek.[8]

Company K

Edward L. Allen, also age 19, enlisted for a year's service on February 9, 1865 and was mustered into **Co. K** that very day. Presumably he was sent directly to the trenches outside Petersburg for the final weeks of the Union siege.

It's possible that Privates Allen and Hadley chose to volunteer in response to encouragement from their towns' Board of Selectmen. Certainly by the time they enlisted, Vermont towns were being notified by the War Department of quotas which, if not met by volunteers, would have to be filled by a draft that local officials were reluctant to impose. Furthermore, as an incentive, late-war volunteers could sign up with a recruiter to fill a vacancy in a specific Vermont regiment, whereas draftees would not have their choice of assignment.

Waitsfield was proud of its ability to encourage men to fill vacancies in the ranks of Vermont regiments. Generous bounties likely were one factor.[9]

Breakthrough at Petersburg

Joseph Wheelan offers this account of an hours-long bombardment on April 1, 1865 that preceded the final infantry assault of Petersburg. We can be confident that Privates Allen and Hadley, and First Sergeant Steinberg experienced this terrifying event.[10]

> [General Ulysses] Grant had initially wanted four army corps [II, VI, IX and XXIV] to attack right away because he feared Lee might strike at Sheridan in a desperate attempt to recapture Five Forks, "risking everything upon the cast of a single die." But nightfall made an immediate attack impracticable: troops couldn't be sent groping in the darkness; better to wait until daybreak. In the meantime, Grant ordered a bombardment of all the Confederate lines north and south of the James River.
>
> No other Union Army bombardment during the war equaled this one. For three hours, 150 guns crashed and heaved, emitting "a constant stream of living fire" on the Confederate lines around Petersburg and Richmond. An awed soldier of the 126th Ohio wrote that the bombardment set "the very earth beneath quaking and trembling at each discharge of those war monsters which sent shot and shell into the enemy's camp." The gunners fired so rapidly that there was "a constant flash as of lightning in intense darkness." It was "indescribably wild and grand," wrote an Ohio officer. Confederate batteries responded with fury....
>
> In the Union ranks on this misty, moonless night some soldiers wrote letters home; others wrote messages that they left with noncombatants in case they did not return. As the hour of attack neared, they discarded nonessential clothing as well as their playing cards—to disassociate themselves from a petty vice that could send them to the fiery regions if they were killed.
>
> In what had become standard procedure for many Union infantry units, the soldiers wrote their names on slips of paper and pinned them to their uniforms so that their bodies could be identified. "All knew that bloody work was before us," wrote General Lewis Grant, commander of VI Corps' Vermont Brigade. Another VI Corps officer, Colonel Hazard Stevens, wrote that he overheard many of his comrades say, "Well, goodbye, boys, this means death."

Grant had positioned the VI Corps just to the west of Petersburg. "The Vermont Brigade was placed at the front of a wedge-shaped attack formation," Howard Coffin writes, "and just before dawn, twelve thousand men rolled forward. The first Union soldier over the works was Captain Charles Gould of Windham, Vermont, who was promptly bayoneted in the face and back."[11]

End of the war for Waitsfield's men in the 5th Volunteer Infantry

Allen, Hadley and **Steinberg** survived that assault on Petersburg and went on to experience the final events of the war in Virginia: the fall of both Petersburg and Richmond; the subsequent chase of the Army of Northern Virginia by Meade's army; and Lee's surrender to Grant at Appomattox Court House.

Those three Waitsfield men mustered out with the remainder of their regiment on June 29, 1865.

Notes

1. Dr. Shaw's commission with the Fifth Vermont Infantry Regiment was dated August 15, 1861, a few days prior to the regiment's mustering-in.

2. Editor of *St. Albans Daily Messenger*, cited in *The Camp Griffin Gazette*, October 18, 1861.

3. Peck (1892), 142-143, cited by Tom Ledoux on the *Vermont in the Civil War* website: https://www.vermontcivilwar.org/events/5/history (retrieved Sept. 17, 2019).

4. The three-year term of service of the Fifth Regiment would not expire until September 1864. Perhaps the reason men were offered this opportunity to re-enlist so early was to ascertain the strength the regiment would be able to muster when the Spring 1864 advance would commence.

5. Andy Ward, licensed battlefield guide, in a zoom presentation to the Green Mountain Civil War Round Table, November 10, 2020.

6. Benedict (1886), I: 201–202.

7. Hadley was mustered-in the same day he enlisted. That suggests he had no "basic training" in Vermont but was transported directly to Virginia to join the regiment.

8. The regiment (as part of the Old Vermont Brigade) participated in a demonstration at Gilbert's Ford (*aka* Opequon Creek) on September thirteenth. Its next action was the much larger Battle of Opequon (Third Winchester) on the nineteenth, in which the Vermont Brigade was supported by the First Vermont Cavalry and the First Vermont Heavy Artillery Battery. The same combination of units fought at the Battles of Fisher's Hill (Woodstock) and Cedar Creek, where they were joined by the 8th Vermont and 10th Vermont Infantries.

9. Jones (1909) writes that by the end of the war the town had distributed $10,433.13 in bounties (p. 94). An online inflation calculator suggests that amount would represent $189,987.25 in 2023 dollars. Town bounties supplemented State and federal enlistment bounties.

10. Wheelan (2015), 180–181.

11. Coffin (2013), 28. Gould survived his wounds.

6th Vermont Volunteer Infantry Regiment

The Sixth Vermont Volunteer Infantry Regiment included an unusually large number of men (35) with Waitsfield connections. One member, **Edwin C. Lewis**, had enlisted as early as May 1861 although his mustering-in was delayed until that fall.

Following an urgent call by the War Department for additional manpower later that year, 25 other Waitsfield men were mustered into the Sixth Regiment on October 15, 1861 along with Private Lewis. Just four days afterwards, the Sixth Vermont Volunteer Infantry Regiment headed to the front. (There seems to have been little or no "basic training" in Vermont for those men.) The regiment reached the nation's capital on October 22nd and two days later marched to Camp Griffin at Lewinsville, Virginia where it joined the Second, Third, Fourth and Fifth Vermont Volunteer Infantry Regiments. With the addition of the Sixth Vermont Regiment, General William Farrar ("Baldy") Smith's long-desired all-Vermont Brigade finally was realized.[1] Thereafter, we see those five Vermont infantry regiments on the field fighting together throughout the war as the [First] Vermont Brigade, at times supplemented by other units.[2]

Nine more Waitsfield men were assigned to the Sixth Regiment between late 1862 and the summer of 1864 as the ranks of that regiment were reduced by disease and battle casualties.

The 35 Waitsfield recruits were distributed across four companies of the regiment, one man each in Companies **D** and **K**, 14 in Company **G**, and 19 in Company **H**. Service records for those men are presented below, grouped by companies.

Company D

Daniel Stoddard, one of the October 1861 Waitsfield enlistees, was assigned to **Co. D**. Born in Waitsfield, Daniel Stoddard appears to have enlisted at age 17 (given his birthdate as shown on the Ledoux & Associates website, our primary source for enlistment data) although he likely had given his age as 18, as that was the minimum age for entering Union service. Even more interesting, Stoddard served under an assumed name, "Daniel Joslyn". He was wounded at Bank's Ford, Virginia during the Chancellorsville Campaign (on May 4, 1863) but recovered to serve out his three-year term, mustering out on October 28, 1864.

Fig. 10. "Vermont Brigade" jacket pin, supplied by the federal government to all members of the First Vermont Brigade once that brigade was formed following mustering-in of the Sixth Vermont Volunteer Infantry Regiment

Photo from Wikipedia.

It's reasonable to assume that unless absent from his company on some of the following occasions—and there is no information suggesting that—he fought in all the engagements of the Sixth Regiment up to the day he was wounded. Those were Warwick Creek, Lee's Mills, Williamsburg, Golding's Farm (2 days), Savage's Station and White Oak Swamp, all on the Virginia Peninsula; in the Antietam Campaign at Crampton's Gap and Sharpsburg, Maryland; at Fredericksburg on December 13, 1862; and the next spring at either Marye's Heights or Salem Heights (both on May 3, 1863, the day before he was wounded at Bank's Ford). Possibly Stoddard also was at Second Fredericksburg (June 5, 1863).[3]

Stoddard likely was with the regiment at Gettysburg on July 3, 1863 and also at Funkstown, Maryland during Lee's retreat; and that fall, at Gainesville and Rappahannock Station, Virginia. Furthermore, he probably was present with the Sixth Vermont Volunteer Infantry Regiment the following spring in the Virginia Wilderness, and at Spotsylvania, Cold Harbor and the Weldon R.R. battle.[4] That summer (when the Sixth Regiment was detailed to roust Confederate General Jubal Early's advance on Washington) he probably was present at Fort Stevens, Maryland and Charlestown, West Virginia as well as the battles at Opequon (Third Winchester), Fisher's Hill and Cedar Creek, all in the Shenandoah Valley of Virginia.[5]

Company G

Fourteen Waitsfield men served in Company G: **Bertrand Delos Campbell, John J. Chase, George W. Fisher, Eli Gilson, James Harriman, Manley Hoyt, John F. Jones, Edwin C. Lewis, Allen E. Mehuron, Benjamin Poland, Emery L. Smith, James H. Somerville, Lyman Brown Stoddard** and **Julius E. Tucker**. One other Waitsfield soldier served briefly with Company

G: **Mason C. Shepherd,** whose record appears with Company H below, was transferred into Co. G on New Year's Day 1865, then was transferred back to Company H five months later.[6]

Service records of the Waitsfield men in Company G

Nine men (Campbell, Harriman, Hoyt, Jones, Lewis, Mehuron, Smith, Lyman Stoddard and Tucker) were mustered into Company G on October 15, 1861. Later they were joined by five others (Chase, Fisher, Gilson, Poland and Sommerville). Service records for these men appear below.

Bertrand Delos Campbell joined the Sixth Vermont Volunteer Infantry Regiment after previous attempts to enlist elsewhere had failed.[7] Persisting, Campbell enlisted with Co. G of the Sixth, where he was mustered in as a Corporal. After a year's service, on October 22, 1862, he received an honorable discharge from a hospital in Philadelphia, Pennsylvania.[8] Less than two years later Campbell went to Barton, Vermont and enlisted with the 1st Vermont Cavalry.[9] After just five weeks with the cavalry, he was killed in action.[10]

James G. Harriman, who was mustered in as a Private, soon was promoted to Sergeant. Harriman was wounded on the first day of fighting in the Wilderness of Virginia, at the commencement of spring campaigning in 1864 by General George G. Meade's Army of the Potomac.[11] Harriman was discharged five and a half months later, in October.

Manley N. Hoyt died in the service on July 18, 1862. He succumbed to chronic diarrhea in a Philadelphia hospital.

John F. Jones. Born in Plymouth, England, the 26-year-old Jones was credited to Waitsfield, suggesting he resided in the Town by October 1861. Jones was mustered in as a Sergeant. Sixteen months after his service commenced, he was honorably discharged on account of sickness. Sometime later, Jones enlisted in a Massachusetts regiment, but while there he again sickened. He died November 28, 1864.

Edwin C. Lewis had served previously in the First Vermont Volunteer Infantry as the only Waitsfield man in that early 90-day regiment.

Lewis later was commissioned as a Second Lieutenant and served in that capacity in Company G of the Sixth Regiment for a time, but resigned his position on June 4, 1862. Some 18 months later Lewis enlisted in the Sixth Regiment once more, this time being mustered in as a Private from Rutland on December 23, 1863. Lewis was wounded at Cold Harbor (June 1, 1864). He was discharged from the Sixth Regiment in August in order to be promoted to Captain of a new unit comprised of two companies (D and K) of the 13th United States Colored Heavy Artillery, based in Kentucky. Lewis was discharged from that regiment on October 21, 1865.[12]

Capt. Lewis was the only Waitsfield man selected to officer a unit of Black soldiers during the war, to my knowledge.[13]

Allen E. Mehuron, born in the Hinesville section of Hinesburg, Vermont, enlisted from Fayston.[14] He was mustered into Company G on October 15, 1861 with others cited here. Private Mehuron succumbed to chills and fever while at Hagerstown, Maryland during the Antietam Campaign and was sent to a hospital in Philadelphia. He was discharged from that hospital on February 4, 1863 by reason of a Surgeon's Certificate of Disability.[15]

Emery L. Smith had mustered in as a Private but was promoted to Corporal within his first year of service. Taken prisoner June 29, 1862 at the Battle of Savage's Station on the Virginia Peninsula, he was paroled on September 13 of that year and returned to Company G to march and fight until wounded in the Virginia Wilderness on the first day's fighting of the Overland Campaign, along with his comrade James Harriman. That wound explains Smith's discharge at the end of October 1864.[16]

Lyman Brown Stoddard gave his age upon enlistment as 18, but calculated by his birthdate, Stoddard appears to have been only 14. He was wounded at Marye's Heights (Fredericksburg, Virginia) on May 3, 1863. Lyman Stoddard was one of the G Company soldiers who re-enlisted. (Even though their term of service would not expire until mid-October 1864, men in the Sixth Regiment were asked in December 1863 if they wished to return home when their service was up, or were willing to sign on for another tour of duty.) Stoddard was wounded a second time in the Wilderness fighting of 1864. Stoddard mustered out on June 26, 1865 with the rest of the Sixth Regiment's veterans. ("Veterans" was an appellation given those who had re-enlisted.)

Julius E. Tucker deserted on August 30, 1862 but returned on March 31,

Fig.11. Poster commemorating a person's service in the Sixth Vermont Volunteer Infantry Regiment

This 2023 photograph documents the service of Allen E. Mehuron.

Courtesy of Kathy and Tom Mehuron of Waitsfield. Photo credit: Jim Dodds

1863. The L&A website shows Tucker as having re-enlisted on December 15, 1863 while serving with Co. G. Tucker was taken prisoner on May 30, 1864 when the Sixth Regiment was engaged in operations along the line of Virginia's Totopotomoy River, and was sent to the Andersonville, Georgia POW camp. He was paroled on April 28, 1865 and was mustered out on May 23, one month before the rest of the Sixth Regiment.

John J. Chase and **Eli Gilson** were the first Waitsfield men added to Company G after the original enlistees. Both mustered in September 22, 1862, just days after Lee's first invasion of a northern state had terminated in the Battle of Antietam. **Gilson** died on April 7, 1864 of chronic diarrhea in a field hospital at Brandy Station, Virginia. He was 23. **Chase** was wounded at Cedar Creek, Virginia on October 19, 1864, but survived to muster out with his company on June 19, 1865.

George W. Fisher, Benjamin Poland[17] **and James H. Somerville** were one-year enlistees who joined the depleted Sixth Regiment in late summer, 1864. **Somerville** served from August 29, 1864; **Fisher** from September 2, 1864; **Poland**, from September 7, 1864. All three mustered out in June 1865.

Company H

Of the 19 Waitsfield men who served in **Company H**, fifteen were mustered in October 15, 1861 along with the original Co. G men and the two "singletons" of companies D and K. Those fifteen were: **Luther Ainsworth, Mitchell Biscorner**[18], **Henry N. Bushnell, Luther Chase, Mark C. Chase, Hiram F. Dike, Ephraim H. Fuller, George S. Kneeland, Ireneaus P. Newcomb, Edwin R. Richardson, Daniel P. Shepherd, Mason C. Shepherd, Lewis M. Spaulding, Solon S. Spaulding** and **Simeon Stoddard**.

Four other Waitsfield recruits joined H company just days after the Battle of Antietam. **Nathan Thayer** and **Almon Walker** would have participated in the Fredericksburg Campaign (December 1862), the infamous "Mud March" (January 1863) and the Chancellorsville Campaign (May 1863). Thayer was disabled shortly after Chancellorsville.

Judson W. Richardson and **William Henry Stoddard** joined H Company in December 1863, almost a year after the Fredericksburg disaster and the Mud March fiasco had ended Ambrose Burnside's command of the Army of the Potomac. (Joseph Hooker, who succeeded Burnside, also was gone by then. The Army of the Potomac was headed by George Gordon Meade when Richardson and W. H. Stoddard entered service.) Joining the regiment so late in the year, it's unlikely either man saw action until the Overland Campaign began in May 1864.

Service records of the Waitsfield men in Company H

The first casualty from **H** company was **Luther Chase**, who died of disease in the Vermont Brigade hospital at Camp Griffin, Virginia on January 31, 1862, just three months after he entered the service. His body was shipped home, where it lies in Waitsfield's Irasville Cemetery next to a cenotaph commemorating his brother Mark.[19]

Mitchell Biscorner was killed in action at Lee's Mills, an engagement on the Virginia Peninsula, April 16, 1862. He was buried [as Basconner] in the Yorktown National Cemetery.

In the same Lee's Mills action **Corporal Ephraim H. Fuller** was shot through both thighs. (The author has no information on Fuller's likely long hospitalization.) He was mustered out two and a half years later, on October 28, 1864, eight months before his term of service would have ended. Although Fuller was buried in Iowa, Waitsfield's Irasville Cemetery contains a cenotaph for him.

Ireneaus P. Newcomb died of typhoid pneumonia at Hampton, Virginia on May 9, 1862, shortly after the Lee's Mill battle, and was buried in the Hampton National Cemetery. There is a cenotaph for Newcomb in Waitsfield's Irasville Cemetery.

Both **Daniel P. Shepherd** and **Mason C. Shepherd** were wounded at Lee's Mills. Nevertheless, they re-enlisted when that opportunity arose later. Mason Shepherd was wounded again May 5, 1864 in the Virginia Wilderness. In January of 1865 he was transferred to Co. G, only to be transferred back to Co. H in May. Both men mustered out with the other veterans of the Sixth Regiment on June 26, 1865.

Luther Ainsworth had been commissioned as a Second Lieutenant eleven days before he was mustered into Company H in that capacity, at age 31. He won two promotions afterward, acceding to Captain before he died of a gunshot to the abdomen on May 4, 1863 at Banks Ford near Fredericksburg, Virginia, in a battle that was part of the Chancellorsville Campaign. His body is thought to lie in an unmarked grave in Virginia.[20]

Hiram F. Dike was mortally wounded the same day his Captain was killed; he, too, died that day.

George S. Kneeland served as a cook in Company H for several months at the beginning of his term of enlistment. The L&A website records that Kneeland was ill from the summer of 1862 until the summer of 1863; nevertheless, he re-enlisted and finished out the war with the rest of the company's veterans.

Henry N. Bushnell, who had mustered in as a Sergeant with the original group of men in October 1861, was promoted to 1st Sergeant in February of 1862. The next spring Bushnell was commissioned as Second Lieutenant, a rank he held for a year before being promoted to First Lieutenant and serving as such in Co. C. (Presumably Bushnell was transferred to fill a First Lieutenant vacancy in Co. C.) Five months later he was promoted to Captain and returned to Co. H. At some time, Bushnell served four months in detached service with division sharpshooters, although when that occurred is not cited in our source materials. Bushnell was mustered out June 26, 1865.[21]

Mark C. Chase had enlisted with his younger brother Luther. Private Mark Chase was discharged May 29, 1862, likely disabled by illness. He re-enlisted 19 months later, and returned to Company H. Wounded in the Wilderness on May 5, 1864, he became a prisoner of war and was sent to Andersonville, Georgia. He died there a month later, of bronchitis. Despite there being a cenotaph for Mark Chase in Waitsfield's Irasville Cemetery, his body rests in the Andersonville POW Cemetery.

Lewis M. Spaulding was killed in action (a head wound) on the first day of Wilderness fighting in the Overland Campaign, May 5, 1864. He was 19. His body rests in the Fredericksburg (Virginia) National Cemetery.

Solon Spaulding was promoted to Corporal upon his re-enlistment in December 1863 or perhaps shortly after. He was mustered out a week before most other Sixth Regiment veterans, on June 12, 1865.[22]

Simeon Stoddard was wounded May 5, 1864 at the Wilderness. He was discharged on October 28 of that year, along with all the others in the regiment who did not re-enlist back in December 1863. I have found no information about the nature of Stoddard's wound or whether he may have spent the May–October interval in a hospital before being discharged.

Edwin R. Richardson, another of the original enlistees in Co. H, was promoted to Corporal in February '62, to Sergeant in July '63, and to 1st Sergeant in January '64, before being killed in action August 21, 1864 at Charles Town, West Virginia during the Shenandoah Valley campaign. He was 21 years old.

Judson W. Richardson entered Co. H in December 1863. He was promoted to Corporal on June 19, 1865 (after the war effectively had ended) and was mustered out soon afterwards with the last of the Sixth Regiment's men. **William Henry Stoddard**, who had reported to Co. H the same day as Judson Richardson, also was mustered out on the same day.

Nathan Thayer was discharged for disability on June 3, 1863, one month after Chancellorsville and just weeks before the start of the Gettysburg Campaign.[23]

Almon Walker was transferred at some point from Co. H into the Veterans Reserve Corps (VRC).[24] The VRC was comprised of men considered permanently disabled—by either a wound or disease—but judged still able to perform some service. Walker might well have been with the VRC, the so-called "Invalid Corps," when it was charged with defending Washington City during the 1864 Confederate attack by Jubal Early's forces. He served with the VRC until being discharged on July 10, 1865.

Company K

Franklin Edwin Spaulding, a former Waitsfield resident, enlisted from Sheldon and was mustered in on October 15, 1861. He was assigned to **Company K**, a company that had no other soldiers from the Town. **Spaulding** would have participated alongside the Waitsfield soldiers in Companies D, G and H both in regimental camp life and military actions during his eight months of service that terminated July 30, 1862 with a discharge attributed to disability.[25]

The Sixth Regiment's march to Gettysburg

Despite a high casualty rate among Waitsfield's Sixth Regiment enlistees, it may be worth noting that none of those casualties was incurred in the deadliest battle of the Civil War, the three days at Gettysburg. There, the Sixth Regiment was stationed at the extreme left of the line on July third but was not called into action that day.

Vermont's Sixth Regiment is famed for having led the line of march when the Army's VI Corps was ordered to Gettysburg: It set a very rapid pace for the Corps and sustained that pace for almost 24 hours. Frank G. Butterfield's account of the regiment's march begins:

> When the battle of Gettysburg opened on July 1 [1863], the regiment, with the Sixth Army Corps, was at Manchester, Md., thirty-five miles from the battlefield. At dusk orders came to move, but it was about 10 o'clock at night before the column started for Gettysburg. It was on this occasion that General Sedgwick issued his famous order, "Put the Vermonters ahead and keep the column well closed up," and before the sun went down on the afternoon of the 2nd the column deployed into line of battle at Gettysburg.[26]

Diversion of the Sixth Regiment to New York City

Following the close of the Gettysburg Campaign, the Sixth Vermont Regiment was sent to New York City as part of a force dispatched to clamp

Fig. 12. The Riots at New York - the Rioters burning and sacking the Colored Orphan Asylum. Source note: *Illustrated London news*. (London : Illustrated London News and Sketch Ltd., 1842-).

down on draft rioters. (The other regiments of the First Vermont Brigade had overlapping riot-control assignments in New York City, Kingston and Poughkeepsie, New York.) The Sixth Regiment was there a full month, from August 14 to September 16, before returning to Culpeper, Virginia.

The last Union campaign of that year, the Mine Run Campaign, occupied the Army of the Potomac including the Vermont Brigade (and, of course, the Sixth Vermont Volunteers) between November 26 and December 2, 1863. The men then returned to their winter camp to await the Spring 1864 campaign.

The Overland Campaign

The First Vermont Brigade suffered tremendous losses in the 1864 Overland Campaign that opened with fighting in the Virginia Wilderness. Soldiers fought and died in the same woodlands that had seen horrors just one year earlier.

As the Army of the Potomac's Overland Campaign progressed, fighting extended to Spotsylvania, Virginia and beyond, with battles throughout May and June. After months of almost constant fighting during which the

Army of the Potomac shifted ever south and westward, shutting down vital railroad lines to Richmond, the campaign evolved into a siege of Petersburg, Virginia. While the bulk of Meade's forces were engaged in that siege, the five Vermont regiments constituting the First Vermont Brigade were detached to repulse CSA General Jubal Early's advance on the nation's capital, marked by an attack on Fort Stevens, part of a 37-mile defensive ring around the city. After that Confederate attack failed and Early's corps retreated into Virginia's Shenandoah Valley, the brigade was ordered to the Valley to support Brigadier General Philip Sheridan's army.

The Sixth Regiment in the Shenandoah Valley; its return to Petersburg and the war's end

Numerous battles in the Valley followed, including Opequon (Third Winchester), the second day at Fisher's Hill and, climactically, Cedar Creek. The Sixth Regiment returned with the rest of the Vermont Brigade to the Army of the Potomac in December, where it resumed life in the trenches around Petersburg, Virginia before participating in the final battles for Petersburg and then at Sailor's Creek which wound up Lee's retreat after Richmond fell.

Henry N. Bushnell of Co. H was specially mentioned in an after-action report for gallant conduct throughout the "breakthrough" day at Petersburg, April 2, 1865.[27]

The Sixth Regiment did not travel to Washington, D.C. for the two days of the Union's Grand Review (May 23–24, 1865), but later there was a VI Corps Review in which the Sixth Vermont Volunteer Infantry Regiment (by then reduced to battalion size) "made a splendid appearance," according to front-page coverage in *The New York Times*, as it marched as part of the VI Corps' 2nd Division, 2nd Brigade (the Old Vermont Brigade) under Lewis A. Grant.[28]

Casualty rates among Waitsfield soldiers in the Sixth Vermont Regiment

The one Waitsfield man who served in Company **D** became a casualty; likewise, the one in Company **K**. The first was wounded; the other, discharged early because of disability.

Eleven of the 14 Waitsfield men who served in **G** Company became casualties. Two died from disease, while three others were discharged early because of illness. Four were wounded, some more than once. Two were taken prisoner.

Fifteen of the 19 Waitsfield men who served in **H** Company became casualties. Three died of disease, including one who died while a prisoner of war. One man was discharged early because of illness while another completed his term of service in the Veterans Reserve Corps as "permanently disabled". One man was ill for a full year before he eventually returned to duty. Four men survived wounds in battle. Five Waitsfield men in Co. H were mortally wounded or killed in action.

Combining these losses across all the Waitsfield soldiers who served in the Sixth Vermont Volunteer Infantry Regiment shows the group suffered a 79.4% casualty rate. One way to contemplate this statistic is to consider that only one in five of the Waitsfield "boys" who served in the Sixth Vermont returned home without outwardly visible evidence of injury.

Notes

1. General W. F. ("Baldy") Smith did not command the Vermont Brigade, however, as he had been promoted to Division command in October 1861. Smith's successor as brigade commander was W. T. H. Brooks, nicknamed "Bully" Brooks.

2. The 26th New Jersey Volunteer Infantry was part of the brigade from the beginning, but only until the New Jersey's 90-day enlistment expired shortly after. Much later, at the time of the Battles of Spotsylvania Court House (May 8-21, 1864), the 11th Vermont Infantry, designated by then as the 1st Vermont Heavy Artillery, joined the brigade.

3. There is no information available about the severity of Stoddard/Joslyn's wound nor his recovery period, so I cannot be sure about Stoddard's presence at this first large action after he was wounded.

4. It's likely Daniel Stoddard alias Joslyn marched over the very battlefield of his May 1863 wounding when the 1864 Overland Campaign commenced.

5. It is notable that Stoddard/Joslyn's record encompasses much of the history of Vermont's Sixth Regiment. After Daniel Stoddard departed from service, the regiment experienced these additional engagements in Virginia in 1865: Petersburg (two battles in March plus one in April) and Sailor's Creek. This information appears in a post-war account of the Sixth Regiment written by Lieutenant Frank G. Butterfield, in Peck (1892), 1, 177-180.

6. I have not been able to find an explanation for those transfers. Perhaps Shepherd had some special skill that was needed temporarily in G Company.

7. The Ledoux & Associates website shows that Campbell had enlisted in Company H of the Third Vermont Volunteers early in June 1861 but was discharged in August. The website does not offer an explanation for that discharge. Campbell then attempted to join Co. H of the Sixth Vermont but was rejected by the regimental surgeon.

8. The L&A record does not tell us when or why Campbell was admitted to the hospital.

9. A photograph of Campbell apparently in his cavalry uniform (part of the John Gibson Collection) appears on the L&A website.

10. Jones (1909), 85.

11. By that time Ulysses Grant had been appointed General in Chief. Grant chose to make his headquarters in the field (rather than in Washington, D.C) and

to travel with Meade's army. This campaign also is known as Grant's 1864 [Overland] Campaign for that reason.

12. Lewis' service as Captain in the 13th U.S. CHARTY is recorded by Peck (1892), II, 710. See the section on 13th Regiment, U.S. Colored Heavy Artillery Battery which appears later in this volume.

13. United States infantry units comprised of Black men (named "U.S. Colored Regiments") all had white officers. Such units were organized after being authorized by the Emancipation Proclamation.

14. Mehuron appears in this work because he was buried in Waitsfield's Irasville Cemetery. It seems he lived in the Town following his military service. He served as a commander of Post no. 36 (the "Ainsworth Post") of the Grand Army of the Republic.

15. Mehuron also may have been wounded somewhat earlier in that campaign, at South Mountain. The author is indebted to Mary Kathleen Mehuron for providing this information *via* a telephone call and an e-mail, September 2021.

16. Peck (1892), I, 203.

17. Poland had enrolled in E. R. Kinney's Warren company and was mustered in at Rutland, according to the Reverend Mr. Dascomb's *The Memorial Record of Waitsfield, Vermont* (1867). Nevertheless, Poland was credited to Waitsfield.

18. Biscorner is cited as "Bascorner" in Peck (1897), 205 and 764; and as "Basconner" in Jones (1909), 84. The author preserves the Ledoux & Associates spelling of his surname.

19. Luther Chase died on January 31, 1862 per the L&A website, although his Irasville tombstone says "January 30."

20. This detail of Ainsworth's death appears on the L&A website. The same site offers a photograph of Ainsworth in uniform which is credited to the VHS Reunion Society Collection.

21. Photos of Bushnell in uniform appear on the L&A website.

22. This early discharge date may suggest a disability was responsible.

23. Less than a month after his wounding, Nathan Thayer began receiving a Union pension that continued until his death in 1915 at age 76. The *Barre Daily Times* of June 4, 1915 stated that Thayer received a pension longer than any other Vermont Civil War veteran, a claim the L&A Webmaster evaluates as, "It is very possible this is accurate." (Information retrieved 6/24/2020.)

24. I have not found information of when or why Walker's transfer into the VRC occurred.

25. Primary sources disagree on the date of Franklin ("Frank") Spaulding's discharge. I use here the date given on the Ledoux & Associates website. Peck (1892) gives Spaulding's discharge date as July third, while Jones (1909) gives it as June 30.

26. Butterfield, cited in Peck (1892), 1, 179.

27. Bushnell's having been singled out for special mention appears in Jones (1909), 85.

28. The VI Corps review received extensive coverage in the June 9, 1865 *Times*, archived and available to readers.

7th Vermont Volunteer Infantry Regiment

Six Waitsfield men served at some time in the Seventh Vermont Volunteer Infantry Regiment, a three-year regiment raised early in 1862. Two men were assigned to Company **C**; one to Company **D**; three to Company **K**. The Seventh was the first Vermont infantry regiment to serve far from the Virginia/ Maryland region where the Union's Army of the Potomac was concentrated.

Company C

Hira Wood was mustered into the Seventh Vermont Volunteers on February 12, 1862. Wood was assigned to Company C but deserted early in March, before the regiment left its Rutland camp bound for the Gulf coast.[1]

Eugene McCarty.[2] Born in Ireland, McCarty was a Waitsfield resident when he enlisted at age 20 and was mustered in the same day, February 9, 1865. Private McCarty served only a few months before being discharged on May 12, 1865 at New Haven, Connecticut.

Company D

Before joining the Seventh Vermont in 1865, **Zimri Lathrop**[3] had served in the state's 14th Volunteer Infantry Regiment, a nine-months regiment that was part of the Second Vermont Brigade. Lathrop was 30 years old when he enlisted in Company K of the Fourteenth from Rupert, Vermont (his birthplace). Lathrop served with the 14th Vermont Volunteer Infantry Regiment from October 10, 1862 until July 30, 1863. Following his release from that regiment after the Gettysburg Campaign, he chose to enlist again (this time from Dorset, Vermont) for a one-year term of service. Lathrop was mustered into Co. D of the Seventh Vermont Infantry on January 18, 1865 and was mustered out on September 29, 1865. Private Lathrop would have been present, then, during the Seventh's actions at Mobile, Alabama with the Army of the

Military Division of West Mississippi and on the U.S./Mexico border with the Army of Observation.

Company K

Company K was organized via a recruiting station in Northfield. Within days it joined the other companies of the regiment at Camp Phelps in Rutland.

Edward A. Burns, **Daniel McCarty** and **Levi C. Peabody** served in Company K. Corporal Peabody was part of the Seventh Infantry from its organization, while Privates Burns and McCarty joined near the end of the war.[4]

Service history of the Seventh Vermont Volunteer Infantry Regiment

Regimental officers came from eight Vermont communities, though none from Waitsfield. Several of those officers, as well as many of the regiment's men, had served previously in the First Vermont Infantry, so they brought ninety days' experience in soldiering; other officers transferred into the Seventh from the Second and the Fourth Vermont Regiments.

Armed with new Springfield rifles, the Seventh departed Rutland by train for New York City on March 10. Upon arrival, the men were treated to a generous supper in their honor, with speeches by state politicians and military officers, at the Fifth Avenue Hotel. On March 14 the men were divided into two groups for travel from Sandy Hook via transport ships *Premier* and *Tamerlane*, and were not reunited until their arrival at Ship Island, Louisiana on the Gulf of Mexico. This proved just the first of many long-range moves, as the men eventually would participate in actions in Louisiana, Mississippi, Florida and Alabama.

The Seventh Regiment, unlike Vermont's earlier regiments, was not assigned to the Army of the Potomac; instead, it became part of a new Department of the Gulf army, in a division headed by the Massachusetts "political general" Benjamin Franklin Butler.

Future historian of the Seventh Regiment William C. Holbrook, citing G. G. Benedict's 1886 history of Vermont soldiers and sailors in the war, observed that the men suffered from sea sickness and confinement in the "close and ill-arranged" transports during their nearly one month aboard. Two men died during that voyage, and were buried at sea.[5]

After 24 days the first five companies of the regiment disembarked the *Premier* and established a camp at Ship Island, with the companies aboard the *Tamerlane* arriving three days later. The regiment was placed adjacent to the camp of the Eighth Vermont Regiment, also newly arrived. Holbrook has described their new home:

> The Vermonters here found themselves on a narrow strip of snow-white sand, thrown up by the waves, about seven miles long and from one-quarter to three-quarters of a mile wide. The only vegetation upon it was a grove of pines at the northeastern end, from which the troops rafted wood for the cook-fires.[6]

Soldiers of the two new Vermont regiments were among some seven to eight thousand men under Butler's command. The Seventh and Eighth Vermont Regiments were brigaded with the Ninth, Tenth, and Thirteenth Connecticut, the Eighth New Hampshire and the Seventh and Eighth Maine infantry regiments, accompanied by three artillery batteries and one company of cavalry.[7]

Provided only with salt rations during their time on Ship Island, the men drew water from shallow wells. They spent their time in company drill, for the most part. Although the men of the brigade could hear cannon fire from federal attacks on Forts Jackson and Saint Philip one hundred miles away, the surrenders of which were followed by a Union occupation of New Orleans in the final days of April, they took no part in that campaign. But beginning on May second a detachment from the brigade, including some companies from the Seventh Regiment, was ordered to occupy two forts previously manned by the Confederates and now abandoned, on Lake Pontchartrain. (The detached companies did not include Waitsfield men.)

It wasn't long before the entire Seventh Regiment left for New Orleans. Traveling on the *Whitman*, a steamer that would sink just months later on the Mississippi, killing its charge of sick and wounded Union soldiers, the regiment arrived at Carrolton, a town six miles up-river from the great southern city.[8] Its task: to guard over three miles of earthworks. The men spent only a month there, but it was a time of great discomfort. Ground flooding due to a levee break left decomposing plants and animals in their camp. Malaria struck. Oppressive heat made daily drills highly fatiguing.[9]

On June 15, the Seventh Regiment was ordered aboard the *Iberville* for immediate departure to Baton Rouge, then as now the capital of Louisiana. The Seventh engaged in a conflict at Hamilton's Plantation near Grand Gulf, Mississippi on June 24. Over the next five weeks the regiment participated in operations against Vicksburg, Mississippi.[10]

David Bastian's account of Union efforts (carried out in large part by 1200 impressed slaves from nearby plantations) to construct a canal across De Soto

Point in order to divert the Mississippi River near Vicksburg which, if successful, would have left that major port city landlocked and thus of no further military value to the Confederacy, notes that Vermont's Seventh Regiment was among the units encamped near or actually engaged in that construction work from late June until the project was abandoned on July 21.[11]

The Union soldiers under Brigadier General Thomas Williams withdrew to Baton Rouge three days later. By then William's command had been reduced by disease from its original force of 3,200 to only some 700 men fit for duty.[12]

It seems certain that Corporal Levi C. Peabody was the only Waitsfield man present in the Seventh Regiment during that operation.[13]

The Seventh Regiment fought at the Battle of Baton Rouge on August fifth, and assisted in evacuating Baton Rouge two weeks later. Throughout that summer the men's health continued to decline. "Having no tents, the men were kept in confined quarters on board the transports," Holbrook writes, "till the number of sick became so great as to require all the room on board, when the portion of the regiment fit for duty was directed to encamp on shore, where, sleeping on the ground and managing with the aid of boughs and drift-wood and a few shelter tents to secure only an imperfect protection from the night damps, their condition was little if any bettered."[14]

Soon the hundreds of stricken soldiers (including many officers and physicians) amounted to fully half the regiment. Holbrook records that 350 sick men were removed in late July from hospital boats of the naval fleet accompanying the troops to a steamer, *Morning Light*, which transported them to Baton Rouge where a hotel had been converted to a hospital. In addition to some men who had died while the steamer was delayed a day before departing, eight more men died during the two-day transit.

Tropical diseases rendered huge losses among the Seventh Regiment and its brigade.

In the summer of 1862 hundreds of men among Williams' infantry brigade which labored on the De Soto Point canal died and more than 100 were discharged for disability. The diseases that struck so many were as various as malaria, swamp fever (leptospirosis), dengue fever and dysentery. Sunstroke, exposure and general disability also contributed to the toll.

In the Seventh Regiment specifically, of 700 men deemed effective [fit for duty] when they left Baton Rouge in June to begin what Holbrook terms an "ill-starred expedition," fewer than 100 remained fit at its close, a loss to the

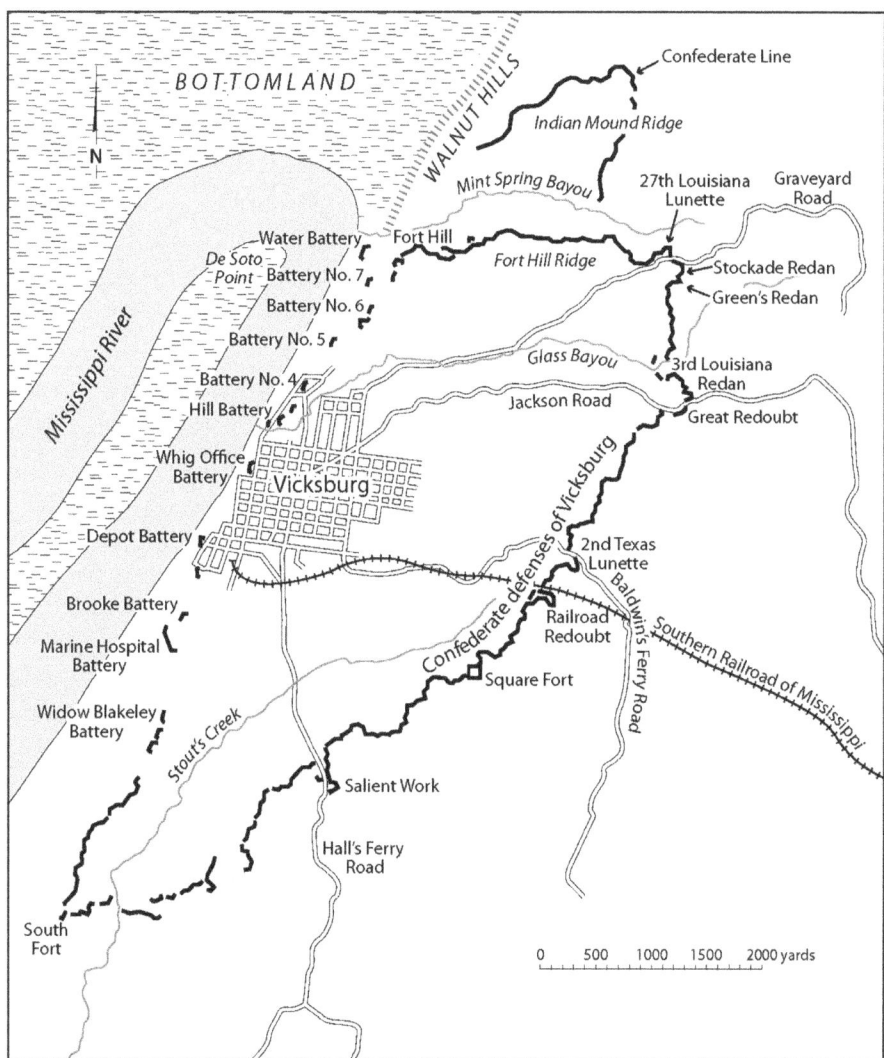

De Soto Point opposite Confederate defenses around Vicksburg

Map 1. Confederate defensive works protecting Vicksburg, Mississippi as of May 18, 1863. Courtesy of Earl J. Hess, Ph.D. from a map on page 16 of his military analysis *Storming Vicksburg*.

ranks of over 600 in 36 days. "It was a terrible, almost a destructive experience," Holbrook states.[15]

The remainder of the regiment returned to Camp Williams at Carrollton, which the men were calling Camp Death by then.

The regiment performed duties near Carrolton until ordered to Pensacola, Florida. Organizationally, it then became part of the army of the District of West Florida. Men continued to succumb to disease there, too, mostly from yellow fever.

With **Colonel Levi Peabody**'s departure just prior to that move (he was discharged for disability) there were no longer any Waitsfield men in the regiment. That continued to be the case until January 1865 when **Privates Zimri Lathrop** and **Daniel McCarty** arrived, followed soon by **Private Edward Burns**.

For this reason, we move ahead in Holbrook's history save for noting that in February 1864 the men remaining in the Seventh were offered the chance to reenlist.[16]

By the time the re-enlistees departed on furlough in August, the Seventh Regiment had left 350 men buried in Mississippi and Florida and more than 200 malaria survivors had been discharged "in shattered health."[12]

The Mobile Campaign and the last actions of the Seventh Regiment

The final campaign for the Seventh Regiment was that of Mobile, Alabama (March 17–April 12, 1865). **Burns, Lathrop** and **Daniel McCarty** would have been present for that campaign. The regiment traveled by steamer to Mobile Point, where they were assigned to Day's Brigade (the Second) of Benton's division in Gordon Granger's XIII Corps. The Waitsfield men found themselves brigaded with men from northwestern states. For the next two months these soldiers had only tents on barren sand as shelter.

Granger's corps, with the XVI Corps under A. J. Smith, comprised a force of some 45,000 federals under E. R. S. Canby, Commander of the Department of the Gulf/Military Division of West Mississippi. An initial campaign objective was the capture of a CSA garrison at Spanish Fort, the strongest of 58 forts protecting the city of Mobile. Benton's division (including the Seventh Vermont Veterans) participated in the first movement against Spanish Fort, taking nine days to march some 36 miles. Heavy rains every day, and quicksand-like ground conditions repeatedly mired their wagon trains and contributed to the men's misery. Finally, on March 27, they were near enough to form a battle line, approaching the fort through a ravine in which they lay down. Only after the men had spent a day there under fire did General Canby revise the attack plan. After dark the men constructed earthworks, offering their first real shelter. The Seventh Regiment, which had been providing skirmish companies, then was rotated a few hundred yards to the rear but quickly found itself under artillery bombardment there, and was forced to change positions several times.

Waitsfield's **Daniel McCarty** was wounded at Spanish Fort that same day, and he may have been among those taken prisoner. McCarty's wound likely accounts for his early discharge from service on July 30, 1865.

Soon the regiment found itself advancing against Old Spanish Fort proper (CSA Battery No. 1) as well as Fort McDermett (CSA battery No. 2), both commanding the channel of Mobile Bay. Holbrook provides this description of the siege:

> It was dangerous work. If a man exposed head or hand it became a target for the Confederate sharpshooters, and each battery that was erected had in turn to sustain heavy artillery fire. The wailing of shells was constant, day and night, and bombs from cohorn mortars were continually dropping into the saps and trenches. At night the burning fuses disclosed the courses of the shells, and the men could calculate with tolerable certainty where they would fall; but during the day it required a keen eye to see their approach and agile muscles to avoid them. The fatigue duty on the approaches was especially severe. In some places the ground was rocky, and in others filled with stumps and roots and covered with large logs. The duty became so wearing on the men that the officers sometimes took rifles and went on duty themselves as sharpshooters, while the men rested and slept in bomb-proofs sunk in the earth behind the outer line and covered with layers of logs, sometimes three thick, over which were from one to four feet of earth.
>
> About five o'clock P.M. of the ninth day of the siege, April 4th, a general bombardment of the enemy's works along the entire line was ordered, and the troops formed behind the earthworks in readiness to assault. The Seventh took position nearly in front of Old Spanish Fort and Fort McDermett, where the artillery fire, for two hours, was very heavy.[18]

At the height of the siege, on the evening of April eighth, Federal artillery comprised 96 pieces operating from the far right of the siege lines, with nine more operating from the center right and center left. Throughout the siege, Union gunboats supplemented that land-based artillery.

Confederate defenders began to abandon the works at midnight. "For thirteen days and nights in succession there had not been a moment that the Seventh was not exposed to either musketry or artillery fire, or both."[19]

Although the men did not know it then, the same date which marked their victory (April 9, 1865, a Sunday) also saw the surrender of the Army of Northern Virginia far to the north, at Appomattox Court House. That very day the Seventh Regiment, with the bulk of the XIII Corps, departed for Blakely, Alabama in expectation of assisting federal troops engaged there.

However, as it turned out, they were not needed. They returned to Stark's Landing, where they boarded transports, debarking at Magnolia Point, then marched six miles before camping a mile from Mobile. A day later Benton's entire division, including the Seventh Vermont with **Privates Burns** and **Lathrop** still present, presumably,[20] hurriedly pursued the retreating Confederates, with the Seventh Regiment keeping to the line of the Mobile and Ohio Railroad in hopes of preventing any destruction by the Confederates of valuable railroad property, including machine shops.

Among the incidents of this final push, the Seventh Regiment saved a bridge that had been set on fire by the Confederates. That action is hailed by Holbrook as "…one of the last two hostile meetings of the war…."[21]

The Seventh was on hand for the surrender of CSA General Richard Taylor's army at Citronelle, Alabama, ending hostilities east of the Mississippi River. Subsequently, it was selected as one of the regiments to form the Army of Observation under General Godfrey Weitzel that was stationed just above the mouth of the Rio Grande to watch for political changes within Mexico that might drag the US into a border war. (France was attempting to install Maximilian as emperor in Mexico.) Throughout July and August of 1865, the regiment moved around in that general area, finally going into camp for the fall and winter.

The Seventh Regiment was mustered out at Brownsville, Texas on March 14, 1866. (The last Waitsfield men were gone by then: Private Lathrop had mustered out late in September 1865 and Private Burns, in February 1866, a year and a day from his enlistment.) The men's trip home was broken up by a few days in New Orleans, where some decided to remain permanently. The regiment arrived at Brattleboro on the fifth of April, where a final reception was provided and the veterans received their last pay. Then they headed out to their hometowns and families.

Notes

1. Hira Wood was credited to Granville, Vermont. His inclusion in this work is justified by his birth in Waitsfield. Note the earlier section, "Who is a Waitsfield soldier?"

2. McCarty's surname is misspelled as "McCarthy" in Jones (1909), 89. Jones' history shows Eugene McCarty as unassigned (perhaps in anticipation of an authorized but never raised 18th Vermont Infantry Regiment), as does Peck's *Revised Roster*, 2, 672. But the Ledoux & Associates website shows McCarty was assigned to Co. C, 7th Vermont Regiment.

3. Lathrop is included in this Waitsfield story because he was working here when he married in the village (1890), and he was buried here. In July 2020 the author located Lathrop's burial marker in Irasville Cemetery, although erosion had rendered it nearly illegible.

4. Peabody was mustered in as a Corporal for the three-year term of the regiment on February 12, 1862. He was discharged for disability on October 24, 1862. Daniel McCarty enlisted for one year's service. He was mustered in January 24, 1865 and was mustered out July 30, 1865. Burns also enlisted for one year's service. He was mustered in February 10, 1865 and was mustered out February 9, 1866. (Peck, 1, 295–296).

Peck's 1892 roster cites a Daniel McCarty in two places—with the Seventh Regiment as noted above (1, 297); and as a sailor who substituted for another man and served nine months before deserting on September 30, 1865 (2, 709). Because the service dates given with those two entries are mutually exclusive, they must reference different enlistees. The Ledoux & Associates website also carries information on two Daniel McCartys, one being the Waitsfield native whose army career is noted in this section.

There's another mystery with respect to the Seventh Regiment. The name of Columbus T. Clough appears in the A.G.'s 1864–65 Report as a Waitsfield resident who furnished a substitute in the last year of the war. (That was entirely legal at the time. A substitute received a federally-set bounty of $300, presumably paid by the man he replaced.) Unfortunately, I have not learned that substitute's identity.

5. Holbrook (1891), cited in Benedict page 4. Five years after Benedict's 1886 history was published, Colonel Holbrook obtained Benedict's permission to republish Benedict's chapter on the Seventh Regiment, to be accompanied by his own preface and extended to include the regiment's 1866 experiences. So, although this work primarily draws upon Holbrook's 1891 version, any direct quotations should be understood as Holbrook quoting Benedict's earlier work.

6. *Op. cit.*, 5.

7. *Op. cit.*, 6. Two of the three artillery batteries were the First and Second Vermont Artillery.

8. At the time Carrolton was still an independent town; only later was it incorporated into New Orleans.

9. Holbrook, *op. cit.*, 9. Morale also was low, Holbrook writes, because the men had not been paid since they left Rutland.

10. Those operations preceded by a year U.S. Grant's siege of Vicksburg that extended from May 18, 1863 to July 3, 1863.

11. Bastian, David F. (1995), 60.

12. The Seventh Vermont Infantry belonged at this time to an infantry brigade commanded by Thomas Williams who reported to Benjamin Butler. Holbrook's account of this period (pp. 19–20) is not completely clear, but it seems that some of the stricken men were sailors of Admiral Farragut's flotilla that was supporting Butler's land force.

13. I have no information as to whether Peabody's later discharge for disability was occasioned by an illness suffered during this first failed canal operation.

14. Holbrook, *op. cit.*, 20. As regimental historian, Holbrook wrote after the war that the expedition to Vicksburg failed because it was ordered and conducted against the advice of experienced naval and military [army] men, and because Butler underestimated the enemy's numbers and resources.

15. *Op. cit.*, 45-46. Holbrook writes: "The seeds of disease, which had been planted in the Vicksburg swamps, now developed with fearful rapidity under the hot summer sun and amid the malarial surroundings of the strip of solid ground between swamps, on which the camps were placed.... The sick list of the Seventh increased with alarming rapidity and the death-rate almost kept pace with it."

16. Their term of service was considered by the War Department as expiring June 1. Those who reenlisted were entitled to the usual 30-day furlough, although that was delayed until August. The regiment thenceforth was known as "Seventh Regiment Vermont Volunteers (Veterans)." Its next duty station: New Orleans. While there, the regiment was drilled in street maneuvers and was employed in guard duty.

17. *Op. cit.*, 60.

18. *Op. cit.*, 70–71. Union artillery pieces were being fired at three-minute intervals. Those pieces included two-hundred-pound rifles, thirty-pound rifles, howitzers and mortars.

19. *Op. cit.*, 72.

20. I am assuming that Daniel McCarty either was hospitalized or in a prisoner of war camp at that time.

21. Holbrook *op. cit.*, 74. The regimental history notes that CSA General Richard Taylor alluded to that action as "the last engagement of the Civil War" in his postwar reminiscence, *Destruction and Reconstruction*. But Holbrook corrects Taylor, stating that the engagement at Palmetto Ranch, Texas a month later actually was the last.

8th Vermont Volunteer Infantry Regiment

Waitsfield claims four men who served in the Eighth Vermont Volunteer Infantry Regiment: **Morris Dumas** and **Victor B. Mix** in Company **A**; **Nathaniel Edwin Annis** and **Henry Ephraim Foster** in Company **C**.

Only **Private Annis** and **Captain Foster** were among the original enlistees of the Eighth Regiment. **Privates Dumas** and **Mix**, 27 and 18 respectively, joined the regiment in late December 1863.

Information about the Eighth Vermont Volunteer Regiment's earliest service comes from a regimental history incorporated into Peck's 1892 *Revised Roster* (vol. 1, 299–303).

Organization of the Eighth Regiment; service in Louisiana

The three-year regiment, armed and equipped by the federal government for service under General Benjamin F. Butler, assembled late in January, 1862 at Camp Holbrook in Brattleboro, Vermont.[1]

> The winter was one of unusual severity; the snow was deep, mercury frequently went below zero, the men were housed in cheap sectional houses, and much sickness and discomfort ensued. [S. E. Howard, Captain, Co. H, Eighth Regiment, cited in Peck, 1, 299.]

The First Vermont Light Artillery reported to Camp Holbrook as well, and accompanied the Eighth Infantry Regiment when the Eighth left the camp early in March for New York City. From there the artillery battery and the infantry regiment embarked on two ships, the *Wallace* and the *James Hovey*, headed for Ship Island in the Gulf. The men endured "a rough passage" during their transit from March 9th until April 5th. At Ship Island, drills were the regiment's main business until U.S. naval forces captured New Orleans in May, when the Eighth Regiment was shipped to that city. "The people of the city were in a state of ugliness and vindictiveness hardly to be expressed," Howard's narrative continues.

In New Orleans, the regiment was quartered at the Mechanics Institute, as described by the Captain of Co. C (the Color Company of the regiment), Waitsfield native **Henry Ephraim Foster**:

> Our quarters are in a large public building called "Mechanics Institute." It affords ample room for both officers and soldiers, and with an abundance of hard bread and meat, good air and water, we flatter ourselves that few regiments are more favored than the Vt. 8th.... The health of Company C has been as good as could have been expected since leaving Camp Holbrook. We exceedingly regret to record the death of one of our number since leaving the snowy hills of Vermont—Alonzo McGaffee of St. Johnsbury, Vt. He was in feeble health at the time of his enlistment, but thinking that a change in climate might prove beneficial, he decided to go south as a soldier. But instead of improving in health he failed constantly from the time we left Camp Holbrook until the 7th inst., when death relieved him from all bodily sufferings. He now sleeps beneath the snow-white sands of Ship Island.[2]

Activities in and around Donaldsonville, Brashear City and Thibodeaux (all in Louisiana) occupied much of the fall and early winter of 1862-1863, and included rebuilding miles of roads and railroads, and constructing two bridges. During that period **Company A** was selected to skirmish at the head of an assault on Confederate rifle pits along Bayou Teche that had disabled the federal gunboat *Calhoun* by forcing it aground. The Eighth's involvement saved the *Calhoun*. There were 91 Confederate casualties in that action of January 14, 1863, including 57 prisoners taken; more than 200 arms were captured.

Highlights of the regiment's service following the occupation of New Orleans in May 1862 were its numerous skirmishes in villages and towns along various Louisiana bayous, with eight engagements spanning June 1862 through June 1863, including three assaults on Port Hudson, Louisiana as part of Ulysses Grant's extended Vicksburg Campaign.[3]

It was at Port Hudson, on May 27, 1863, that **Captain Henry Ephraim Foster** received the severe shell wound that led to his resignation in August. For the rest of the regiment, life after that first Port Hudson assault continued "in trenches with its horrors". There were non-productive reconnaissances and a second "disastrous" assault on Port Hudson (June 14th). Of the latter, S. E. Howard writes:

> The Eighth Vermont led the assaulting column on this occasion...and it

accomplished prodigies of valor, reaching the enemy's breastworks, but the ground over which it passed was strewn with its dead and wounded, and it was obliged to fall back. Its losses in this fruitless affair were twenty-one killed and seventy-five wounded, of whom seven afterwards died of their wounds.[4]

Following the surrender of Port Hudson's garrison on July 9 (five days after the surrender of a Confederate army locked down inside Vicksburg), the Eighth Regiment immediately marched to Donaldsonville, reaching there the next day and fighting again the day after that. The regiment was ordered directly from the battlefield after that engagement, marching to Thibodeaux and making camp there.

In August 1863 a detail was sent to Vermont to recruit men to fill vacancies in the regiment. A second recruiting detail that included a sergeant from each company of the regiment was sent to Vermont a month later.

In September the regiment moved to Algiers, Louisiana, moving from there by sea to Sabine Pass, Texas where it engaged in yet another unsuccessful expedition. By that time, General Nathaniel Banks had replaced General Butler as commander of the force that included Vermont's Eighth Volunteer Infantry.

Re-enlistees receive furloughs

Although their terms would not expire for many months, 321 men of the Eighth Regiment agreed In January 1864 to re-enlist.[5] As a reward for reenlisting, those men left winter camp on April 7th for a thirty-day furlough, arriving in Montpelier on April 16th. Those who did not elect to remain in the service sailed for home on June 6, 1864 and were mustered out at Brattleboro sixteen days later. Privates Mix and Dumas, having joined the regiment just a month before reenlistments of longer-serving men had been solicited, were not eligible for that furlough, of course.

The Eighth moves to the Shenandoah Valley of Virginia

A major change in fortune was soon to come to the so-far not particularly renowned Vermont Eighth Volunteers. On July 5, 1864 the regiment left from Algiers on the steamer *St. Mary* for Fortress Monroe, Virginia. From there it was hurried to Washington to assist in throwing back Confederate forces under CSA General Jubal Early that were impinging on the nation's capital. During July and August, the regiment made a series of marches and maneuvers that often "…were forced and severe."

Under Major General Philip Sheridan the Eighth Regiment fought at

Winchester (*aka* Opequon) where it successfully repelled a Confederate advance, then took a position in front of their opponent's center, stationed on a wooded crest, S. E. Howard writes. The Eight Regiment held its position for some hours, with considerable loss, until it was ordered to charge alongside the Twelfth Connecticut Regiment. As Squire Howard remarked on that September 19th action,

> When Sheridan's dispatch was published saying that Early had been sent 'whirling up the valley,' the Eighth Vermont and Twelfth Connecticut felt that they had borne no small part in producing the result.[6]

Before that victory, however, the Eighth Vermont men had been exposed to a horrific sight as they moved to the front through a narrow ravine. James Michael LaMonda, in a Norwich University honors thesis on Vermonters in the Shenandoah Valley, quotes Captain Howard on what they saw there:

> In this defile was established a hospital; and as the regiment passed, we saw the surgeons taking out and examining the bright, keen knives; and on a table was a victim undergoing amputation of the leg, while other mangled men, and pools of blood, showed too plainly what was going on at the front…I believe that it was a mistake, locating the hospital where the men must see these sights before going into action.[7]

The Eighth was party to the Union success at Fisher's Hill (September 22) and in a pursuit that night near Woodstock, the regiment captured 250 prisoners. The Army of the Shenandoah (Sheridan's command) followed Early's shrinking army south on the Valley Turnpike (now Route 11) to Harrisonburg, then turned back north, camping at Cedar Creek.

On October 19, 1864 the regiment's sacrifice at Cedar Creek set the stage for Union victory. During Sheridan's Valley campaign, Colonel Joseph Thoburn commanded a division in the Army of West Virginia.[8] In an early morning surprise attack, General Early's Confederates attacked Thoburn's division, sending them reeling north. Thoburn was mortally wounded while trying to rally his men.

Captain Howard describes the fighting of the Eighth Vermont Regiment at Cedar Creek in these words:

> Our line was not fairly formed in the fringe of timber before we were in most desperate fighting. It was so dark the enemy could hardly be seen, but the timber was ablaze with the flash of his muskets, the air full of bullets, and above all rose the din of his victorious yells. The Eight Vermont held the left of the brigade and was much more exposed than any other troops.

Charge after charge of the enemy was repulsed. The colors of the regiment were taken away from us three times and as often re-taken....There were hand to hand conflicts, "bayonets dripped blood and skulls were broken by clubbed muskets," but the little band held on until, almost exterminated, it fell back, still showing its teeth and still fighting. During the day the brigade lost more than one third of its fighting men, the greater part of them on this "horrible hill of sacrifice."[9]

There are two monuments to the Eighth Regiment on the Cedar Creek battlefield. The older memorial marks the spot where the regiment advanced to meet the enemy in the woods in pre-dawn darkness, losing before sunrise 110 men killed and wounded out of the 148 men engaged, and 13 of the 16 commissioned officers with them. A more recent memorial was dedicated on the sesquicentennial anniversary of the Battle of Cedar Creek.

Over the next two months, even while what was left of the Eighth Regiment was in winter camp, the regiment engaged in several skirmishes, some with CSA General John Mosby's formidable cavalry raiders.

The regiment's final assignment

The day after President Abraham Lincoln was assassinated, the Eighth Regiment was ordered from its winter camp at Summit Point, Virginia to Washington, where it was posted outside the capital city to prevent the escape of John Wilkes Booth, the President's suspected assassin.[10]

The regiment returned briefly to Summit Point before being posted again to Washington. There it remained until the Grand Review in May, finally being mustered out of service on June 28, 1865. Privates **Victor Mix** and **Morris Dumas,** the only Waitsfield men left in the regiment, departed then.

Notes

1. The camp was named for then-Governor Frederick Holbrook. The Governor's son William became Colonel of the Seventh Vermont Regiment, and wrote a regimental history cited extensively in the Seventh's section of this work.

2. H. E. Foster to the Editor of *The Caledonian* (May 29, 1862), cited on the Ledoux & Associates website (retrieved July 9, 2020).

3. The Vicksburg Campaign culminated with the surrenders of Vicksburg itself (July 4, 1863) and Port Hudson five days later.

4. Howard, cited in Peck's *Revised Roster* (1892), 1, 301.

5. No Waitsfield men would have been among those re-enlistees, as Dumas and Mix's December 1863 enlistments made them ineligible for that option, and Annis and Foster already had departed. Captain Foster had resigned in August as a consequence of his May wound. Annis had been mustered out five months into his enlistment (July 16, 1862), although I have not found the reason.

6. Howard, cited in Peck (1892), 1, 302.

7. Howard, cited in LaMonda, 78.

8. That field army, which included the Eighth Vermont Volunteer Infantry Regiment, functioned as a corps in Sheridan's Army of the Shenandoah.

9. Howard, cited in Peck (1892), 1, 302. Howard does not identify the author of the material he quotes in this passage.

10. Booth escaped, of course. He was killed on the Garnett farm in Port Royal, Virginia on April 26, 1865 by a Union soldier who shot him as he emerged from a barn which pursuing soldiers had set afire after Booth refused their command to surrender.

9th Vermont Volunteer Infantry Regiment

Eleven men from the Town of Waitsfield enrolled in **Company I** ("eye") of the Ninth Vermont Volunteer Infantry Regiment. Early in its career, the Ninth Vermont Infantry acquired the unwelcome distinction of being the only Vermont unit captured whole. The men of the Ninth were captured at Harpers Ferry on September 13, 1862 after they had fled there to avoid military defeat and possibly even annihilation by a Confederate army that was sweeping all before it in the Shenandoah Valley. The Ninth's leaders had expected to be protected by Miles' troops in the Harpers Ferry garrison, but as an officer later wrote, "...by treachery or incompetency, [they were] surrendered into the hands of the rebels."[1] The Ninth became part of more than 12,000 men captured when the garrison was taken.

The men became parolees. A biography of George J. Stannard, commander of the Ninth Regiment at that time, gives this picture of the demoralized prisoners:

> Tuesday, September 16, found the 9th Vermont, now paroled prisoners, marching down to the pontoon bridge that would lead them through Maryland to Annapolis, via Frederick and Baltimore. Virginia planters stood by the bridge looking for Negro slaves who might be trying to escape with the Yankees... A telegram was sent to Washington as the men passed through Frederick that stated, "They are ordered to encamp near the Monocacy Bridge about three miles from the town. They... are greatly chagrined at the surrender of Harper's Ferry, which they consider entirely unnecessary and do not hesitate to charge treachery....All agree that the position could have been held against any force that the enemy could bring against it, and while in our hands they could not have crossed the river with any considerable force."[2]

They marched for five days from Harpers Ferry to Annapolis (a distance of some 100 miles). From Annapolis Valentine Barney, Captain of

Company A of the Ninth Regiment, wrote a letter home on September 22nd that began with a description of his company's march from Harpers Ferry; that letter includes details of the battle and ultimate surrender.[3]

> Dear Wife,
> I arrived here last eve with my co after a fatiguing march we came over 20 miles yesterday and when we got here I had but 25 men in the co and I left Hap Ferry with 96. I found the rest of them here for as they fell out they were put on board the cars and got here before us We have had a very hard march and had I not been very tough I could not have stood it but I am here safe and feel finely this morning... I found 3 of my men here who were left at Winchester...the rest are there yet and I have heard nothing from them yet, but I hope soon to see one of my Lieuts here before long for I am kept so clost to my company. It is thought that we were sold at H. Ferry and I am inclined to the same opinion, but what they will do with us I cant tell Some say we are to be sent west to fight the Indians and others that we are to be Sent to our own State but what to believe I cant decide I am perfectly reconciled to any thing that comes and if we are ordered to Cape Horn I am willing to obey though I would much prefer to be exchanged and fight the Rebels for a while. I will give you a little account of the part I took in the engagement at H. Ferry Well[,] after the Rebels had driven our forces from Maryland Hights and were planting Batteries there as well as on Loudon Hights I was at about noon of Sunday ordered out with my Co to Reinforce the Pickets as there was fear of their being driven in So off we started and while on the way out the Rebs opened fire on our camp from 4 different points our Batteries returning the fire After I arrived at my post I stationed a part of my men in the edge of the woods to watch the movements of the Enemy and their pickets could be seen just across a field and near enough so our boys might have Shot some of them but the orders were not to fire but to keep watch of the moves and report often I kept the rest in the rear of the woods as a reserve. this was hardly done when a Battery opened fire on us from the opposite woods and our guns opened on them but as they did not elevate their pieces enough we were exposed to both fires I changed our position quite often and thereby kept out of range of their Shells though many came very near to us but lucky for us none were hit at about 5 oc. a column of Rebels advanced on our left and as we were in danger of being cut off from camp we fell back to a cross roads and remained there till the fight was over the next morning at dark the canonading ceased, and all night it was no very pleasant Job to be around Stationing men at different points as often to be abandoned by them by some appearance of rebel scirmishers at day light we got orders to return to camp but after about ½ of our men had gone in with a Lieut the order was countermanded and I remained very soon the ball opened and with 7

Rebel Batteries and ours together the Shells flew pretty thick and kept up a continual roar till about 9 oc when after the Ohio pickets abandoned their posts and the Rebel Scirmishers advanced to our rear and fired on us I then had my men fall back towards camp to keep from being flanked but in a good line well spread we had not gone far when the white flag was raised to my great Surprise and cheer after cheer went up from the rebels. we went into camp and though not many were killed it was an awful sight to see a few dead who were struck by shells and lay in the ditch....Some of the rebel Batteries continued Shelling us for some time after the flag was raised as they could not see it for smoke. I never had such feelings come over me as at that time and I could hardly suppress the tears. I expected to have to go to Richmond after giving up my side arms and many threw away their revolvers and swords, and many of the boys broke their guns over Stumps but happy for us the terms of Surrender were to parole all and respect private property.

From Annapolis the paroled men of the Ninth took a boat to Baltimore and, finally, a train to Chicago, arriving at Camp Tyler on the 28th of September. Camp Tyler lay a quarter mile from Camp Douglas, a prison camp used for Confederates captured by Union forces. Tyler was considerably smaller than its neighbor, "consisting primarily of horse stalls." The Ninth, including ten men from Waitsfield,[4] was housed in the horse stalls until it moved into winter quarters at Camp Douglas on the first of November.[5]

Regarding the latter place of confinement, George Mahary writes, "Camp Douglas was a hellhole. Everyone recognized it, but officials in Washington refused to do anything about it."[6]

An officer charged with prisoners' care had written to the Union Quartermaster General back in July about conditions there:

> Camp Douglas is located on low, swamp ground without any possibility of drainage. . . . The sinks [pits that served as open sewers] which have been dug and dug again are overflowing and when the hot weather sets in there must be much sickness. The barracks are too much crowded for health and some changes must be made to bring about a good sanitary state of things.[7]

Quartermaster General Meigs rejected that request for improvements.

Waiting for an exchange

At this still-early period of the war, prisoners of war were exchanged for counterparts in the enemy's ranks; *i.e.*, a CSA Corporal taken prisoner by a federal force could be exchanged for a captured Union Corporal, while a Private could be exchanged for a Private, *etc.*

The officers and men of the Ninth Regiment being held at Camp Douglas were eager to be exchanged. Finally, a date was scheduled: An exchange was to occur on January 10, 1863. But a large influx of Confederate prisoners was expected to arrive on January 26th following battles at Arkansas Post, Arkansas and Murfreesboro, Tennessee [*aka* the Stones River battle], so the Ninth Regiment was held another four months at Camp Douglas to serve as their guards.[8]

The Ninth Regiment was still at Camp Douglas when (in March 1863) its Colonel, George J. Stannard from St. Albans, was called away. He had been appointed a brigadier general, and was to lead the Second Vermont Brigade.[9]

In April 1863 detachments from the Ninth Vermont accompanied batches of Confederate prisoners to City Point, Virginia where they handed them over to Confederate officers designated to accept them.[10]

Soon after, the exchanged Ninth Infantry Regiment was assigned to a reserve brigade of the VII Corps, serving in the Department of Virginia. A jurisdictional change in federal military departments subsequently assigned the regiment to the Department of Virginia and North Carolina (based in Yorktown, Virginia from July '63; Beaufort, North Carolina from October '63; and New Berne, North Carolina from July '64).

Not until September 1864 was the Ninth Vermont Volunteer Infantry given a place in a corps which readers may recognize as part of the rapidly-enlarging federal army: The regiment joined the Second Brigade, Second Division of the XVIII Corps, which soon after was merged into the Second Brigade, Third Division, XXIV Corps.[11]

From a prisoner of war camp in Illinois, to coastal North Carolina and eventually to the gates of Richmond, Virginia, the Ninth Vermont became one of the most traveled regiments in the Union army, historian Donald Wickman has written.[12]

Company I

Ten Waitsfield men mustered into **Co. I** on July 9, 1862: **Alexander Baird, Oliver C. Campbell, Isaac H. Elliott, Herman Ralph French, William H. H. Greenslit, George Burton Hall, Philip Hoffman, John H. Quigley, Daniel Russ**[13] and **Thomas Sanders. Alba B. Durkee** joined them in January 1864.

The first to die among this Waitsfield group was **Private Greenslit**, who took his own life August 21, 1862 while the Ninth Regiment was camped just north of Winchester, Virginia.[14] (The regiment had arrived there July nineteenth.) Col. Stannard's regiment was ordered to entrench and hold that city against a return of CSA General Thomas Jonathon Jackson—widely known as "Stonewall" Jackson—whose force had routed Banks' federal army from the area only three months earlier.

Company I and the other companies of the Ninth Regiment were engaged throughout August 1862 in constructing a bastioned fort, armed with heavy guns. Baker's account in Peck's (1892) *Revised Roster* describes the men's earliest encounter with arduous duty in a hostile civilian environment:

> The men soon became drilled to hard service, and the frequent fights with bushwhackers at night, and the skirmishing often, and sometimes daily, with small bodies of irregular rebels who infested the region, developed the men rapidly into veteran soldiers.[15]

Details from the service records of the other Co. I members appear below

Isaac H. Elliott was taken prisoner at Winchester, Virginia on September 3, 1862, and was held for 20 days. Elliott was discharged soon after (September 25th) "by reason of ill health."[16]

Oliver C. Campbell had been commissioned as a Second Lieutenant a week before the regiment was formed. He served in that capacity with Co. I until July 6, 1863 when he was transferred to the Veterans Reserve Corps (VRC).[17] The L&A website notes that Campbell served in Rutland and in Concord, New Hampshire and Boston, all while with the VRC, presumably. He resigned the service November 15, 1865.

George Burton Hall stayed with the company until January 15, 1863 when he was discharged so that he might enter the 17th United States Infantry ("the regulars"). The transfer was effective that same day. Hall was with the 17th U.S. Infantry until discharged on June 1, 1863. Nevertheless, he wasn't finished with a military career. Nine months later, he joined Vermont's Third Light Artillery. (Hall's service record continues with sections on those units later in this work.)

A number of Waitsfield men who remained in the company changed ranks.

Philip Hoffman was promoted to Corporal (January 15, 1863), then to Sergeant (July 1, 1864).

John H. Quigley, born in Ireland, was credited to Waitsfield. He was mustered in as a Sergeant and at the beginning of 1863 was promoted to 1st Sergeant. However, he served as the company's 1st Sergeant only until June of that year when he was reduced in rank.

Thomas Sanders, the other Ireland-born member of I Company, was mustered in as a Corporal although he, too, later was reduced in rank.

Alexander Baird was promoted from Private to Corporal in March 1865.

Quite late in **Herman Ralph French**'s service (February 4, 1865) he was promoted away from Co. I to Hospital Steward, a regimental non-commissioned staff position. French's final four months of service were served in that capacity.

Daniel Russ, who had been promoted to Sergeant (March 26, 1864) and then to First Sergeant (March 16, 1865), was discharged June 8, 1865, five days prior to the general mustering-out of the regiment. That earlier discharge date, and the service record's use of "discharged" rather than "mustered out," may indicate Russ was suffering from an illness.

Alba B. Durkee, age 21, enlisted from Waitsfield although he had been born in Fayston, suggesting that he was living in the Town when he enlisted. He joined Co. I in January of 1864. Private Durkee died of typhoid fever nine months later in an army hospital at New Berne, North Carolina.[18] His body lies in the New Berne National Cemetery. There is a cenotaph in the North Fayston Cemetery.

Ninth Regiment Waitsfield men in combat, April 1863–June 1865

The history of the Ninth Regiment as written by First Lieutenant Joel C. Baker continues through the re-enlistment of some members (though none from Waitsfield) until the final disbanding of the regiment, reduced by then to battalion-size, in December 1865. Our account, however, references only that portion of Baker's history which refers to actions while there were any men from the Town still present. Confederate General James Longstreet's forces laid siege to Suffolk, Virginia in April 1863. Baker writes:

> The skirmishing was almost constant for several weeks, and there was seldom an hour when the rattle of musketry and the roar of artillery was not heard in all parts of the besieged camps, and the Ninth regiment had its full share of the hard work, and detachments of it did brilliant service in encounters with the enemy, especially in the capture of Battery Huger, at Hill's Point, the reconnaissance on the Edenton Road, and the pursuit to the Blackwater.

When Longstreet abandoned that siege in June,[18] the Ninth moved to Yorktown where it remained until October, "languishing with all kinds of miasmatic diseases and writing dismal letters," in Baker's words. Interventions by Vermont's Governor and one of its U.S. Senators resulted in a War Department order to move the regiment to a healthier environment. On October 24th, the Ninth embarked with a part of a NYS regiment for Morehead City, North Carolina. Reaching that destination after "a tempestuous voyage," the men were directed to take possession of Newport Barracks.

For the next several months the Ninth was engaged in guarding a railroad from Morehead City to Croatan. There were few Confederate detachments in the area although bushwhackers, roving guerrilla bands of four to ten men, often were encountered.

On January 27, 1864 the regiment, now closer to a healthier status and enlarged by new recruits, made a forced march of thirty miles overnight which resulted in the capture of a garrison of Confederate cavalry at Young's Cross Roads, North Carolina. It's likely Alba Durkee had arrived in a crowd of 350 men newly-recruited from Vermont that boosted the regiment's size to 844.[19]

Very soon after, George Pickett (one of Longstreet's division commanders) sent a full brigade of infantry, supplemented by cavalry and artillery, to capture the Ninth Regiment in its camp at Newport Barracks. After the Confederates drove away Companies **B** and **H** of the Ninth which had been posted as outliers, "The fight became general and lasted until dark, the Ninth being pressed back by mere force of numbers... At night the Yankee boys had been crowded back to the Newport river, and, to prevent annihilation or capture, passed over the railroad and highway bridges and set them on fire, and made a night march to Beaufort unmolested and unpursued."[20]

Encounters with Confederate forces began to occur more frequently, Baker continues. Outposts were re-established and the Newport Barracks position was strengthened. Details from the Ninth captured a fishing expedition engaged in gathering food for the CSA Commissary and seized three boats and 500 pounds of sea trout. Two days later another detail captured 18 men from the Seventh North Carolina Cavalry. Because our source doesn't identify the make-up of those details, we don't know if any Waitsfield men were involved.

Subsequent actions included a foray to Jacksonville on the New River, North Carolina that involved a march of 80 miles over four days with several skirmishes on the way.[21]

Mid-September 1864 found the Ninth Vermont Infantry in Petersburg, Virginia, assigned to the XVIII Corps commanded by Major General E. O. C. Ord. On September 29 the Ninth fought at Chapin's Farm, Virginia on the north side of the James River. The Ninth was sent unaided to take Battery Morris at Fort Harrison; it made a charge that carried the works, writes Baker, and drove off rebel defenders of that battery.

One more battle involving the Ninth (a federal loss on October 27 at Fair Oaks, Virginia) was deemed important enough to be inscribed later on the regiment's colors. Immediately afterwards the Ninth was sent to New York State in expectation that riots might break out during the upcoming presidential election. While most companies of the regiment went to New York City, one company was sent to Troy, New York. Those Waitsfield men still with the regiment certainly went to one or the other of the two cities.

The Ninth's service draws to a close

Upon their return to the trenches around Petersburg, men of the Ninth settled into the Union's winter siege. "As the time drew near for the collapse of the giant rebellion," Baker writes, "both sides prepared for the struggle."[23]

Baird, French, Hoffman, Quigley, Russ and **Sanders** presumably were present in the trenches of Petersburg right through to the fall of Richmond.

The Ninth Vermont is cited on the roster of General Edward O. C. Ord's XVIII Corps that broke through the Confederate inner defense line on April 2, 1865. Marching towards Richmond, Ord's men came in sight of other Union troops on a converging road. For the next mile and more they raced, much of the time at the "double quick step," vying to be the first to enter the burning city.[24]

The Ninth Vermont Infantry Regiment subsequently constituted part of a Provost Guard that remained in Richmond for two weeks after the surrender of that city. The regiment's former colonel (E. H. Ripley, now a breveted brigadier general}, continued in charge of federal troops in the former Confederate capital for a much longer time.[25]

On June 13 the five Waitsfield men still with the Ninth (the men named just above minus Russ, who had been discharged five days before) were mustered out and headed home.

Notes

1. First Lieutenant Joel C. Baker, cited in Peck (1879), 1, 339.

2. Official Records, series 2, vol. 4, 527-528, cited in Mahary (2001), 104-105.

3. Valentine G. Barney to wife Maria, cited in Marshall, ed. (1999), 107-108. Original spelling and punctuation are preserved with the exception of my insertion of one comma to clarify Barney's meaning.

4. The eleventh Waitsfield man in the Ninth Regiment, Alba Durkee, was not with the 10 taken prisoner at Harpers Ferry as he did not join the regiment until December 1864.

5. Benedict (1886), 209, cited in Mahary (2001), 106.

6. Mahary (2001), 107.

7. Official Records, series 2, vol. 4, p. 110, cited in Mahary (2001), 107.

8. Mahary, op. cit., 111.

9. The 12th, 13th, 14th, 15th and 16th Vermont Volunteer Infantry Regiments constituted the Second Vermont Brigade. There were Waitsfield soldiers in all those regiments except the Sixteenth Regiment.

10. Those officers represented the Confederate Commissary of Prisoners. That system of exchanges was ended later in the war by Ulysses Grant.

11. Dyer (1959), I, 233.

12. Wickman's account of the Ninth Vermont (1862-1865) is cited in The Camp Griffin Gazette (XXI, 7), September 2014, 3.

13. Russ' enlistment was credited to Moretown, Vermont. But because he had been born in Waitsfield, he is included here as a Waitsfield soldier.

14. Although there is a cenotaph in the Warren Cemetery marking the death of Private Greenslit at age 22, his actual place of burial is unknown—perhaps somewhere near the regiment's former campground in Winchester?

15. Baker, in Peck (1892), 339.

16. Jones (1909), 86. Note that Jones spells Elliott's surname "Elliot". It appears that Jones' record of Elliott's capture and discharge contains some errors as no combination of capture and discharge dates yields a 20-day interval.

17. The city's name now is spelled "New Bern".

18. General Robert E. Lee ordered Longstreet to return with his men to the Army of Northern Virginia, as he was preparing for an invasion of Pennsylvania.

19. Baker, in Peck, 1, 340.

20. Ibid.

21. Op. cit., 341.

22. The colors of the Ninth Vermont Infantry carry these names: Harpers Ferry; Newport Barracks; Chapin's Farm; Fair Oaks; Fall of Richmond.

23. Baker, in Peck, 1, 342.

24. In August 2022 I stood at the intersection of Osborne Turnpike and New Market Road where those forces converged. Richmond's mayor had driven out to that spot to surrender his city. He implored Union generals to enter Richmond and restore order as his 65-man police force was unable to contain looting by drunken mobs. This intersection now is occupied by a 7-11 convenience store.

25. Baker, op. cit.

10th Vermont Volunteer Infantry Regiment

Five Waitsfield men served in the Tenth Vermont Volunteer Infantry Regiment, all in **Company B**: **Chester Stephen Dana, Edwin Harvey Dana, Daniel T. Foster, Hiram Andrew Luce** and **Willard M. Thayer.**

All five were born in Waitsfield, although Thayer and the two Dana recruits were living outside the town at the time they enlisted (Thayer in Warren, Chester Dana in Fayston, and Edwin H. Dana in Waterbury).

The then-Governor, Frederick Holbrook, had selected Daniel Foster to head a recruiting office in Waitsfield for the 10th Vermont Volunteer Infantry Regiment. In a press statement referencing President Lincoln's call for an additional 300,000 men, the Governor announced his appointment of Foster and other recruiting officers across Vermont, and noted: "The 9th Regiment now in camp in this State, will form part of our quota," as well as two new regiments being raised. The Governor's appeal for enlistees featured current pay rates and a state bounty.[1]

The Tenth Vermont was considered a "sister regiment" to the Eleventh Vermont as those two infantry regiments were raised concurrently in different parts of the state. Military service commenced for four of the five Waitsfield men on September 1, 1862 when the 10th Regiment was mustered into the service of the United States. Just five days after its mustering-in, the Tenth Vermont Volunteer Infantry Regiment left Brattleboro and two days after that, arrived in Washington. The regiment went into camp the next day at Camp Chase near Arlington Heights, Virginia. Its first assignment was to guard fords on the Potomac River. The ten companies of the Tenth were dispersed along the Maryland side of the river from Muddy Branch to Edward's Ferry, with **Company B** stationed at Conrad's Ferry.

That work occupied the regiment until mid-October, when the various companies were brought back together in a camp at Seneca Creek, a marshy spot in the Poolesville, Maryland area that proved to be "a camp of fever and death," in the words of the Tenth's chaplain and historian, the Reverend Dr. Edwin M. Haynes.[2]

The regiment remained in the Poolesville camp for nine months, performing picket and guard duties. All that time, it had no encounters with the enemy, Dr. Haynes reports. During that period **Hiram Luce** died of (an unspecified) disease on April 22, 1863 in Armory Square Hospital in Washington, D.C., becoming the first casualty among the Waitsfield men of the Tenth Vermont Infantry.[3]

On June 22nd the Tenth Vermont was ordered "to march at once" to Harpers Ferry, West Virginia where it was incorporated into the Army of the Potomac.[4]

The regiment seemingly took no part in the October 1863 Bristoe Campaign (characterized by Dyer as "a campaign of maneuvers" [5]) but in a follow-up to that campaign it joined the First Vermont Brigade in an advance to the line of the Rappahannock River over two days early in November. It fought at Brandy Station, Virginia on November eighth.

The Brandy Station engagement was a preliminary to the Mine Run Campaign, the last of that year.

General Meade's Mine Run Campaign

The regiment's first engagement that rose to the dignity of a battle, in the words of regimental historian Haynes, occurred during that last Union campaign of 1863, at Locust Grove (*aka* Orange Grove), Virginia.[6] There, on November 27, 1863, the regiment engaged with Confederates holding a position on the crest of a hill. Advancing "in gallant style," the men took that hill, behaving "with determined bravery" despite never before having been under fire.[7]

Until that engagement, the Waitsfield youth were unbloodied. However, in that engagement of November 27 **Willard M. Thayer** was mortally wounded. Unlike most "mortally wounded" men who died within hours or days after a battle, Thayer lingered 10 months, presumably hospitalized the whole time, before he succumbed to his wound in September of the following year.[8]

The fifth Waitsfield enlistee, **Edwin Dana**, was mustered in on New Year's Eve, 1863.

Fighting in 1864 and 1865

The Army of the Potomac took up winter quarters in and around Brandy Station. Dyer records the 10th Vermont Infantry as having participated in two days of demonstrations on the Rapidan River early in February 1864, perhaps in skirmishes at Culpeper Ford.⁹

When Ulysses Grant arrived at Brandy Station in March 1864, now as Lieutenant General and general-in-chief of all Union armies, he reorganized the five corps there into three, one of which—the VI Corps—was headed by John Sedgwick. The VI Corps already included the First, or "Old," Vermont Brigade (the Second through the Sixth Vermont Regiments) as part of Getty's Division. One division from the now-disbanded Third Corps was assigned to the VI Corps: That division (Rickett's) included a brigade of which the 10th Vermont Regiment was part. Thus, when Grant's Overland Campaign began, the 10th Vermont Infantry was serving in the same corps, albeit not in the same division, as the First Vermont Brigade.¹⁰

The campaign included skirmishes, raids, cavalry engagements and multiple extraordinarily brutal encounters over the next five weeks as the Army of the Potomac advanced from the Rapidan River to the James River. The campaign's first battle came almost immediately, in a part of Virginia denoted on maps as "the wilderness."

That battle commenced May 5 with Union cavalry units including the First (and only) Vermont Cavalry Regiment engaged in combat at Craig's Meeting House and Todd's Tavern. Howard Coffin writes: "Early that morning, as the cavalry moved into action, the men of the 10th Vermont Regiment had been roused from sleep along the south bank of the Rapidan [River] at Germanna Ford."¹¹

Coffin's account continues with this statement by the Tenth Regiment's surgeon: "Our division remained at and near the ford, where we had crossed, until General Burnside, with the Ninth Corps, arriving from Warrenton, appeared on the other side of the river. The division was then ordered to move by the Germanna Plank Road, to the old Wilderness Tavern."¹²

Meanwhile, the First Vermont Brigade was likewise moving toward the Wilderness Tavern, as part of Getty's Second Division. The division remained there, awaiting orders. When those came, around noon, Getty moved his division to a position south of the Tavern where the Orange Plank Road and the Brock Road met. General Meade had ordered Getty to hold that crossroads "at all hazards" until Hancock's ll Corps could arrive.¹³

Coffin describes the fearful toll among men of the Old Brigade who fought all day to maintain that crucial Wilderness position. Among the losses Coffin cites were three Mad River Valley men, all shot in the head.¹⁴

Coffin writes that the Vermonters held the crucial crossroads position all day until withdrawn for a rest in the woods, with Hancock's corps coming to their relief.

Yet the fight for the crossroads had been but one violent part of a far larger battle.... [North of the crossroads position] the battle seesawed along the Orange Turnpike. The 10th Vermont, in Rickett's Sixth Corps Division, had marched down from the Rapidan in the morning and was positioned near Wilderness Tavern, away from the action. In the afternoon, the regiment was marched west along the turnpike and quickly came under artillery fire.... Soon the 10th was moved into woods on the south side of the turnpike, to support a part of Sedgwick's line." [15]

Lemuel Abbott from Barre, a Second Lieutenant in the Tenth Regiment at the time, describes an incident that occurred during that march under artillery fire before the regiment reached the relative safety of the woods:

> Before Capt. H. R. Steele had hardly finished dressing his company [Co. K] after forming line, a shell...exploded in the ranks of Co K, killing a private and wounding others. The shell had burst actually inside the man completely disemboweling and throwing him high in the air in a rapidly whirling motion above our heads with arms and legs extended until his body fell heavily to the ground with a sickening thud... We were covered with blood, fine pieces of flesh, entrails, etc., which makes me cringe and shudder whenever I think of it. The concussion badly stunned me. I was whirled about in the air like a feather, thrown to the ground on my hands and knees—or at least was in that position with my head from the enemy when I became fully conscious—face cut with flying gravel or something else, eyes, mouth and ears filled with dirt, and was feeling nauseated from the shakeup.[16]

The Tenth Regiment, arrayed in line of battle, maintained its position through the night of May 5/6. The next day the regiment was moved further into the woods and again formed a line of battle. There they came under desultory artillery fire until mid-afternoon. Hours later Colonel William W. Henry ordered the 10th to *run* [move even faster than at a double-quick pace] deeper into the woods, to reach a position behind where the firing had come from. They were halted there and ordered to give a "war cry" repeatedly, which had the effect of stopping the enemy's advance. "With the coming of darkness, the battle in the northern section of the Wilderness died away."[17]

The Battle of the Wilderness had produced 1,420 Vermont casualties.[18]

In the darkness of the night of May 7 the VI Corps marched east, toward Chancellorsville (site of a Union defeat one year earlier) before turning south. The Old Brigade brought up the rear of the Corps' line of march, with the 10th Vermont somewhere ahead of it in the column. The Reverend

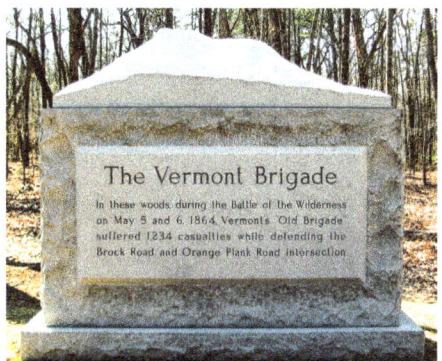 

Fig. 13. Obverse and reverse of "The Vermont Brigade" monument at the crossing of the Orange Plank Road and the Brock Road, the Wilderness battlefield in Virginia

Photo credit: Gail Blake

Dr. Edwin M. Haynes, Chaplain of the Tenth Regiment, describes the regiment's experience:

> In crossing the battlefield of Chancellorsville we saw many signs of the desperate conflict that raged there just a year before... The field was a sepulcher, silent, and full of dead men's bones. It seemed worse even than the one we had just left... Here was all the debris of battle, white and moldy; splintered gun carriages, torn saddles, broken muskets, battered canteens, shriveled cartridge boxes and knapsacks, blankets stripped into shreds and hanging upon the bushes, skeletons of horses and men scattered about the field and mingling in the common dust... Scores of human skulls were kicked over and went rolling away from the path we were treading to other scenes of carnage.[19]

The Tenth Vermont passed through Chancellorsville and came onto the field at Spotsylvania mid-afternoon of May eighth. Meade's Army of the Potomac and Lee's Army of Northern Virginia each had driven hard to be first, but Lee's men won that race, "just barely," according to Howard Coffin. As Union cavalry were driven away (to entrench about a mile northwest of Spotsylvania village), infantry of the two armies dug in. The 10th was the first Vermont infantry unit on the field, although it was held in reserve with the rest of Rickett's division. Accordingly, the Tenth Regiment incurred no casualties at the Bloody Angle fighting at Spotsylvania Court House. Chaplain Haynes, who toured that area the next day, observed:

> The mutual carnage was frightful. Here it may be said without exaggeration that the dead lay in heaps and the soil was miry with blood. The slain

were piled upon each other—packed up so as to form defences with a mass of quivering flesh.[20]

Union losses at the Bloody Angle salient were estimated after the war as 8,500.[21]

Private Oscar Wait(e) of Sheldon left a detailed first-person account of 10th Regiment activities during this period. Waite recounted the Tenth's movement to Cold Harbor, Virginia after thirteen days at Spotsylvania, followed immediately by fighting on the North Anna River and beyond. Fighting around Cold Harbor itself lasted twelve days.[22]

Edwin Harvey Dana was grievously wounded June 1, 1864 by a gunshot to the right leg, in the first day's battle at Cold Harbor. It seems likely Dana was hospitalized (perhaps in a division hospital?) for many months before being transported to Vermont where he became a patient at the Sloan General [Military] Hospital in Montpelier.[23]

Coffin's 2002 history includes Oscar Waite's account of how the particularly disastrous third day at Cold Harbor had opened for other soldiers of the Tenth Vermont:

> At half past three this morning [Friday, June 3, 1864] the orderly sergeants quietly told the men to fall in for roll call; the names were called and the answers given in tones not louder than ordinary conversation, and the men dismissed for breakfast of pork, hardtack and coffee, made over tiny fires in some sheltered ravine. Then the companies were formed into regiments; from these came brigades; and from the brigades divisions... Some of the men were just leaning on their guns; others quietly pinned tags to the coats, with the names and addresses of friends at home: but at the same time, all were watching a gray streak of light creeping along the horizon, and were listening for that bugle call which, whatever its military significance, means to us boys, "More childless parents; more weeping maidens; widows and orphans."[24]

A ten-minute Union artillery barrage had opened the Union's infantry assault.

The VI Corps, led by Rickett's division, went into action with the first wave of that assault. Its fighting commenced at 4:40 A.M. and lasted just minutes. Lemuel Abbott, now a First Lieutenant in Co. G of the Tenth Regiment, remembered it this way: "We never even reached the enemy's works. We advanced under a murderous fire in our front from the enemy's artillery [and] sharpshooters, and when in range of its main line of battle... were simply slaughtered."[25]

Map 2. Red arrow added to this National Park Service map points to the location of the 10th Vermont Volunteer Infantry Regiment troops on the Cold Harbor, Virginia battlefield, June 3, 1864

Three advances by Union infantry were made before 8 A.M. that day; all were brutally repulsed. When Ulysses Grant wrote his memoirs in the final weeks of his life, he wrote of Cold Harbor, "I have always regretted that the last assault at Cold Harbor was ever made.... [N]o advantage whatever was gained to compensate for the heavy loss we sustained."

A Confederate brigadier general there that day wrote: "I had seen the dreadful carnage in front of Marye's Hill at Fredericksburg, and on the old railroad-cut which Jackson held at the Second Manassas, but I had seen nothing to exceed this. It was not war, it was murder."[26]

After Cold Harbor, there were only two of the five Waitsfield enlistees remaining with the Tenth Vermont Volunteer Infantry Regiment: **Chester Dana** and **Daniel Foster.**

The 10th Regiment, with the rest of the VI Corps, joined in the earliest assaults on Petersburg before settling into a siege of that city. For a time, the regiment was ordered to Bermuda Hundred to assist the Army of the James under Benjamin Butler, but that assignment was a brief one. The Tenth Vermont participated in the Battle of Monocacy, Maryland (helping prevent Jubal Early's invasion of Washington, D.C.) before being sent to Virginia's Shenandoah Valley where the regiment would share in Phil Sheridan's operations. Those included Winchester (where **Daniel Foster**, now serving as a Second Lieutenant, was wounded on September 19th), Fisher's Hill and Cedar Creek.[27]

Sheridan's troops didn't just fight. They conducted a campaign to destroy crops that otherwise would have sustained the Army of Northern Virginia. Food crops and animal forage were their targets, whether in warehouses and barns or standing in fields.

A long-after-the-war account by a member of the 10th Regiment makes that damage clear. "Everything in the shape of barns, grain, forage, or mills was destroyed. Nothing was left south of Strasburg which would be of any use to the rebel army. It was rough on the non-combatant, but Virginia had made her bed, and now she was lying in it… We all considered Early so thoroughly whipped, demoralized, and destitute of artillery that there was little prospect of our ever being called upon to face his followers again." [28]

The Tenth regiment remained in the Shenandoah Valley near Cedar Creek until December fifth, then was moved to the vicinity of Warren Station, Virginia.

After engagements at Hatcher's Run and Weldon Railroad, the regiment was occupied throughout the winter primarily with picket duties before it was returned to duty in the trenches outside Petersburg.

The Tenth was the first regiment in its division to plant its colors inside Confederate lines during the breach at Petersburg on April 2, 1865. The whole VI Corps pursued Lee's army to its surrender a week later. By the end of April it was traveling by way of Danville, Virginia to D.C.

The Tenth Vermont Volunteer Infantry Regiment was mustered out from Burlington on June 27, 1865.[29]

Chester Stephen Dana had been mustered out May 22, 1865; **Daniel T. Foster**, not until June 29, 1865.[30]

Notes

1. The *Daily Green Mountain Freeman* (Montpelier) of August 8, 1862, 3-4.

2. Dr. Haynes' history of the regiment appears in Peck's (1892) *Revised Roster of Vermont Volunteers in the War of Rebellion*, 1, 379-381.

3. Peck's 1892 *Revised Roster* associates the April 22, 1863 date with a discharge of Luce for disabilities. That doesn't necessarily contradict the Ledoux & Associates record of his death on that date: Luce may have died in the D.C. hospital the same day he was discharged from service. Luce's body is buried in Riverbank Cemetery, Stowe, Vermont.

4. Just two days earlier the new state of West Virginia, carved out of 48 Virginian counties, had come into existence.

5. Dyer, II, 923.

6. Dyer (*op. cit.*, 928) names this engagement "Payne's Farm".

7. Haynes, in Peck, I, 379.

8. Thayer had been promoted to Corporal some time before that battle, according to the Ledoux & Associates website, but that promotion is not recorded by Peck. The *Revised Roster* and the L&A website both give the date of Thayer's death as September 23, 1864 although Thayer's headstone in the Warren, Vermont Cemetery gives his death date as the twenty-second.

9. Dyer, *op. cit.*, 929-930.

10. The Overland Campaign began May 4, 1864.

11. Coffin (2002), 98-99.

12. *Op. cit.*, 99.

13. *Op. cit.*, 100.

14. *Op. cit.*, 116. Those three were James Maynard, Lewis Spaulding and Horace Stoddard. Their stories are told in other sections of this work.

15. Coffin, *op. cit.*, 120-121.

16. Abbott, cited in Coffin, *op. cit.*, 121.

17. Coffin, *op. cit.*, 140-141.

18. The Old Vermont Brigade alone accounted for 1,269 of those casualties, per Gordon C. Rhea (1994), 436. Rhea writes, "Lewis Grant's Vermonters held the dubious honor of losing more men…than did any other Union brigade" at the Battle of the Wilderness." (For years before Rhea published his work that uses casualty figures from the Union's Official Records, Old Brigade losses were given as 1,234, a

number that is inscribed on the First Vermont Brigade monument on the Wilderness battlefield.) When casualty lists were published in Vermont newspapers over the next week the whole state was said to have been thrown into mourning.

19. Haynes, quoted in Coffin, *op. cit.*, 155.

20. Haynes, quoted in Coffin, *op. cit.*, 180.

21. Dyer, *op. cit.*, II, 934.

22. Cold Harbor lay on a direct line between *White House* on the Pamunkey River, where Grant placed his main supply base, and Meade's army camps.

23. Among the effects of a gunshot wound to Edwin Dana's right leg, muscles that control foot movement were severed, according to a medical report prepared by Dr. Henry Janes, then serving as commander of Sloan General Hospital in Montpelier, Vermont. Surgeon Janes testified that Dana's wound left him "unfit" for transfer to the Veteran's Reserve Corps. Accordingly, Dana was discharged from the Sloan hospital (and from service) on January 27, 1865.

Dr. Henry Janes of Waterbury, Vermont had been appointed by President Lincoln to direct all medical care in Gettysburg, Pennsylvania after the July 1–3, 1863 battle there. When three hospitals were opened in Vermont for wounded soldiers, Dr. Janes was recalled to Vermont to head one of those hospitals, Sloan General Hospital in Montpelier. (The other two were located in Burlington and Brattleboro.) Dr. Janes' detailed report on Edwin Dana's injury appears on the Ledoux & Associates website, https://www.vermontinthecivilwar. Note that Dr. Janes' report gives Dana's first name as "Edward."

24. Waite, cited in Coffin, *op. cit.*, 297.

25. Noah Andre Trudeau (1989), 286.

26. Both Ulysses Grant's and CSA Brigadier General Evander Law's words are cited in Coffin, *op. cit.*, 298–299.

27. Don Wickman, ed. (2006) includes Oscar Wait's vivid eye-witness account of 10th regiment fighting at Cedar Creek and many other battlefields. Wait adds pungent commentary of officers' mismanagement on many of those fields.

28. Oscar Waite's unpublished ms, cited by LaMonda (2003), p. 119.

29. Peter T. Washburn, *Report of the Adjutant and Inspector General of the State of Vermont, From Oct. 1, 1864, to Oct. 1, 1865.*

30. Perhaps Foster's retention until then was necessitated by hospitalization for his Winchester, Virginia wound. Foster had been promoted in the service several times, finishing as a Captain. His war-years' correspondence is archived in a collection, University of Vermont Libraries.

11th Vermont Volunteer Infantry Regiment

When an urgent call from the War Department went out for a half-million new recruits in the late summer of 1862, Vermont's response was to raise two new regiments concurrently. The first group to fill up became the Tenth Vermont Volunteers, considered a sister regiment to the second group, denominated the Eleventh Vermont Volunteers. However, in October the Eleventh regiment was equipped and drilled as an artillery unit, the First Vermont Regiment, Heavy Artillery. Two companies of the new Heavy Artillery Regiment that are of interest to readers of their section were separated for their training early in their service before being united more than a year later to garrison Fort Massachusetts outside the nation's capital. [COMPANY B was trained at Fort Massachusetts originally, then at Forts Totten and Stevens before returning to Fort Massachusetts. COMPANY D was trained at Fort Saratoga for its first two months of service before being assigned to Fort Massachusetts where it joined Co. B and (briefly) Co. I.] The other companies of the regiment were sent to a variety of other forts. Much later in the war, the Eleventh reverted to infantry service.

The Eleventh had another distinction. It was the largest unit among Vermont's contributions to the war effort. It encompassed 12 artillery "batteries" instead of the usual 10 infantry "companies" and each battery consisted of 150 men. Additional officers needed to be named because of the regiment's size, 1,315 men.[1]

Waitsfield supplied three men to the 11th Vermont Volunteer Infantry Regiment, **Thomas Burke** and **George P. Welch** to **Company B**, and **Charles H. Ryder**[2] to **Company D**.

Company B

Thomas Burke was born in Montreal, Canada about 1843. He enlisted at age 21 and credited to Waitsfield, so it's to be assumed that he had moved from Canada to the United States sometime prior to that. He was mustered in August 6, 1864.

George P. Welch, also 21 at his enlistment, was born March 29, 1843 in Ossipee, New Hampshire. He, too, was credited to Waitsfield. Welch was mustered in August 3, 1864.

Both soldiers were mustered out August 25, 1865. Burke died less than two years after leaving the service.

Company D

Charles H. Ryder enlisted at age 25 and was mustered into Company D at the regiment's creation [September 1, 1862]. He had been born in Waitsfield, but was credited to Morrisville upon his July 14th enlistment. He fulfilled a three-year commitment and was mustered out June 24, 1863. Ryder lived until 1925 and was buried in the Thayer, Kansas Cemetery where a gravestone shows him as having served with Co. D, "1VT H.A.", per the L. & A. website.

Private Ryder had accompanied the Eleventh Regiment to duty in the "Northern Defenses" of the nation's capital. During its year and eight months of service outside Washington, the regiment built and garrisoned Fort Slocum, Fort Stevens and Fort Totten.[3]

A regimental history recorded in Peck (1892) notes that the camps of the 1st Vermont Heavy Artillery (H.A.) during that period "were well-built structures, with a fine hospital" and were visited almost daily by persons from the capital city. "No more pleasant or cheerful experiences were ever the lot of soldiers in actual war," opined James M. Warner and Aldace F. Walker, co-authors of that history.[4]

That apparent idyll ended when the 11th Vermont Regiment/1st Heavy Artillery was called upon to reinforce the Army of the Potomac. "Marching from Washington *via* Belle Plain and Fredericksburg, it reached the front and joined the [Old Vermont] brigade on Sunday morning, May 15th [1864]," writes G. G. Benedict. "It was, as it were, a brigade in itself,… a larger number than was now left of the other five regiments put together."[5]

The size of the H.A. required its division into three battalions, each supervised by a major. From then on Vermont's 11th Regiment/1st Heavy Artillery fought as part of the First [or Old] Vermont Brigade under Lewis A. Grant.[6]

Private Ryder would have been present through the latter part of the Overland Campaign, participating in VI Corps operations on the lines of the North Anna River (May 22–26), Pamunkey River (May 26–28) and Totopotomoy River (May 28–31), and battles around Cold Harbor (June 1–12).

Later, the 1st Vermont H.A. played a role early in the siege of Petersburg, being engaged in actions for control of the Jerusalem Plank Road (that is, along the Weldon Railroad) before being ordered by Ulysses Grant to Virginia's Shenandoah Valley.

Disaster strikes the regiment; many perish in Southern prisons

Five companies of the 11th Regiment were cut off from a larger Union working party in wooded country along the Weldon Railroad on June 23, 1864. Surrounded by Confederates, 261 of those men were captured, as well as 139 from the Fourth Vermont and one from the Fifth Vermont, units which had been stationed as skirmishers to protect Eleventh Regiment men tearing up that portion of the railroad. Thus, 401 Vermont Brigade men went off to prisoner of war camps that day.[7] Additionally, thirteen men of the brigade were killed in that action and 45 wounded, 14 of them mortally. In the Eleventh Regiment alone, losses were 9 killed and 31 wounded, 11 of them mortally.

Private Charles Ryder from Waitsfield presumably was present that day but was not a casualty. (Note that Privates Burke and Welch had not yet joined the regiment.)

An after-war account by G. G. Benedict reads:

> A sad sequel must be added to this disastrous episode. Of the 401 men thus captured, over one half died within six months after their capture, a few in Confederate hospitals, but most of them in the prison pens of Andersonville and Columbia, S. C. The names of two hundred and thirty-two Vermonters, most of them strong and vigorous men when taken that day, who thus died by a lingering death in the hands of the enemy, are elsewhere given.... A number who lived to be exchanged, came home mere wrecks of men and died soon after, and it is probably no exaggeration to say that 70 per cent of the men so captured died in prison or from the results of their captivity.[8]

A much more recent accounting (2003) by David Faris Cross, M.D. gives the disposition of each individual captured that day, first the officers, then the men listed by company within regiment.[9] Cross' *A Melancholy Affair at the Weldon Railroad: The Vermont Brigade, June 23, 1864* chronicles by name those who were sent to POW camps in Charleston, Columbia and Florence, South Carolina; Goldsboro and Salisbury, North Carolina; Richmond, Virginia; and Millen and Andersonville, Georgia. Dr. Cross's interest in medical conditions in those camps leads him to document from C.S.A. records the wounds many of the soldiers had suffered in the battle prior to their capture, as well as amputations performed in the prisons and the various diseases prisoners acquired there, with an emphasis on scurvy. He cites "starvation" as the sole cause of death for one Vermont Brigade soldier and as contributing (with disease and exposure) to the deaths of three others.[10]

Murders of Vermont prisoners at Andersonville

According to various prisoners' accounts, Cross states, Stephan H. Nelson of Co. I, Fourth Regiment, who died at Andersonville in December 1864, was "…stomped to death by Captain Wirz." This is the only known account of a prisoner dying at the commandant's hands *versus* the many whose deaths can fairly be ascribed to his neglect and maladministration.[11]

Two officers of the Eleventh Regiment captured at Weldon Railroad were killed in escape attempts.[12]

Company A's Captain Edwin J. Morrill was fired on while attempting to escape from Andersonville six days after being captured. He died the next day (June 30, 1864) of gunshot wounds so received.

Company B's Second Lieutenant Edward B. Parker died of wounds at Columbia, South Carolina on October 13, 1864, one day after he was set upon by bloodhounds as he tried to escape.

It's likely that Waitsfield's Private Charles Ryder had known both of those men prior to their capture. Whether he ever learned of their deaths in separate escape attempts is unknown.

Effects of imprisonment in POW camps on soldiers' religious beliefs

Writing of soldiers' perceptions of God during the Civil War, David Goldfield (2011) describes a growing sense among soldiers on both sides as the war continued into the winter of 1863 and beyond, that God had no hand in it. "Rather than the personal, interventionist God of evangelical Christianity, this Supreme Being was more detached and more inscrutable… . Any soldier who participated in battle and looked out over the field afterward found it difficult to fathom what God had in mind." But "if God was out of it, then what was the purpose of all this misery?" Goldfield continues:

> If the answers were elusive in the camps, they were even less clear in places where soldiers languished in more horrid conditions. The battle for life over death continued in the hospitals. The contest was more desperate in the military prisons. If it was difficult to imagine a divine presence on the battlefield, it required an immense leap of faith to think of a God who would countenance a Civil War prison.

A large army lived in prisons. More than 410,000 soldiers (200,000 Union and 210,000 Confederate) spent time as forced guests of the enemy. Of these, 56,000 died, mostly from disease. These deaths accounted for nearly 10 percent of all fatalities during the war.[13]

Southern civilians' awareness of conditions in prisoner of war camps

John B. Jones' *A Rebel War Clerk's* Diary (1866) details life in the Confederate capital throughout the war from his perspective as a clerk in the Confederate war department, employed to read military communications. Although his diary entries make clear that Richmond civilians, not just Confederate administrators, were aware of the many Union prisoners of war held there, he doesn't record instances of civilians attempting to relieve prisoners' sufferings as some residents of Savannah, Georgia did.[14]

In *Saving Savannah: The City and the Civil War* (2008) Jacqueline Jones writes of Savannah's black community collecting donations of bread that they tossed over the walls of the prison stockade despite the risk of being jailed. And when hundreds of Andersonville prisoners were transferred from Sumter, Georgia to Savannah,[15] Savannah citizens "brought clothing and bread to distribute to the men." However, their contributions were rejected by prison guards. Ms Jones writes of a white boy who tried to hand a loaf of bread to one prisoner, Union soldier Daniel Kelley, as he was being herded onto a railroad car for transfer to a camp at Millen, Georgia. "When a guard intervened, a black man stepped up, seized the loaf, and threw it into the railroad car full of prisoners." (That man immediately was arrested.) Her narrative continues: "Within a few weeks Confederate officials had brought Kelley and others back to Savannah, and this time white and black women gave them water and wheat bread while they were incarcerated." Furthermore, she recounts a report by one of the prison guards of another occasion when "between 500 and 1000 women and children visited the stockade carrying baskets of provisions."[16]

Late-war enlistees from Waitsfield

Privates **George P. Welch** and **Thomas Burke** joined **Company B** of the Eleventh Infantry Regiment/1st Heavy Artillery in early August of 1864.

Welch had served a three-year enlistment in the Tenth Vermont Infantry Regiment before he joined the Eleventh Regiment. It's likely both of these men (as well as Private Ryder) participated in the Shenandoah Valley engagements—at Charlestown, West Virginia and at Gilbert's Ford, Opequon, Fisher's Hill and Cedar Creek in Virginia—before the regiment returned to siege operations outside Petersburg.

"Scorched Earth" policy in the Shenandoah Valley; Confederate reprisals involving the Eleventh Regiment

During the years of the Sesquicentennial of the Civil War, the Vermont Humanities (VH) organization produced online essays weekly under the title *a look back at the war.* One of those essays dealt with the Union policy of burning foodstuffs throughout the Shenandoah Valley (the so-called "Bread Basket of Virginia") during the period now under discussion, and retaliations by unauthorized guerrillas.[17]

The online essay of October 3, 2014 cited the following letter that specifically mentions the murders of two men from the 11th Vermont Regiment. The writer's original spelling and punctuation are preserved. I have added a few clarifications; those appear within brackets.

> …We have done a business for the confederacy during this campaign th[r]ough the Valley of Va that 'I Recon' wont be forgotten very soon Upon our advance, and when near Charlestown after a skirmish near that place in which corpl Jackman of Co K of this regt [the 5th] was killed and partially buried by Rebls during the night time; leaving his head above ground; and inserting a head board into his mouth in which cond[it]ion his remains were found….
>
> While in camp near Berryville I am told by members of the 11th Rgt VT Vols that two men belonging to that regt were found murdered a short distance out of camp… One of them was lieing upon the ground lifeless with his throat cut from ear to ear
>
> Another was found also lifeless hanging from a tree by his feet head downwards his mouth filled with pulled wool… .
>
> And now when I tell you that we have burned; by fire from Staunton to Strasburg [Strasburg, Virginia], the principal property of those persons who are engaged in this rebellion (and that includes every available male from the ages of 11 years (eleven) to nearly seventy years of age) and all such property as can be of immediate use to the Rebel government I think you can hardly call us very bad names in view of the atrocities committed by these infernal traitors….
>
> Some few dwelling houses burned by design; others caught fire by accident lit by sparks escaping from the general conflagration around, . . all commingling in one grand, vast and gigantic conflagration which can be better understood when I state that its area comprised … a distance of 75 miles

with a breadth of about 5 miles across The time of the burning principally commenced on the 4th [of October, 1864] after the foul murder of Capt Meigs.[17] The angry flames illumed high up the dark heavens of that moonless night... .But little distruction was perpetrated on the 5th preparatory to our greater work which began on the sixth ending on the 9th The work of those three [four] days will long be remembered by us as well... .

Ah! Those three hundred thousand fresh soldiers graves in these slave states call for redress at our hands; and as true as God has a principal they shall have it, and woe to those unhappy people of this rebellions conspiracy if they do not soon return to their allegiance ....[18]

Closing out the war

The Eleventh Vermont Infantry/1st Heavy Artillery Regiment participated in action at Fort Fisher (Petersburg) on March 25, 1865, and the assault and capture of CSA lines before Petersburg on April second which necessitated the evacuation of Confederate forces and government officials from Richmond, Virginia.

The three Waitsfield men of the Eleventh Regiment, as part of the Old Vermont Brigade with the VI Corps, pursued the remnants of the Army of Northern Virginia to Appomattox Court House. Subsequently the Corps marched a hundred miles in four days to Danville, Virginia where it remained until after the last Confederate army surrendered in late May.

Welch and Burke both were mustered out of service on August 25, 1865, two months later than Ryder.[19]

Notes

1. Peck (1892), I, 455.

2. Peck, *op. cit.*, spells Charles H. Ryder's surname as "Rider", 427.

3. At a later period of its service, the Eleventh Infantry Regiment/1st Vermont Regiment, Heavy Artillery garrisoned four more forts, finally covering a seven-mile front that ran from East Creek to Rock Creek in the District of Columbia, per Peck, *ibid.*

4. *Ibid.*

5. Benedict (1886), I, 451.

6. Organizationally, the Eleventh Regiment joined the vastly depleted Old Vermont Brigade under L. A. Grant in Getty's division of the VI Corps, headed by Horatio G. Wright after John Sedgwick was killed during the Spotsylvania fighting. The Tenth and Seventeenth Vermont Infantry Regiments and the Third Battery, Vermont Light Artillery already had been fighting alongside the Vermont Brigade since the Overland Campaign began.

7. Some sources suggest as many as 410 Vermonters (including a few not in the Vermont Brigade) were captured. Maps of that day's action can be found at *The Siege of Petersburg Online*: https://www.beyondthecrater.com/maps/. Readers will find the maps of the Jerusalem Plant Road and the Weldon Railroad actions are the most relevant maps at that site for this topic.

8. Benedict (1886), 1, 481–482.

9. Cross (2003), Appendix C. The list of Eleventh Vermont casualties appears at 202-228. Cross writes that 407 Vermonters from the 4th and 11th Vermont Regiments but none from the 5th Regiment were captured that day.

10. Those four men were: Harrison W. Varney of Co. D, Fourth Regiment, Francis W. Doying and Franklin Woodard, both of Co. F, Eleventh Regiment, and Thomas Babcock, Co. K of the Eleventh. Babcock, Doying and Varney died in Andersonville; Woodward, in Florence.

11. Cross, *op. cit.*, 200.

12. Source: The Ledoux & Associates website, https://www.vermontinthecivilwar.org

13. Goldfield (2011), 320-321.

14. John B. Jones (1866), II: See accounts of famine in Richmond as early as April 1864, and insufficient food for CS armies and the prisoners held in POW camps (February 1865).

15. Because the Confederate administration feared General William Tecumseh Sherman might lead his invading army to Sumter to liberate Andersonville prisoners, in late summer of 1864 they sent many Andersonville prisoners to prison camps elsewhere in the state and even outside Georgia.

16. Jacqueline Jones (2008), 196.

17. Explanatory material inserted by the VH editor states that Lieutenant John Meigs, chief engineer on General Philip Sheridan's staff, and two others were surprised by a Confederate cavalry patrol on the night of October 3rd, and Meigs was killed. That editor notes that Northerners believed Meigs was murdered by civilians, and Sheridan ordered some houses burned in retaliation.

18. George Howard to wife, October 9, 1864, in Marshall, ed. (1999), 264–266, cited in *Civil War Book of Days* (5, 40), October 3, 2014, at https:www//civilwarbookofdays.org.

19. Private Ryder, having been among the initial enrollees, had been mustered out on June 24, 1865.

12th Vermont Volunteer Infantry Regiment

The Twelfth Vermont Volunteer Infantry Regiment was the first of five new infantry regiments to be raised in Vermont in response to Lincoln's August 1862 call for 300,000 members from states' militias, all to serve for nine months. The Twelfth Infantry Regiment as described by G. G. Benedict in Peck's (1892) *Revised Roster of Vermont Volunteers* included "many citizens of property and standing" in their communities (and "of earnest loyalty," in Benedict's words) "whose professional and business engagements forbade their enlisting for a longer term."[1]

Men from ten towns' militias, each comprising a company, constituted the core of the Twelfth Regiment. Seven of those companies previously had served in the First Vermont Volunteer Infantry Regiment. **Company F**, which **John G. Lewis** joined, was one of those experienced companies but the companies which **Benjamin Henry Adams** and **Lucius W. Nourse** joined (**Companies D** and **I** respectively) were not.[2]

Officers and early service of the Twelfth Regiment

The Twelfth gathered in camp at Brattleboro in late September, while it awaited its mustering-in ceremony.[3] No doubt drilling and learning camp routines occupied its 996 officers and men in that interim. On October seventh the regiment departed for the District of Columbia where it camped on East Capitol Hill for the next three weeks, being assigned to the Reserve Army Corps in defense of Washington. With the arrival by October 30 of the Thirteenth through Sixteenth Vermont Regiments, the Second Vermont Brigade was constituted.

Asa Blunt from St. Johnsbury, who had served previously as Lieutenant Colonel of Vermont's Sixth Regiment, was the Twelfth's first Colonel. Blunt (as the ranking Colonel among the five regimental commanders) assumed brigade command for a time. He served in that capacity until Brigadier General E. H. Stoughton arrived.[4]

Under General Stoughton the brigade shifted over from the inner defenses of the nation's capital into Virginia, near Munson's Hill. From there, the 12th and 13th Vermont Regiments moved on November first to Camp Vermont, located on the road to Mount Vernon about two miles south of Alexandria, Virginia.[5]

Those first regiments of the brigade were joined by the other regiments one week later. Over the next six weeks, while the brigade primarily performed picket duty, 300 men were detailed each day to work on the construction of Fort Lyon.

The Second Vermont Brigade (including the 12th Regiment, of course) moved to Fairfax Court House in Virginia on December twelfth. There it performed picket duty along Cub Run and Bull Run, the latter a site of major battles in 1861 and 1862.

The first engagement of the 12th Regiment with Confederate forces came at Fairfax Court House on December 28, 1862 when the regiment helped repel a cavalry raid headed by CSA General J. E. B. Stuart.

On January 20, 1863, once again paired with the Thirteenth Regiment, the Twelfth moved to Wolf Run Shoals, Virginia where the two units picketed on the outer defensive line of the capital over the next three months, guarding fords of the Occoquan River, a tributary of the Potomac. On May first the Twelfth was sent to Warrenton Junction, Virginia to guard the Orange and Alexandria Railroad.[6]

Subsequent moves within Virginia were to Rappahannock Station, to guard a railroad bridge there; then (in detachments) to Bristoe Station and Catlett Station; then to Manassas; and finally, to Union Mills. It was from Union Mills that the Twelfth Vermont Volunteer Infantry Regiment marched away on June 25, 1863 in a pursuit of Confederate forces that concluded at Gettysburg, Pennsylvania.

Service in a supporting role at the Battle of Gettysburg

Privates **Adams**, **Lewis** and **Nourse** marched with the Twelfth Regiment in the Second Vermont Brigade's rear guard of Union columns as Major General George G. Meade ordered the Army of the Potomac to follow the Army of Northern Virginia (ANV), holding to an inside track in order to defend Washington and Baltimore from any sudden attack. The ANV was invading Northern territory for the second time and Robert E. Lee already had some Confederate units in Pennsylvania.[7] Surprised at the rapidity of Meade's reaction, Lee ordered those units to reverse their routes and converge with the rest of his army which was moving across Maryland towards south central

Pennsylvania, headed for the state capital, Harrisburg.

The Twelfth Regiment crossed the Potomac River at Edwards Ferry on June 27, which happened to be only the second full day of Meade's command. Moving *via* Frederick City, Maryland, the regiment neared Gettysburg, Pennsylvania on July first. There, the Twelfth Regiment was assigned to guard the trains (*i.e.*, supply wagons) of the I Army Corps, a task it shared with the Fifteenth Vermont Regiment.[8]

Two companies (B and G) of the Twelfth Regiment were detached and sent forward to guard a I Corps ammunition train parked on Gettysburg's Taneytown Road, where they remained through July third.[9]

The eight companies of the 12th Regiment not detailed to the ammunition train on Taneytown Road, along with Vermont's 15th Regiment, were assigned to the railroad depot at Westminster, Maryland (some 25 miles southeast of Gettysburg) to guard baggage and supply wagons associated with seven Union corps. The Vermont men arrived there around midnight on July second and soon found themselves subject to conflicting orders issued by Generals Meade and Sickles. In the ensuing confusion, Meade's orders prevailed—the Vermonters remained there with more than 2800 wagons plus the horses and mules required to pull all those, and the teamsters (drivers) who were responsible for the animals. Additionally, 900 Confederates taken prisoner on July third were afterwards escorted to Westminster and they also became the charge of those Vermonters.[10]

The regiment's term of service expired on July fourth. On the first leg of its travel home (*via* rail from Baltimore) the Twelfth Regiment was tasked with guarding 2,500 Confederate prisoners. Once back in camp at Brattleboro on July 9th, while awaiting their mustering out, many members of the Twelfth volunteered for a final service: They were willing to go to New York State to help suppress draft riots. Their service was deemed not needed, however, and the Twelfth Regiment, including its three Waitsfield privates, was mustered out on July 14, 1863.[11]

Information from the Waitsfield men's service records

Benjamin Adams and **Lucius Nourse** both were born in Waitsfield but had moved away at some time, as they were credited to other Vermont towns upon their enlistments (Chelsea and Rockingham, respectively). Each was 19 when he enlisted. Thus, it's unlikely those privates had had time to attain the social status ascribed by Benedict to many other Twelfth Regiment enlistees.

A year after Adams' nine-months' service with the regiment, he enlisted in the 2nd Vermont Battery, Light Artillery. Later he was transferred to the 1st Vermont Company, Heavy Artillery. See those sections of this work for a continuation of Adams' record.

John G. Lewis was somewhat older (23) than Adams and Nourse. His enlistment was credited to Northfield, Vermont where he had moved from his birthplace, Concord, New Hampshire. Lewis meets our definition of a Waitsfield soldier by virtue of his 1918 burial in the Waitsfield Common Cemetery.

Notes

1. Benedict, in Peck (1892), II, 456. Benedict claims there that "[N]o Vermont regiment in after years furnished more men of prominence in civil life." It should be noted that Benedict himself served in the Twelfth Regiment.

2. *Ibid.* Company F had been known as the New England Guard of Northfield.

3. A mustering-into federal service of a state's regiment required a regular army officer be present. For the 12th Vermont Volunteer Infantry Regiment that happened October 4, 1862.

4. Stoughton served from December 7, 1862 until March 9, 1863 when he was captured in his headquarters at Wolf Run Shoals, Virginia by CSA General John Mosby. Colonel Blunt then resumed brigade command temporarily until relieved by Brigadier General George J. Stannard in April.

5. Eric Ward, editor of George G. Benedict's wartime letters to his hometown newspaper, the *Burlington Free Press*, notes that Benedict and five 12th Regiment companions made the trek from camp, "a two-hour walk," to tour Mount Vernon and pay their respects at the graves of George and Martha Washington. Because two men at a time from each company of the Second Brigade were released for a day during this period to take in the capital's sights (Ward, 94), it is possible that Adams, Lewis and Nourse visited the Capitol building, the White House and/or the Smithsonian Institute, all popular tourist destinations at that time.

6. Benedict, *op. cit.*, 457.

7. The first time had been in mid-September 1862 when Lee took his army into Maryland, an advance that culminated in the Battle of Antietam.

8. Benedict, *loc. cit.* The Second Vermont Brigade was part of the Third Division, I Corps. Major General John F. Reynolds commanded the I Corps from March 9, 1862 until his death on the first day of battle at Gettysburg (July 1, 1863). Reynolds was succeeded immediately by Abner Doubleday and a day later, by John Newton.

9. Ward (2002), 207.

10. *Ibid.*

11. Benedict, *loc. cit.*

Fig. 14. Ford's Old Mill at Wolf Run Shoals, Virginia near where the 13th Vermont Volunteer Infantry Regiment camped the first three months of 1863.

Fig. 15. Campground of the 13th Volunteer Infantry Regiment at Wolf Run Shoals, Virginia

13th Vermont Volunteer Infantry Regiment

The Thirteenth Vermont Volunteer Infantry Regiment is remembered with particular esteem by Vermonters because of the role that regiment played at the Battle of Gettysburg. Thirty Waitsfield men served in the Thirteenth Regiment, all in **Company B**:
   John Baird, Albert D. Barnard, Charles D. Billings, Fordis O. Bushnell, Samuel Jackson Dana, Myron M. Davis, Henry Albee Dewey, Julian J. Dumas, Edward Anson Fisk, David Gleason, Daniel Grandy, Edgar A. Hastings, Eaton A. Heath, John Hines, Ziba H. McAllister, Alson D. Page, Edwin Franklin Palmer, Dexter F. Parker, Loren B. Reed, Oscar C. Reed, John W. Richardson, Levi W. Seaver, Oscar A. Stearns, Dorric Smith Stoddard, Lathrop Thompson Stoddard, Cyrus G. Thayer, James M. Thayer, Harvey M. Wait, Edmund Whitcomb and **Orcas C. Wilder**.[1]

Histories of the Thirteenth Regiment

Besides Vermont Adjutant General Theodore Peck's 1892 report, generally known by its shortened title of *Revised Roster*, two volumes in the collection of the Joslin Memorial Library in Waitsfield hold accounts of the service of the Thirteenth Vermont Volunteer Infantry Regiment. Those are Eli Nelson Peck's *Supplement to the History of the Thirteenth Regiment Vermont Volunteers* (1911) and Sturtevant & Marsh's *Pictorial History of the 13th Regiment Vermont Volunteers, 1861–1865* (1910). As the title of the latter suggests, it includes photographs of many members of the regiment.

Additionally, the regiment's **Edwin Franklin Palmer** wrote a book after he returned from the regiment's nine-month enlistment *(The Second Brigade; or, Camp Life)*, based on a diary he kept during his service. Palmer, who had enlisted as a Sergeant, was elevated to Second Lieutenant in November 1862. His account of the regiment's 1863 march to Gettysburg and its participation in the fighting is quoted extensively below.

13th Vermont Volunteer Infantry Regiment, Company B

John Baird
CO. B., 1861

Albert D. Barnard
CO. B., 1862

Charles Billings
CO. B., 1861

Corp. Fordis O. Bushnell
CO. B., 1862

Samuel J. Dana
CO. B., 1862

Sergt. H. Albee Dewey
CO. B., 1862

J. Julian Dumas
CO. B., 1902

Edward A. Fisk
CO. B., 1862

David Gleason
CO. B., 1862

Daniel Grandy
CO. B., 1862

Edgar A. Hastings
CO. B., 1862

Eaton A. Heath
CO. B., 1863

John Hines
CO. B., 1860

Ziba McAllister
CO. B., 1862

Lieut. Edwin F. Palmer
CO. B., 1862

Dexter Parker
CO. B., 1863

Loren B. Reed
CO. B., 1860

Oscar C. Reed
CO. B., 1860

John Richardson
CO. B., 1862

Levi W. Seaver
CO. B., 1860

Oscar A. Stearns
CO. B., 1860

Dorric Smith Stoddard
CO. B., 1900

James M. Thayer
CO. B., 1865

L. Thompson Stoddard
CO. B., 1862

Harvey M. Wait
CO. B., 1862

Edmund Whitcomb
CO. B., 1862

Capt. Orcas C. Wilder
CO. B., 1862

Portraits not available for three Waitsfield men: Myron M. Davis, Alson D. Page, and Cyrus G. Thayer.

The regiment's early months in military service

The 30 Waitsfield men of Company B were mustered in for nine months service on October 10, 1862. The men of the company elected **Orcas C. Wilde**r, a 34-year-old hometown "boy," as their Captain. Their regimental commander was Francis V. Randall from Montpelier.[2] The Second Vermont Brigade, to which the Thirteenth Regiment belonged, was under the command of Asa Blunt initially, then Edwin Stoughton, and later (from April 20, 1863), George J. Stannard.

The Waitsfield men in Company B seem to have been a singularly youthful group. Only three recruits were older than 30. Sixteen were under 21. This, at a time when the average age of all those in the 13th Regiment was 24 years.

The regiment's earliest assignment was in defense of Washington City, where the men camped on East Capitol Hill. They performed picket duties along the Potomac, later passing months at various northern Virginia sites. The regiment also performed railroad guard duty for a time.

Misery caused by inadequate shelter

Albert Clarke's regimental history records severe weather in the winter of 1862–63, causing intense misery. For almost two weeks beginning November 26, the 13th Regiment (as well as the 14th and 15th regiments, all under the command of Colonel Randall at the time) guarded the railroad along Bull Run. "Although they had tents, there was much suffering from severe cold and storms."[3]

Daily, the men anticipated raids by CSA General J. E. B. Stuart's cavalry. When relieved on December 5, the men returned to Camp Vermont just south of Alexandria, Virginia, traveling on flatbed train cars open to a heavy wet snowstorm. "When they reached camp in the evening, it was still snowing, their tents had not arrived and they were without food, fuel or axes.... Many... took colds and some of them never recovered." [4]

The regiment was moved frequently, setting up camp at times in Centreville and Fairfax Court House, Virginia and performing railroad guard duties in those places. The 13th VT camped at Wolf Run Shoals, Virginia from January 20 to April 2 before it established Camp Carusi five miles away on the Occoquan River (a tributary of the Potomac), where the regiment was charged with guarding fords in the vicinity.

Lieutenant Clarke's history describes the Carusi site as a delightful camp with a fine parade ground.[5]

Fig.17. The Old Mill near Camp Carusi (also known as Camp Widow Violet), the Occoquan, Virginia home of the 13th Vermont Volunteer Infantry Regiment after early April 1863, and before it marched to Gettysburg.

Company B put *hors de combat* by disease

In January an epidemic of measles had struck down 25 members of Company B. The rest of the company were relieved of all other duties for two weeks to provide nursing care to their sick comrades.[6] **Charles D. Billings** and **Cyrus Thayer** presumably were hospitalized for months with complications of measles, as they died in camp from that disease, both on May 19, 1863.

Oscar Reed had been the first Waitsfield man in Co. B to die: He had succumbed to typhoid fever on Christmas Day, 1862. **Loren Reed** (Oscar's brother?), who had been detailed away from the company to play cornet in the brigade band, died of measles at the Occoquan camp on May 30, 1863.[7]

The regiment in the months before Gettysburg

With the coming of spring and the regiment established at Camp Carusi, the men were close enough to Chancellorsville, Virginia to hear cannonading from that battlefield. However, the regiment took no part in that May 1863 battle. When Hooker's Army of the Potomac (defeated at Chancellorsville) began crossing the Occoquan on June 13, headed northward in pursuit of Lee's Army of Northern Virginia, an order came down for the 13th Vermont to join the other regiments of the Second Vermont Brigade at Union Mills preparatory to the brigade's also marching north.

The "first battle" of Gettysburg

As the regiments of the Second Vermont Brigade began their trek toward what would become the Gettysburg battlefield, Confederate troops under Jubal Early already were raiding in the area. (Early wrote out a list of supplies he expected Gettysburg's Town Councilmen to gather from their citizens.) Meanwhile, one of his brigades was busy pillaging railroad cars there: After emptying the cars of any materials they could use, Early's men set the cars on fire.[8]

The 13th Regiment's march to Gettysburg and participation in the battle there

Edwin Palmer notes that on June 25, 1863 his brigade was ordered to report to General John Reynold's First Corps which was moving to stop Lee's second invasion north over the Mason–Dixon line. The Thirteenth Regiment began a seven days' march to Gettysburg, Pennsylvania. It departed camp at 8:00 that morning, stopped briefly four times, and arrived at Union Mills at one o'clock. Given an hour's halt there for food and rest, the men mingled with friends in other regiments of the brigade.

Rain began to fall, and continued intermittently throughout the rest of that day's march. When the men camped for the night, "Wet as everything is, fires are started, and all have hot coffee and hardtack for supper."[9]

Continuing Palmer's narrative, we read:

> (June 26) Near by us we find bivouacked the old brigade, and the rest of the sixth corps, who came from Bristoe Station, and marched till two o'clock in the morning. Centreville is abandoned, and all the government property that cannot be carried is burned.... [A] few now are got into the ambulances before starting. After the artillery, teams, and all the troops have passed us, we fall in, and bring up the rear.
>
> As we start off in the morning, there is much fun, and jokes fly as lively as in camp; but this grows less and less, till dark, when you hear but a little, and this seems somewhat forced. At night we pitch our tents in a mowing near a station on the Alexandria and Loudon railroad.
>
> (June 27) At daybreak the bugle is blown. The blankets are rolled; and by five we are tramping. Up to nine o'clock the brigade rested three times....At one time we made a long stop, for hundreds of teams belonging to the army

of the Potomac to pass .At two we came in sight of Edward's Ferry.....Here we find many soldiers; and here we halt an hour,—during which time many wash their feet, some of them blistered and almost bleeding. We encamp for the night a few miles north of the river, expecting to start early in the morning for [either] Harper's Ferry, or Hagerstown.

(June 28, Sunday) We remained till all the troops around the ferry passed....At eight we are marching—the hottest day we have seen. Frequently you will see soldiers falling out to throw away their blankets, or all their clothing, except what they are wearing, and then run to take their place in the ranks; and at each rest, the ground is strewn with blankets, blouses and shirts. At noon we have reached the mouth of the Monocacy river. Here we halt just long enough to boil coffee and 'cloy the hungry edge of appetite' with hard tack. Then we push on, rest, —on, rest again, —on, —on, no rest, —on, up a rising land. 'I'd like,' said the soldier by my side, 'I'd like to be General just one half day, and load some of these officers with my knapsack, gun, and equipments strapped to their backs.' His face is fiery red, and sweat running down it like rain on window panes; but still we push on; the front regiment has gained the height. 'Halt,' cries the General; and 'halt' comes down the long line, repeated by the other officers. Down go the guns, —down goes everything that weighs down, and then the panting soldiers. Five minutes more, and the bugle is sounded for us to march. 'The General has changed horses, we've tired out one,' I hear a good natured soldier saying, as he is bending over to pick up his rifle. A mile and a half more brings us to the foot of a small mountain a little north of Adams's Station, on the Baltimore and Ohio Railroad; and here we bivouac for the night....

(June 29) Beeves were shot and dressed last night, so we have fresh meat with hard tack for breakfast this morning. Some of the soldiers' feet are in a bad condition. I saw one round blister an inch in diameter on the bottom of the heel. 'Can't go far tomorrow,' said many a boy, as we closed our march yesterday. But they washed them in cold water, and all start off in far better spirits than last night, although it rains hard, and we in the ranks actually know nothing at all where we are going. We suppose the enemy somewhere in Maryland or Pennsylvania....[T}oday noon, after plodding through mud and rain as fast as we can, we find ourselves at Frederick City. Here the brigade leaves ninety soldiers, unable to go farther....We have heard that Gen. Meade is in command of the army, not knowing whether to believe it.

(June 30) We commence marching at six; and halt at Lewistown in about two hours....We also halt at Mechanicstown. Here we find that a brigade of cavalry passed us in the night. These, too, wear out as well as infantry. I saw six sleeping in a field, whilst it was raining, and no rubbers [rubber blankets] over them. Our regiment is in the rear, and arrives at Emmettsburg [Emmitsburg, Maryland] just at dark; but still we must pitch our tents and have our coffee. The march this afternoon has been exceedingly hard. Two soldiers are left in houses on the way. At one time, near evening, as we had been exerting every chord for near two hours, splashing, splashing through the mud, faster, faster every moment, 'it seems,' said an old soldier, whose lips has never uttered a complaint before, 'it seems as though the General meant to kill the whole of us.' Soon one drops down in his tracks, and is thought to be dying; but stimulants are given him, and he survives, but unable to go farther....'I'd rather fight than stir another step,' has fallen from many a lip today.

(July 1, Wednesday) Early we are informed that we shall not march today. ...But unexpectedly about nine o'clock orders came for us to fall in. We move on rapidly through the mud and rain, (it clears off in the afternoon,) when, suddenly, at four, the smoke, like a vast, dark, snow-drifting cloud rolls up before us from the field of Gettysburgh [sic], five or six miles away....As we are approaching the field we meet women and children going back into the country, now and then looking around with terror on every face; but one middle-aged woman stands nearly still, bareheaded, whilst the brigade is passing her, screaming till she can hardly speak, 'Go-ahead, boys; the rebels are off there,' and swinging her large naked arms in all directions, causing general and hearty laughter among all the soldiers that see her.

As most Vermonters know, the 13th Vermont Volunteer Regiment did not participate on the first day of the Battle of Gettysburg. Not only did they camp that night in a wheat field to the rear of the I Corps (placed to the right of the center of the federal line of battle along Cemetery Hill), but they remained there until about 11:00 the next morning. Then they were ordered up and marched a hundred rods, Palmer writes, where they stacked arms in a clover field to the rear of the highest point of Cemetery Hill.

Historian Harry W. Pfanz fills in the story from there, explaining how the Thirteenth was ordered to move from its position on the reverse slope of Cemetery Hill (behind the I Corps battle line) to an exposed position facing CSA General William Barksdale's brigade of Mississippians, in support of Hancock's II Corps.[10]

Picking up Palmer's narrative once more:

The forenoon [of July 2nd] wears away, the enemy here and there feeling our strength; and then nearly four hours of almost unbroken silence; but such silence!—such as is wont to hang over the sea, foretelling furious storms—before the iron globes begin to be hurled on their merciless errands. Now suddenly a heavy fire is opened on Cemetery Hill. The ambulances, which had been collected near, and some teams, rush back in great haste. Before it is continued a quarter of an hour, a few soldiers of the eleventh corps actually run away; and half our regiment (the other half is supporting a battery further at the right) is ordered up nearer the brow of the hill to take their places. They move steadily the short distance, and lie down under the flying shells. For two hours now a most terrific cannonade is kept up at this point, and along to the left; for two hours the destructive missiles come, whizzing, whizzing, bursting, bursting, sending down their death-bearing pieces amongst us, and crushing through the little strip of woods to our right—but not a soldier flinches. In the midst of the furious storm, Gen. Doubleday rides along, and says in a pathetic voice: 'Boys, you will fight—won't you? The honor of your State is in your hands. This battle is to decide whether Lincoln or Davis is President.' [11]

[....]

Soon comes a pause—a few moments of silence, all save the groans of the dying and the cries of the wounded—more painful than the unearthly clangor that preceded—and in a moment, long, dark lines of infantry—three columns—forty-five thousand under Hill and Longstreet, are seen moving down on our left—steadily, and seemingly irresistible as a planet in its course. The blow is most directed against the fifth corps on the extreme left; but Gen. Sickles and his brave command are not daunted at the mighty host now forming in their front. On they come, and instantly all the air is filled with the ten thousand rifle cracks, and the louder roar of artillery....

The rebels for awhile waver, and then spring on with increased numbers. The carnage here is terrible; but our troops stand the shock as though every man cared nothing for his life. Gens. Hancock and Gibbon are both wounded.[12] As our thinned lines begin to tremble considerably and show signs of giving away, the fifth corps is thrown in and more than fills up the breach. A heavy battery is wheeled on to an eminence a way to the left, and sends down its destructive contents into the ranks of the enemy, shaking the hills at every discharge. For a moment, at last, the foe seemed stunned and about to stagger off before the awful tempest. But no, —through the dusky air and under the serried peaks of smoke just lifted up from the lines, behind can be seen the officers dashing along, urging on the men; that they too are being reinforced. In a few minutes their whole columns rush on with greater force and more fury than before. The sixth corps has just arrived on the field of battle, and almost at the same instant a division from the right wing has been sent to the support of the left….Our line of battle had been broken, and the rebels dragged off a battery near the centre. Instantly the five companies of our regiment are deployed in the midst of the unabated storm of bursting shells, and thrown into the breach. . . .[13] They now charge down the sloping hill, over the dead and dying, shouting, firing into the foe. . .[I]t seemed but a moment, till the rebel lines were breaking all along and flying back in dismay. The victory is complete.

Palmer's memoir takes note of the wounded being taken to field hospitals in the rear of Cemetery Hill as the exhausted men tried to get some sleep even as Confederates continued to wage war over to their extreme right. Fighting continued there until ten P.M. and resumed at daybreak the next morning (July 3) with an advance by the Union's XII Corps.

> The fighting bids fair to be raging along the whole line from flank to flank. We in the centre almost at the same time are awoke by the crackling of the skirmishers' rifles a little way to the left, and before we have time to pick up our blankets, and lie down between the batteries, in the front line, the hostile bombs are bursting fast and furious over our heads. For three hours now the cannonade continues at this point—we lying on our faces,—and still the savage engagement goes on to the right, not at all abated; but rather the wondrous fury that broke at once, seems much increased as more artillery are brought into play, and the musketry fire is partially drowned by their thundering peals....But as the battle is growing thus fearful, reinforcements arrive, and are posted to send an enfilading fire, which quickly causes disorder in the ranks of the enemy, and soon rout, too, follows.
>
> It is nearly noon; firing soon ceases all over the field, and the sun, which has been obscured much of the day by clouds, now shows his splendor, as if to smile on this signal triumph of the friends of liberty over slavery. It would seem that three such repulses and defeats would be sufficient to convince the foe of the futility of attempting to break through our lines. But no, before two o'clock, a hundred cannon, in a circular line, are concentrated and sending their horrid bombs on Cemetery Hill, thick as hail, and swift and crashing as thunderbolts. We have three heavy lines of battle in the center, a few rods apart, gracefully curved as a rainbow, one behind the other. Our brigade has not moved during the day, and is the front line, in the open field, on the left side of the hill....For two hours, I say, they lie there,—the shells tearing up the earth, filling the air with the splinters of trees and fences, killing and wounding many; but no stragglers go to the rear. Now they rush down the slopes forty or fifty rods to the lowest spot between the contending batteries, and about midway. Here in a strip of low brush they construct a small breastwork out of an old rail fence the best they can. But the enemy saw us move and turned some of their guns upon us here and wounded a few; but most fortunate for us, the most part of their shells and grape-shot came crashing down a few feet in the rear. Soon the enemy are seen moving over the hill and forming directly in our front. They have marched but a

short distance before the order comes, 'Fire, Fire!' A sharp firing is continued till the rebel line wavers and to our right, staggering and falling rapidly from flank to flank. No cooler, braver man can be seen on the whole field than Gen. Stannard, who is down among his boys, to fight with them and share their fate. The front line of battle to our right did not advance when we did; so the thirteenth and sixteenth regiments are marched into the open meadow by the flank and as quickly as possible; for they are moving in a terrific storm of shell grape and musketry. Here they change front forward, forming the new line of battle at right angle to the old, bringing them on the flank of the advancing foe, and but a few feet from them. A destructive fire is now poured into them, and before they have faced many volleys, the rebel column is broken to pieces....[14]

Casualties among Waitsfield men of Company B

Battlefield injuries

Edward Anson Fisk was wounded on Day 2 of the Battle of Gettysburg (July 2, 1863) when a fragment of an artillery shell struck his right knee.[15] (The same shell had just hit a Duxbury man in the foot: It struck Fisk as it rebounded.)

Samuel Jackson Dana, Dexter F. Parker, John W. Richardson, Dorric Smith Stoddard and **Lathrop Thompson Stoddard** were wounded on Day 3 of the battle (July 3, 1863). Only Parker's wound (in a hand) was believed severe; the other men's, slight. They all returned to the firing line after receiving first aid.[16]

Other known casualties

Per the Ledoux & Associates website, **Daniel Grandy** spent "several months" in a Washington, D.C. hospital, and **David Gleason**, "most of [his] time" in a hospital.

The 26 Waitsfield survivors who remained in Company B (including Gleason and Grandy) were mustered out of service on July 21, 1863. Casualties continued after that date, however.

When **Albert D. Barnard** was discharged at Brattleboro on July 21st, he already was suffering from fever and exhaustion. He never recovered, and died in his family's farmhouse on North Road three weeks later, at age 21.[17] Barnard's marker in the Waitsfield Village Cemetery carries his parents' heartbroken inscription: "We have laid thee on our country's alter [sic]."

John Baird, like Albert Barnard, died soon after his Gettysburg service.

Baird's record shows he died (at age 21) two months after the company was mustered out. In the absence of any record of a specific illness or wound suffered during his military service it is not possible to state definitively that Private Baird's death was caused by that service. However, Orcas Wilder, his captain, made that connection in an account of Company B that he wrote for inclusion in Sturtevant & Marsh's 1910 volume.

Moreover, **James M. Thayer**, who had been discharged by reason of disability in January 1863 (after a possible nine-day hospitalization at the Wolf Run Shoals camp), died on November 29th that year. It was measles that had led to James Thayer's early discharge and it seems likely that complications from that disease took his life, as he, too, was mentioned in Captain Wilder's postwar account (along with Barnard and Baird) as being debilitated and dying soon after the company's service ended.[18]

Thirteenth Vermont Regiment memorials on the Gettysburg battlefield

While all the military units from the State of Vermont that fought at Gettysburg are memorialized on a single large monument on the battlefield, the 13th Vermont Regiment also has its own particular monument there. That memorial, near the Vermont monument, is accompanied by a 13th VT position marker across a present-day road from those others. The position marker is accessible by a path which the National Park service keeps mowed through a grassy field. It bears the inscription, "Erected by 193 survivors in 1899." This marker also references a monument to the 13th Vermont's Colonel, Francis Randall, that had been erected six years earlier in his hometown of Northfield, Vermont.

Of peculiar interest among Gettysburg statues is that of First Lieutenant Stephen F. Brown, Co. K of the 13th Regiment. His statue notes that he arrived on the field without a sword,[19] "but seizing a camp hatchet, carried it in the second day's battle until he captured a sword from a Confederate officer." Brown's battlefield action caused General Stannard to restore him to honor.

Re-enlistments by three Waitsfield men

Three Waitsfield veterans of Co. B, 13th Vermont Volunteer Infantry Regiment, enlisted later in other units. Two of those men, **Henry Albee Dewey** and **Lathrop Thompson Stoddard**, died in their subsequent units while the third, **Ziba H. McAllister**, survived a wound incurred in his later service. Those men's army careers after their time with the 13th Regiment are described in sections on the **17th Vermont Volunteer Infantry** (L. T. Stoddard), the **1st Vermont Cavalry** (McAllister) and the **U.S. Signal Corps** (Dewey).

Notes

1. Names of the Waitsfield men are given as they appear on the Ledoux & Associates website, https://www.vermontcivilwar.org. That website uses names as shown in men's enlistment papers. The names of some men In the Thirteenth Vermont Volunteer Infantry Regiment differ from their names as given in Jones' 1909 Town history and/or Peck's 1892 report. Samuel Jackson Dana's name is given as Samuel J. Dana by Peck and as Jackson Samuel Dana by Jones. Peck cites Dewey as H. Albee Dewey, while Jones lists him as Albee Henry Dewey. Peck gives Dorric Smith Stoddard's name as Dorick S. Stoddard, while Jones gives Stoddard's first name as Dorie. Jones gives Cyrus G. Thayer's first name as Cyron. The author includes this information in the belief it may assist the research of local genealogists.

2. Colonel Randall had served previously as Captain of F Company in the Second Vermont Volunteer Infantry. Randall resigned that position when offered a promotion to Colonel of the new 13th Regiment. Also see Randall's subsequent career as Colonel of the 17th Vermont in a later section of this work.

3. Clarke, in Peck (1892), II, 479.

4. *Ibid.* While stockades soon were erected, the regiment was ordered after just one week to Fairfax Court House where they camped for five weeks, picketing along Bull Run.

5. Clarke, *loc. cit.* The camp site took its name from the Carusi farm. Soldiers also called that the "Widow Violet" farm.

6. Sturtevant & Marsh (1910), 449–51, cited at the Ledoux & Associates website.

7. The Ledoux & Associates website notes that the WPA Graves Registration database describes Loren Reed's burial marker in Waitsfield's Common Cemetery as a cenotaph. However, the WPA entry is at odds with other information on the L&A website which states that Ziba McAllister (a comrade in the 13th's Company B) returned to Virginia to locate and bring back Reed's body for burial.

8. "The First Battle of Gettysburg, June 26, 1863," a talk delivered by Peter C. Vermilyea to the Central Connecticut Civil War Round Table on November 8, 2021.

9. Palmer (1864), 168.

10. Pfanz (1987), 415–416. Meade's order traveled by way of Captain John C. Tidball to John Newton, heading First Corps at the time. Newton selected two divisions to move to Hancock's support, one being Abner Doubleday's division that contained Stannard's Second Vermont Brigade. The Thirteenth Vermont Regiment was the first regiment in that brigade to receive the order, with Colonel Francis

Randall being hailed by Doubleday himself. "Colonel what regiment do you command?" "The 13th Vermont, Sir," replied Randall. "Where is General Stannard?" asked Doubleday. Randall pointed to a clump of trees in the distance, too far for Doubleday to reach in a short time. [Stannard was there conversing with the First Corps commander, it seems.] Doubleday, who did not yet know the Vermonters, then asked, "Colonel will your regiment fight?" Randall answered, "I believe they will sir." Doubleday then ordered Randall to take his men and report to General Hancock. After Randall was on his way, Doubleday went on to give Stannard orders for the rest of the brigade to follow.

In the selection above, Pfanz incorporates material he credits to G. H. Scott's *Thirteenth Vermont*, 62–63. The latter includes the information that Colonel Randall proceeded with only five companies of his regiment, **Co. B** being one of them. The other five companies were posted in support of an artillery battery on Cemetery Hill, under the direction of the regiment's Lieutenant Colonel, William Munson.

11. Abner Doubleday, the division head who had replaced John Reynolds very briefly as head of the I Corps after John Reynolds was killed on Day One of the Battle of Gettysburg, was again commanding his division. Whether Doubleday made the speech Palmer cites seems dubious; quite possibly this is apocryphal.

12. Winfield Scott Hancock was in command of the II Corps, and John Gibbon led Hancock's second division.

13. Palmer's memoir doesn't identify the five companies, but Peck's *Revised Roster* (II, 480) names them as A, B, C, E and G. That battalion recovered a Union battery that had been captured by Confederates just before, and drew the guns back into Union lines. It also took as prisoners 83 Confederates sheltering in the Peter Rogers house on the battlefield.

14. The excerpted material appears in Palmer, *op. cit.*, 168-196.

15. Fisk described his wound and a subsequent illness in an account he wrote for inclusion in Sturtevant & Marsh's *Pictorial History of the 13th Regiment Vermont Volunteers* (1910), 461-2, as cited on the L&A website: "At Gettysburg I was slightly wounded by a piece of spent shell, which struck my right knee, just as the regiment started on its charge of July 2nd. Though bruised and lamed I did not leave the field and took part in all the movements of the regiment to the last… [By July 21st, the regiment's muster-out date] I was utterly exhausted by these hardships and was sick at Brattleboro with what proved to be typhoid fever when I reached home. This nearly cost my life but careful nursing brought me through."

16. Parker was being helped off the field supported on either side by two Co. B. comrades, Corporal O. G. Miles of Middlesex and Private James H. Wilson of Warren, when an artillery shell struck rocks near the three men. A rock fragment pierced Wilson's heart. (He was the only Company B man killed in action.) Wilson's body was buried on the battlefield. Subsequently, Waitsfield's Samuel Jackson Dana traveled back to Gettysburg to retrieve Wilson's remains, which are buried in the East Warren Cemetery beneath a headstone which records his surname as "Willson".

17. Jones, *op. cit.*, 84; Coffin (2013), 399.

18. Wilder's account as given in Sturtevant & Marsh, *loc. cit.*

19. Brown had been deprived of his sword by General Stannard for disobedience during the June 25–July 1 march. Stannard had ordered that no one could leave the march column. Brown, seeing his men were in desperate need of water, had collected canteens, filled those, and distributed them to his men.

14th Vermont Volunteer Infantry Regiment

Two companies of the Fourteenth Vermont Volunteer Infantry Regiment each saw the service of a single Waitsfield enlistee. When the regiment was organized **Augustine E. Manum**), age 23, was assigned to Company **G** while **Zimri Lathrop**, age 30, was placed into Company **K**.[1]

The Fourteenth Vermont Volunteers were part of a Second Vermont Brigade comprised of five regiments, numbered 12 through 16. (All those regiments except the Sixteenth enrolled Waitsfield men.) The Second Vermont Brigade regiments were recruited for nine months service under an urgent call by President Abraham Lincoln in August 1862. Second Brigade men were destined for Union-occupied areas of northern Virginia in order to free up more experienced soldiers from routine, less dangerous duties so the latter might fill losses in veteran fighting units.

An account titled *Life in Camp* by J. C. Williams, a Company B corporal from Danby, describes the movement of Vermont's Fourteenth Regiment toward the Eastern seat of war.[2] That trip differed from the more usually-pleasant experiences of Vermont regiments which had passed that way earlier in the war. Perhaps what the regiment experienced in traveling through New York City was reflecting changing Union sentiments on the home front at this later date.

Opening with a brief account of the regiment's gathering at Brattleboro, Vermont for two weeks of orientation to camp and extensive drilling, Williams describes a morning review—open to the public—by commander E. H. Stoughton and Governor Holbrook, followed by the regiment's mustering-in ceremony (October 21, 1862). The 960 men of the 14th Regiment left Brattleboro by train the following afternoon. At New Haven, Connecticut "[We] found the splendid steamer *Continental* waiting for us. Our journey thus far had been a pleasant one, and we shall ever remember the kind people of Northampton, Williamstown, and other places, for the generous feeling and liberality manifested towards us, in furnishing us with apples, pies and cake, as we passed through." [3]

However, their reception was altogether different the next day. Williams records:

> Today we are in New York City, having left New Haven about one o'clock, and arrived here at eight this morning. Such contemptible treatment as we received in this city—the greatest in America—is outrageous and shameful, and calls forth the greatest indignation of the Soldiers. The food presented to us was not fit even for a dog to eat. Great God! what a dish to set before human beings—soup alive with maggots! No cheers were given, for our treatment did not demand them, for we had no accommodations whatever.[4]

Given what Williams writes about "no accommodations," one wonders if the men spent the night on the floor of the dining hall, or perhaps outside on the ground.

The regiment left New York City the next morning on two boats headed for Amboy, New Jersey. "Long after dark" on the 23rd, the men arrived.

> If there is ever a want of comfort attendant upon such a journey as this, we experienced it last night. It would be impossible for the Government to treat cattle and hogs any worse than it does its soldiers in transporting them to the seat of war, considering our treatment a specimen. At Amboy we took the [railway] cars for Camden, where we arrived just at daylight this morning, and such a night of suffering and misery is far beyond the power of any pen to portray. Suffice it to say the night was extremely cold, and being greatly fatigued from want of rest and refreshments, and there being no fire aboard of the cars, our sufferings were almost beyond human endurance.[5]

The regiment's receptions in Philadelphia and Baltimore were more cordial. Finally arriving at Washington, "having had little or no rest since leaving Brattleboro," the regiment was directed first to East Capitol Hill, then briefly to Camp Chase in Arlington, Virginia where it joined Vermont's 12th Infantry and some regiments from Maine. Williams describes the men's arrival at Camp Chase: "This is a very warm day, and while awaiting orders, three soldiers were sun struck.[6]

It appears the Fourteenth Vermont Regiment was there only two days before it returned to East Capitol Hill. On October 30 the regiment was officially attached to the Second Vermont Brigade; it was marched to Munson's Hill that same day.[7]

The first duty of the regiment was picketing at Alexandria, Virginia, part of the Union's defensive ring around western and southern approaches to the nation's capital.

Following three weeks at Hunting Creek, Virginia (November 5–26), the regiment performed picket duty at Occoquan Creek for the next 10 days.[8]

From mid-December of 1862 the 14th Vermont, consolidated months earlier with the 12th, 13th, 15th and 16th Vermont regiments as the Second Vermont Brigade, was stationed near Fairfax Court House where it assisted in repelling a cavalry raid led by Confederate General J. E. B. Stuart. Its camp on the Occoquan River (a tributary to the Potomac) was part of Washington's outer defensive ring, and the regiment's picketing responsibility there was augmented by digging rifle pits and constructing corduroy roads. The Reverend Dr. William S. Smart, the regimental chaplain and historian, wrote: "The duty, while not particularly dangerous, was arduous and involved much exposure and hardship in winter weather." [9]

Exposure to the elements takes its toll

In January a Medical Inspector visited the regiment in camp. He deemed 36 members of the regiment unfit for duty and ordered them returned to Brattleboro, presumably to the United States General Army hospital there.[10]

In mid-April the Fourteenth Vermont Volunteer Infantry Regiment, with the rest of the Second Vermont Brigade, was incorporated into the field army. It would serve henceforth with the I Corps of the Army of the Potomac. At the same time all the regiment's sick (50 men) were sent to hospitals in Alexandria.

The 14th Vermont marches to Gettysburg

George J. Stannard took command of the Second Vermont Brigade on April 20, 1863. It was under Gen. Stannard that the 14th Regiment was ordered at the end of June to march northward through Maryland. The brigade's weeklong march terminated outside the small shire town of Gettysburg, Pennsylvania. Neither the Confederate Army of Northern Virginia nor the Union Army of the Potomac had expected to come to blows there.

Williams' memoir describes that rigorous march, each soldier carrying three days' rations in a haversack and having seven days' rations aboard a supply train. General Stannard permitted the men to bring their knapsacks although "unnecessary" items such as changes of clothing were left behind, to be forwarded to Alexandria for storage. Departing at 3 p.m. on June 25 the 14th Vermont marched in rain much of the way until it arrived at its first night's campsite. Subsequently, the regiment moved through Centreville, Virginia, past *Frying Pan*, a site Williams notes as having been the scene of many cavalry skirmishes and "a favorable retreat for guerrilla bands," to Herndon Station, where the regiment made camp the second night.[11]

The next day (June 27) reveille sounded at 3 A.M. The regiment commenced marching at 5 A.M. and it reached Guilford Station, Virginia about an hour later. A brief rest, then on to Broad Run where the men were detained two hours by the passage of a baggage train. They arrived at Edwards Ferry at 3 P.M., crossing over to the Maryland side of the Potomac River *via* pontoon bridges. Their camp that night was near Poolesville.[12]

Resuming at 7 A.M., the march took the regiment across the Monocacy River near its mouth on the Potomac about noon. An hour's rest for a meal—likely hardtack and coffee—then on past Adamsville to a campsite two miles beyond that place. From 7 A.M. the next day (June 29) the men marched all morning through rain, arriving at Frederick City, Maryland about noon. There they discovered the entire Army of the Potomac was moving towards Emmitsburg, Maryland. After some three hours the men again were ordered forward. Camping that night close to Creagerstown, Maryland, the men learned that Major General George Meade had been appointed head of their army just days before.[13]

On June 30th the regiment arrived at Emmitsburg, Maryland, having marched 120 miles in six days. The next day the pace was quickened when "the sound of guns to the north told that a battle was going on and we were needed."[14]

The Second Brigade reached the Gettysburg battlefield late on the first day of fighting there and lay down for the night in a wheat field. Chaplain Smart describes their march as having been "severe," and writes that of 722 men who had left Wolf Run Shoals only 500 remained, the others having fallen out, "unable to bear the killing pace."[15]

The following account by Smart details actions by the 14th Vermont Regiment on July 2nd and 3rd.

> Late in the afternoon of the 2nd, the brigade was called into action on the left center, to repel the attack of Gen. A. P. Hill. A battery had already been captured and was re-taken by the Thirteenth Vermont. Another was in peril and was saved as the Fourteenth double-quicked to its rescue. The regiment remained in this position during the rest of the engagement. In the opening cannonade of the third day the Fourteenth had several non-commissioned officers and men killed by the explosion of a battery caisson, near which they were lying. Colonel Nichols obtained permission to move his regiment

forward about ten rods from the main line, where they lay during the terrific cannonade of the third day.[16] When the gray line of Pickett's massive charge, seventeen thousand strong,[17] moved down upon the position of the Fourteenth, they lay concealed on the ground, until the line was within sixty yards. The men rose at command and gave a staggering and unexpected volley in the face of the charging column. The direction of the advancing charge was changed, and swung off to the north, until their right flank was beyond the right of the Fourteenth. It was at this time that General Stannard's quick eye saw his chance for a flank movement, and delivered it with such fatal effect upon Pickett. The Fourteenth moved a short distance by the flank to the north, and obliquely from the main line. The Thirteenth, followed by the Sixteenth, changed front on the first company and moved out at right

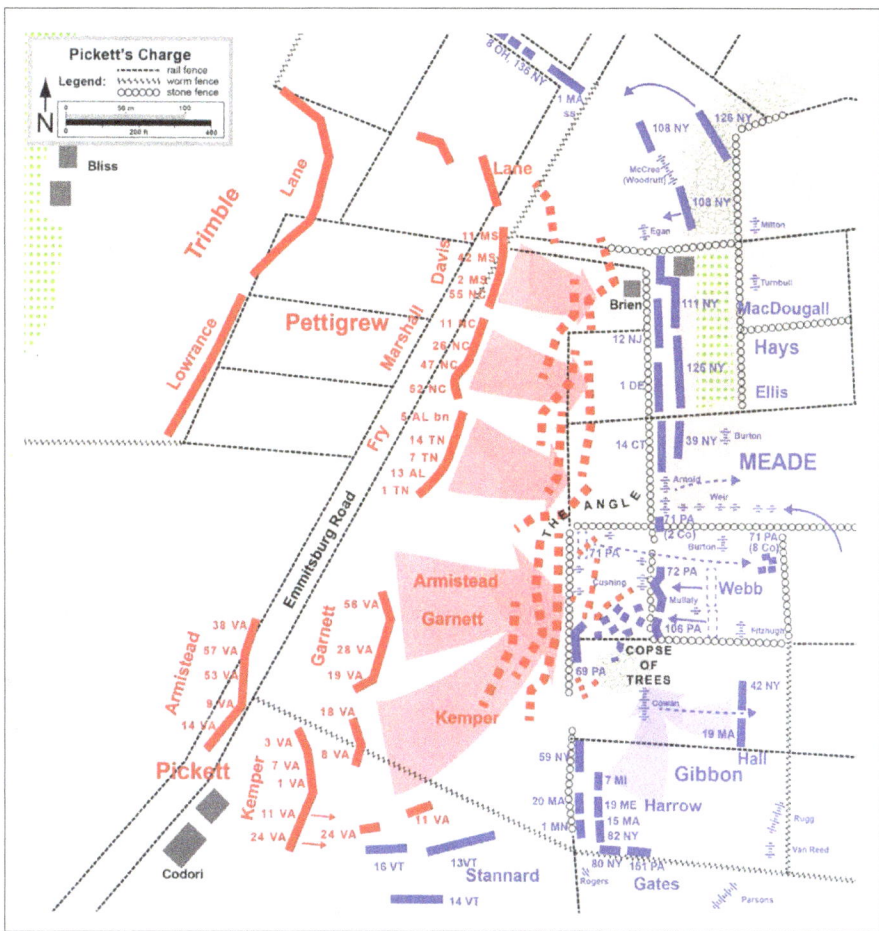

Map 3. "Pickett's Charge, July 3, 1863." Map adapted from material provided by Jen Murray and Peter Carmichael to attendees at the 2022 Civil War Institute, Gettysburg College.

angles, from the line and charged forward. The Fourteenth kept up a rapid fire at close range and closed up the pen in which Pickett's right wing was caught and crushed.

After the main charge was repulsed, [Confederate] General Wilcox's Brigade was seen coming down in front of the position of the Fourteenth. The Sixteenth was coming back to get into line to receive the charge, but Colonel Veazey [Colonel of the 16th Vermont] saw an opportunity to strike them on the front, which he did in splendid style. Four companies of the Fourteenth, A, F, D and I, under Lieutenant-Colonel Rose, formed on his left and assisted in capturing most of the Rebel Brigade.[18]

After the Battle of Gettysburg

The 14th Vermont Volunteers joined the pursuit of Lee's army, which again involved hard marching. Leaving the Gettysburg battlefield on July sixth, the regiment made it to Emmitsburg, Maryland before stopping for the night. The next day's march was remembered by Chaplain Smart as particularly hard: It consisted "of thirty-five miles continuously, ending in rain, mud and darkness, on the top of the Catoctin Mountain, after midnight." [19]

The regiment marched over South Mountain, through Boonesboro to Williamsport, Maryland by July 14. It continued on to Harper's Ferry, then back to South Mountain again, and camped near Berlin [present day Brunswick], Maryland from which place it traveled by train to Baltimore and on to New York City. Draft rioting there had been raging for four days prior to the men's arrival. Despite pleas by General Edward Canby and their own Colonel William T. Nichols to remain in New York and assist in quelling those riots, the regiment refused.[20]

The Fourteenth Vermont Regiment had been released from service on July 18 (following its nine months period of service, and two days before it arrived in New York City) and the men were chafing to get home. They proceeded to Brattleboro, arriving there on July 21. Regiment members, including **Privates Lathrop** and **Manum,** were mustered out July 30, 1863.[21]

Subsequent service by one of the Waitsfield soldiers

Private Zimri Lathrop[22] chose to enlist near the end of the war for a one-year term in the Seventh Vermont Volunteer Infantry Regiment, where he was assigned to Company D. He served there from January 18th until September 29th of 1865, when he was mustered out. During that period Lathrop would have participated in Seventh Regiment actions of the Mobile

Campaign, including a siege of Spanish Fort and battles at Fish River, Blakely and Whistler, Alabama. At Whistler, the Seventh Regiment notably saved from destruction machine and repair shops belonging to the Mobile and Ohio Railroad. (Confederates fleeing before advancing Union soldiers had attempted to destroy those.) All those actions hastened the fall of Mobile and the subsequent surrender of a Confederate army under Richard Taylor.

Notes

1. A comment on Augustine Manum's civilian occupation: Manum, a local beekeeper, manufactured equipment for that trade and gained national recognition when he designed a unique hive design, soon sold across the country.

2. John C. Williams had enlisted in Company B as a Corporal when the Fourteenth Regiment was organized but was reduced in rank to Private at his own request on March 1, 1863 and transferred to Company K. His seemingly odd request for demotion also was made by three other Corporals in Company B.

3. J. C. Williams (1864), 13.

4. *Op. cit.*, 13-14.

5. *Op. cit.*, 14-15.

6. *Op. cit.*, 17.

7. Munson's Hill surmounting the Bailey's Crossroads plain is located very near present-day Fairfax, Virginia. Confederate cavalry commander J. E. B. ("Jeb") Stuart had made Munson's Hill his base the previous year.

8. That move and subsequent ones by the Fourteenth Regiment up to its departure from Wolf Run Shoals at the commencement of the Gettysburg Campaign, are cited in correspondence by Anthony J. O'Connor to Virginia Gage dated October 22, 2015, which the latter has shared with me. Per O'Connor (a Newport, Vermont publisher of Civil War books), the regiment's bases were Camp Chase at Arlington Heights, Virginia, Camp Vermont, Camp Seward, and then back to Camp Vermont in the first week of December 1862.

9. Smart, in Peck, II, 503.

10. Williams, *op. cit.*, 67 and 110.

11. *Op. cit.*, 133-134.

12. *Op. cit.*, 134-135.

13. *Op. cit.*, 136-137.

14. Smart, *op. cit.*, 503.

15. *Ibid.* Another description of the Second Vermont Brigade's march to Gettysburg appears in the Thirteenth Vermont Volunteer Infantry section of this work.

16. This counter-intuitive move forward apparently protected his men without weakening the Union battle line as the Confederates' cannons were overshooting the new position.

17. Smart's recollection of the attacking Confederates as numbering 17,000 is

consistent with the range of estimates (17 to 20 thousand) which "veterans on both sides" tended to cite "for a few decades after the war," according to historian Carol Reardon. "For many more years after that, [Confederate General James] Longstreet set the standard with his comment that no 15,000 troops ever arrayed for battle could take Cemetery Hill. Modern histories of the attack have reduced the number to a range somewhere between 10,500 and 13,000." Reardon (1997), 6.

18. Smart, *op. cit.*, 503.

19. Smart, *op. cit.*, 504.

20. Canby, a federal officer, was charged with putting down the NYC draft riots. Source of this refusal by the 14th: A. O'Connor, correspondence with V. Gage as noted above.

21. An intriguing entry in Peck (2, 520) notes that a 14th Regiment private, Henry Drum from Charlotte, was murdered July 26th while on furlough. His murder must have occurred while the men were in Brattleboro awaiting their formal discharge.

22. Lathrop was born in Rupert, Vermont in 1835. Sometime after he served in the Seventh Vermont he came to Waitsfield where he was working as a farmer when he married for the second time. A certificate of Lathrop's marriage on October 18, 1890 to Leonora Dano is recorded in Waitsfield's Town Hall. Lathrop died August 25, 1900 and is buried in the Irasville Cemetery, where a crumbling gravestone incised "Co D/7 VT INF" led to the discovery of this previously-unacknowledged Waitsfield Civil War soldier.

15th Vermont Volunteer Infantry Regiment

The Fifteenth Vermont Volunteer Infantry Regiment was raised in the fall of 1862, shortly after the 12th, 13th and 14th regiments were subscribed. Subsequently, when the Sixteenth Vermont was raised, those five regiments (all nine-month units) were designated the Second Vermont Brigade.

Waitsfield contributed two recruits to the 15th Regiment: **John D. Donahue** and **Rollin O. Joslyn**. Neither man is cited in Jones' 1909 accounting of local "boys" who went to war for the Union; service records for these two men were located through the Ledoux & Associates website.[1]

Private Donahue was assigned to **Company C** while Private Joslyn went into **Company I** ("eye"). The regiment, mustered in October 22, 1862, was commanded by Colonel Redfield Proctor.[2]

Early actions, including frequent moves, by the Fifteenth Vermont Volunteer Infantry Regiment

A post-war regimental history co-authored by Colonel Proctor and Lieutenant-Colonel William W. Grout for inclusion in Peck's *Revised Roster* records the earliest days of the 15th Vermont Volunteers. The regiment started for Washington on October 23rd and arrived there three days later, in drenching rain.[3]

The men spent their first night in the capital at the *Soldiers' Rest*, as many Vermont troops before them had done, then went into camp on Capitol Hill. Soon after, the brigade crossed over into Virginia but the Fifteenth remained there only briefly before returning to Capitol Hill for a few days until it could move into Camp Vermont near Hunting Creek, Virginia.

Camp Vermont had been established by the Twelfth and Thirteenth Vermont Infantry Regiments about November first. Proctor and Grout describe that camp's location as "in a low malarial place" that was responsible for many deaths during the six weeks the Fifteenth Regiment was there, and even afterwards.[4]

The regiment initially was assigned to construct a stockade around the tents of the new camp. There was drill, of course, as well as picketing and fatigue duty at Fort Lyon.[5]

Proctor and Grout write:

> November 25 [1862], on a dark, rainy night about ten o'clock, Colonel Randall of the Thirteenth, with his own and the Fourteenth and Fifteenth regiments started for Bull Run, then the outer picket line in the defenses of Washington, for the purpose of more effectually guarding the Orange & Alexandria railroad. They made a slow, weary march amid darkness and drizzling rain till about four o'clock A.M., when the rain had turned to snow and the command bivouacked on the left side of the turnpike about two miles short of Fairfax Court House.[6]

Over the next few days, the Fifteenth covered a small area near Fairfax Station, relieving the Garibaldi Guards.[7] On December 4th the Fifteenth itself was relieved and returned to Camp Vermont. (The distance was about 30 miles, which the regiment traveled in a day, stopping only once to make coffee.)

Eight days later the regiment returned to the chestnut grove where the men had taken their coffee break. This time they constructed a camp: They would not be returning to Camp Vermont. Stuart's Confederate cavalry raided nearby areas late in December, causing the regiment to fall out several times to protect Fairfax Court House and Centreville, Virginia. After Stuart's troopers returned to Virginia (riding through Union lines!), the regiment returned to its chestnut grove camp, but it was there only a few days before moving once more to Fairfax Station where it remained until spring. At the latter place the regiment "engaged in drill, both battalion and brigade, and fatigue work on rifle pits southeast of [that] station." [8]

Officers Proctor and Grout continue:

> May 7, the Fifteenth regiment went to Bealeton Station, and on the next day General Stoneman's cavalry came out at that point from their extensive raid in rear of Lee's army. Here the regiment and Stoneman's cavalry did picket duty together for several days, when the regiment returned to duty on Bull Run, camping at Union Mills.[9]

Notable activities in the next month included an attack upon one of the regiment's supply trains by CS General John Mosby's independent cavalry (May 30, 1863) and a creative improvisation of transportation for their own camp equipage which salvaged materials left behind by Confederates at Catlett's and Bristoe Stations on the Orange and Alexandria Railroad when CS Lieutenant-General T. J. "Stonewall" Jackson's forces had burned Union supply trains at those places the year before.

Role of the 15th Regiment in the Gettysburg Campaign

The most remarkable aspect of the brief service by Vermont's Fifteenth Volunteers began, of course, when the Second Vermont Brigade commenced its long march into Pennsylvania (June 25) as part of the I Corps, Army of the Potomac. Citing Proctor and Grout's account of the latter part of that march:

> [At Emmitsburg, Maryland on June 30] the Twelfth and Fifteenth had been detailed to guard the corps' train, which they accompanied July 1, to within about two miles of Gettysburg, where, under an order from General Sickles, whose corps was moving rapidly to the relief of Howard, the Fifteenth went upon the field, and, a little after dark, joined the Thirteenth, Fourteenth, and Sixteenth in a wheat field to the left of Cemetery Hill. Next morning the four regiments were placed in support of the batteries on Cemetery Hill.
>
> Just about 12 o'clock M., General Doubleday, commanding the First Corps, learning the Fifteenth, which had been assigned by Reynolds the day before to guard the train, was on the field, and being disquieted also, by reported attacks upon the train by Stuart's cavalry, ordered the Fifteenth to overtake the train with the least possible delay and rejoin the Twelfth in guarding it. Two companies of the Fifteenth, with two from the Twelfth, were left in charge of First Corps' ammunition train near the field.[10]
>
> The regiment found the [supply] train at Westminster [Maryland] the next forenoon. From Westminster the regiment went with the train via Frederick City and South Mountain towards Hagerstown, and rejoined the brigade in front of Funkstown.
>
> . . . .
>
> [Pursuing Lee's army following the Battle of Gettysburg], On Sunday, July 12, the army formed in line of battle in front of Hagerstown, the Vermont Brigade taking position on the right of First Corps, and Lieutenant-Colonel Grout, of the Fifteenth, with 200 men of the Sixteenth, went upon the skirmish line.
>
> Two days later, Lee crossed the Potomac,[11] and a few days after that at Berlin, Md., the regiment took the cars for home.

It reached New York in the midst of the draft riots.

Its term of service was then up, but at the request of General Canby, commanding in New York,[12] it remained until quiet was restored.[13]

John Donahue and **Rollin Joslyn** both survived their service without wounds, it appears, and they mustered out with the regiment at Brattleboro on August 5, 1863.

Notes

1. Tom Ledoux & Associates, ©2020: https://www.vermontinthecivilwar.org

2. Proctor later served as Governor of Vermont, U.S. Secretary of War and U.S. Senator. Proctor's Lieutenant Colonel, William Wallace Grout, served as a U.S. Representative variously representing Vermont's 2nd and 3rd congressional districts for 20 years.

3. Note that there was no "basic training" in Vermont for this regiment.

4. Proctor and Grout, in Peck, 2, 524.

5. Fort Lyon (named for Brigadier General Nathaniel Lyon who had died at the Wilson's Creek, Missouri battle) was the next-to-largest of 68 Union forts and batteries that constituted defensive rings protecting Washington. It was destroyed by a massive explosion of its powder magazine June 9, 1863—seven months after Privates Donahue and Joslyn labored there.

6. Proctor and Grout, *loc. cit.*

7. The 39th New York Infantry, one of the earliest Union regiments, was called colloquially the Garibaldi Guard (or Guards) as a tribute to Guiseppe Garibaldi, the revolutionary general and patriot who helped birth the state of Italy. Frederick D'Utassy (who was in command at Fairfax Station when the Fifteenth Vermont arrived) organized recent immigrants in New York City into the 39th NY Volunteers. That regiment comprised three companies of Hungarians, three companies of Germans, one company each of Italians, Swiss and French, and one that combined Spaniard and Portuguese recruits; most men had military experience. It was engaged from May 1861 through July 1865. Besides serving in the defenses of Washington, the Guard fought as part of the Army of Northeastern Virginia under McDowell, then in the Army of Virginia under Pope and finally, in the Army of the Potomac under McClellan, Burnside, Hooker and Meade successively.

8. Proctor and Grout, *loc. cit.*, 525.

9. *Ibid.*

10. The regimental historians specify the two companies from the 15th Vermont detailed for that duty as H and K, so it seems clear that neither Donahue nor Joslyn was on the battlefield at Gettysburg on July 2 or 3; rather, they would have been with the other companies of the 15th that were hastening back to support the supply train at Westminster. However, that seemingly-straightforward assignment was derailed temporarily by III Corps pickets under the command of General Daniel Sickles, according to an account by Howard Coffin in *Nine Months to Gettysburg* (1997). The men of the 15th managed to get breakfast with the other Second Brigade regiments early in the morning of July second before they were ordered to

Rock Creek Church (some 2½ miles from the battlefield). Two companies of the regiment remained with the ammunition train there while the other companies marched 23 more miles to the supply trains at Westminster, Maryland, arriving there about noon on July third.

11. The crossing of Lee's army back into Virginia on July 14, 1863 is considered the end date of the Gettysburg Campaign.

12. Major General E. R. S. Canby. Later in the war, Canby took the surrender of Richard Taylor's army at Mobile.

13. Proctor and Grout, *ibid.*

17th Vermont Volunteer Infantry Regiment

The Seventeenth Vermont Volunteer Infantry Regiment was the last State of Vermont infantry regiment called to service during the Civil War. Headed by Colonel Francis V. Randall, formerly commander of the Thirteenth Infantry Regiment (disbanded by then), the Seventeenth included many veterans of earlier Vermont regiments. It was part of the Second Brigade, Second Division, Ninth Army Corps, commanded by Major General Ambrose Burnside. The IX Corps was an independent command within the Army of the Potomac, and the only corps that reported directly to U. S. Grant rather than through George Meade.

Overview of wartime service by the Seventeenth Infantry Regiment

Recruiting for the 17th Vermont Regiment had been a difficult task, according to Marius Péladeau, who has written of the role of Colonel Francis V. Randall in raising the Seventeenth Regiment soon after Randall's men (the nine-month Thirteenth Regiment) were mustered out. At the time, there was a dearth of Vermont men signing up for duty: Only men not already enrolled in the Union's forces, or men who had served previously and had chosen not to re-enlist, were available to be called upon, it seemed. Nevertheless, the need for a new state regiment was great. (If enough volunteers could not be found, Vermont would have to resort to a draft, something no one wanted.) Slowly a unit was assembled. Before it was at full strength—even before a single battalion-size drill was conducted—the Seventeenth Vermont Volunteer Infantry was rushed to the front lines, according to Péladeau's account.[1]

That regiment fought in every battle of the 1864–1865 Overland Campaign: The Wilderness, Spotsylvania, North Anna River, Totopotomoy, Bethesda Church,[2] Cold Harbor, Petersburg, the Mine explosion (July 30), Weldon Railroad, Poplar Spring Church, the first battle of Hatcher's Run and the final assault on Petersburg (April 2, 1865). At least one Waitsfield man had been present in the regiment all that time. Subsequently (although no Townsmen then were left with the regiment), the Seventeenth joined in the pursuit of Lee's Army of Northern Virginia.

Throughout its term of service, the regiment lost 14 officers killed in action or mortally wounded, more than any other Vermont regiment.[3]

Five Waitsfield men enlisted for three years' service in the Seventeenth Vermont Volunteer Infantry Regiment, each in a different company. All became casualties of the war.

Company B

John B. Atherton, born in Canada, enlisted from Essex, Vermont at age 22.[4] He was mustered in March 1, 1864. It is likely that Atherton participated with the 17th Regiment in the campaign from the Rapidan River to the James River that spring, including its battles at the Wilderness and Spotsylvania Court House, operations on the lines of the North Anna and Totopotomoy Rivers, and battles at Cold Harbor and Bethesda Church before he was wounded at Petersburg on June 17, 1864. (It is not known if Atherton was hospitalized for any period following that wounding.) He was mustered out July 14, 1865 with most of the members of the 17th Regiment.[5]

Company C

Lathrop Thompson Stoddard, who had departed with his mates from Co. B of the Thirteenth Infantry Regiment back in July 1863 (just after the close of the Gettysburg Campaign), enlisted in the Seventeenth Regiment eight months later on the day before his 20th birthday. He was assigned to Company C as a Corporal and was honored by being chosen as Color Bearer.

Stoddard was severely wounded and taken prisoner during the July 30, 1864 Battle of the Mine, a disastrous action in the early days of the Union siege of Petersburg, Virginia.[6] Lieutenant General Ulysses S. Grant wrote shortly afterwards: "The loss in the disaster of Saturday last foots up about 3500 of whom 450 were killed and 2000 wounded. It was the saddest affair I have witnessed in this war. Such opportunity for carrying fortifications I have never seen and do not expect again to have." Grant wrote that the Confederate loss in killed at the Mine must be greater than his own, although he acknowledged that Union losses in wounded and captured were four times as great.[7]

According to local historian M. B. Jones, Lathrop Stoddard died August 4, 1864 "while in the hands of the enemy." [8] The Tom Ledoux & Associates website further specifies that Lathrop Stoddard died in prison at Petersburg. A postwar obituary gives a different death date for him, while offering these gruesome details:

> [At the Mine's explosion, Stoddard] carried the State colors 'till [it was] cut and torn in pieces by shot and shell and [he was] wounded in the shoulder while trying to get back to the Union lines, and taken prisoner; [he was] spared the horror of long confinement in Southern prisons [because he] died 8 days after the explosion, August 7, '64 while in the hands of the enemy.[9]

The Waitsfield Village Cemetery has a Stoddard family stone that includes Lathrop's name as well as the name of a brother, Horace B. Stoddard, but that marker is a cenotaph. Neither body ever was recovered.[10]

Howard Coffin's *Something Abides* describes a Waitsfield frame house still standing in 2013 that had been the household of William Tell Stoddard, father of four sons who went to the war. Two sons, Horace and Lathrop, died, whereas Harlan "survived a wound at Savage's Station and imprisonment to return to Waitsfield"; only William [William Henry] "came home unharmed." Coffin writes further of another Waitsfield location where Dr. Simeon Stoddard, the father of William Tell Stoddard, had lived. That grandfather of the brothers just named had ten grandsons who served in the Civil War, Coffin writes. One of those ten, George Walker, "died of disease in Louisiana." [11]

Company E

William Palmer was born in Scotland, perhaps in 1843, suggesting he was 20 or 21 years old when he enlisted on August 2, 1864. He was mustered-in that same day as a substitute for a man from Sutton, Vermont. Palmer was assigned to Company E of the 17th Vermont Infantry Regiment but deserted soon: There's no record that he joined the company.[12]

Company F

Wesley Emerson Dana enlisted in the 17th Regiment on January 2, 1864 at age 18, but he was not mustered in until April 12, 1864. (That happened to be the third anniversary of the opening date of the war, when South Carolina militia directed by General P. G. T. Beauregard, acting by order of Confederate President Jefferson Davis, began shelling Fort Sumter.) The long delay in Dana's mustering-in seems to have been caused by the fact that recruitment into the regiment was slow and there were not yet enough men enlisted in Company F for that company to be sworn in. Once it was,

Company F was rushed to Alexandria, Virginia as part of an *ad hoc* battalion that received only the most minimal introduction to warfare. "Its third attempt at battalion drill was on the bloody field of the Wilderness to the sound of the enemy's guns," records the regimental historian.[13]

Company I

Henry A. Miner[14] was 22 years old upon his enlistment from Reading, Vermont in late May of 1864. He was not mustered in until July 6, 1864. (It has been noted above that the later companies of the regiment were slow to be filled, which delayed mustering-in ceremonies.) Private Miner was wounded during the Union break-through at Petersburg, Virginia (April 2, 1865) and was discharged "for wounds" on July first. Apparently, Miner spent the three months between those dates convalescing, as a 1927 obituary noted that after being wounded, Miner "…was sent to the general hospital in Washington" and sometime later was "transferred to the Sloan Hospital in Montpelier, where he remained until honorably discharged because of wounds." [15]

The 17th Regiment at the Wilderness and Spotsylvania Court House

The regiment began active service almost immediately after its companies rendezvoused at Alexandria, Virginia. With its brigade,[16] it began a march to Bristoe Station, Virginia on April 27, 1864, arriving days later. Following the Orange and Alexandria railroad, the brigade reached Bealeton Station on May 4. The next day it crossed the Rappahannock River at Rappahannock Station and that same day, crossed the Rapidan River at Germanna Ford.

Measles had broken out in the new regiment. The effect of that epidemic, combined with the hard marching, caused the ranks of the 17th Vermont Volunteers to be reduced from its original size of 869 to about 400 when the men halted that night near the VI Corps position on the Wilderness battlefield. "Ignorant of the extent of the carnage of the first day's fight [May 5], as well as of what the morrow held in store, tired, foot-sore, exhausted, they threw themselves on the ground for rest and sleep," Joel Lucia, a First Lieutenant in Company H, wrote after the war.[17]

They were awakened soon after midnight. At 2:00 A.M. of May 6 the regiment led the corps' advance along the Germanna Plank Road. Their division was placed in the center of the Union line. Their brigade (Griffin's) was in line of battle at sunrise. The Seventeenth held the right of the brigade line. It

Fig. 18. Union breastworks in the Wilderness, 1864
Photo courtesy of the Library of Congress.

advanced through woods and open fields until its skirmishers were driven back by the enemy.

> About 9 A.M., the Seventeenth advanced through the pine undergrowth, at times crawling on hands and knees, drove the enemy's line from behind a rail fence and occupied its position. This it held during the forenoon, although disconnected and without support on the right, and until after the regiment on its left had gone back. Here, alone and exposed, it repulsed an attack upon both flanks, holding its position until noon...About 2 P.M., Griffin's brigade was ordered to attack the enemy occupying some log breastworks in the wood beyond a swampy ravine. It moved out rapidly and passing over troops lying in front, charged and drove back the enemy's line. Two hundred prisoners, some of them officers, were taken by the brigade in this advance.[18]

When Confederate reinforcements attacked the brigade hours later, it fell back almost to its former position, but it held that new position the rest of the day and that night until withdrawn. Thus ended the 17th's first battle of the war. It took no other active role in the Wilderness fighting.[19]

It seems that **Lathrop Stoddard**, **Henry Miner**, **Wesley Dana** and **John**

Atherton escaped injury in the Wilderness fighting and moved on with the regiment towards Spotsylvania.

> May 10 the regiment moved with the corps towards Spottsylvania [*sic*] Court House, crossing and recrossing the Ny River. On the 11th, it took up position before the enemy's entrenchments north of the Court House. For three days some of the other corps had been engaged in severe fighting here without definite result or advantage.[20]

Wesley Dana was wounded at Spotsylvania on May 12, 1864, just one month into his military service, becoming one of 72 casualties of about 250 men of the Seventeenth Regiment who fought savagely at the salient that day.[21] Given that Dana was discharged "for wounds" on July 17, 1865, three days after his regiment was mustered out, it is likely he was hospitalized throughout the entire time after his wounding right up until that date.

Battlefield attrition among the Waitsfield men in the Seventeenth Regiment

Wesley Dana's wounding had left only Atherton, Miner and Lathrop Stoddard with the regiment after May 12, 1864.

The next to fall was Atherton, wounded June 17 at a time when Dyer (1909) places the regiment as present in three days of assaults on Petersburg, Virginia that marked the commencement of a Union siege.

On July 30 Stoddard was wounded and taken prisoner at the Crater explosion, and died soon afterwards in a Confederate prison camp, as described earlier.

Only Henry Miner moved forward with the 17th Regiment towards the Weldon Railroad. A post-war obituary reproduced on the Ledoux & Associates website (https://www.vermontinthecivilwar) notes Miner's involvement in actions at the Weldon RR and several subsequent battles prior to his being wounded April 2, the day Union forces broke through the Petersburg defenses. As Miner was discharged "for wounds" on July 1, 1865, he may have been hospitalized throughout the whole April 2–July 1 period.

No Waitsfield men remained in the Seventeenth Regiment after April 2, 1865.

Notes

1. Péladeau (2002), 361.

2. The Seventeenth Vermont Regiment was separated briefly from the 10th Vermont and the Old Vermont Brigade and was the only Vermont infantry unit engaged at the Battle of Bethesda Church, Virginia (June 1-3). After that action the Seventeenth rejoined its earlier comrades in assaults on Petersburg (June 16-18) which marked the commencement of siege operations there. During the siege itself, the regiment was engaged from July 9, 1864.

3. Joel H. Lucia, cited in Peck, 2, 569.

4. Atherton merits inclusion as a Waitsfield soldier because his body was buried in the Waitsfield Village Cemetery upon his death in 1888. Presumably he had moved to the town sometime after the war.

5. Peck records that the regiment marched in the Grand Review at Washington, D. C. on May 23, 1865 and remained in the city until July 14, when it left for Burlington. The men lodged at the Marine Hospital there until they received their final pay on July 24 and were free to go home (2, 574).

6. The Mine is called "the Crater" in many Civil War accounts.

7. Grant (1869), 1062–1063. Grant's message was sent by cipher on August 1, 1864 to Major General Henry Halleck who functioned as Grant's Chief of Staff in the capital while Grant himself traveled with Meade's army during the war's last year.

8. Jones (1909), 92.

9. That obituary, published in *Hemenway's Historical Gazetteer (1892), iv, 799*, appears on the *Vermont in the Civil War* website (retrieved April 9, 2020).

10. Horace B. Stoddard's story appears in the section on the Second Vermont Volunteer Infantry Regiment. Horace was just shy of 22 years old when killed; Lathrop was 20 years old.

11. Coffin (2013), 399. In a search of the Ledoux & Associates website I found a "George Walker" born in Bethel and credited to Randolph upon his enlistment at age 25. That George, presumably a cousin to the four Stoddard brothers cited by Coffin as living in Waitsfield, served as a corporal in the 8th Vermont Infantry and died at Ship Island, Louisiana of "rheumatic fever and dysentery," according to the website. (He is not included as a Waitsfield soldier in this work.) Furthermore, it is possible that George Aaron Walker, whose story does appear in a later section of this work about Waitsfield-born men who served in state units beyond Vermont, may have been another of Dr. Simeon Stoddard's grandsons. Other Stod-

dards named in Jones' 1909 town history are Daniel, Dorric, Franklin, Lyman and Simeon. Their service records appear in this work with their respective regiments.

12. Once more we see a soldier whose name appears in this work based on the criterion of burial in Waitsfield (in his case, in the Village Cemetery). Palmer was hired as a substitute for William F. Ruggles of Sutton. (Dyer, II, 586).

13. Lucia, in Peck, 2, 569.

14. Miner is included here as a Waitsfield soldier because his body is buried in the Waitsfield Village Cemetery. Miner's listing in Peck (2, 594) spells his surname as "Minor".

15. *Barre Daily Times* (June 20, 1927). The obituary gives Miner's discharge date as June 28, 1865, a discrepancy from the July 1 date shown on the L & A website. Either way, he was discharged almost a full month before the 17th Regiment was dismissed at Burlington. That same obituary specifies that Henry A. Miner took part in these 1864 battles: Petersburg Mine (*aka* the Crater), Weldon Railroad, Poplar Springs Church and Hatcher's Run.

16. When the Seventeenth Vermont Infantry joined Burnside's Ninth Corps, it was brigaded with two Maine and three New Hampshire regiments.

17. Lucia, *loc. cit.*, 569.

18. *Ibid.*

19. *Ibid.*

20. Lucia, *loc. cit.*, 570.

21. *Ibid.*

1st Vermont Cavalry Regiment

When Vermont's Governor Fairbanks was asked on September 16, 1861 to raise a volunteer cavalry unit as well as additional volunteer infantry regiments, the Secretary of War announced he already had designated his choice to become Colonel of that First Vermont Cavalry, Lemuel B. Platt from Colchester.

Colonel Platt, the first of seven men who would head the Vermont Cavalry over its time of existence, was authorized to purchase horses and equipment; $160,000 was budgeted. On November nineteenth, the regiment—fully mounted and equipped—was mustered in at a camp of instruction in Burlington.[1]

In a little under a month, the regiment was on its way to the nation's capital, requiring 153 train cars for the journey.[2]

Vermont's volunteer cavalry was the first full cavalry regiment raised in New England.[3]

Only one Waitsfield man, **Alonzo James Cady**, was part of the original group of Vermont troopers who enlisted for three years. Other Waitsfield men would join the regiment later.

Companies in which Waitsfield men served within the First Vermont Cavalry Regiment

Company A

While no Waitsfield men were assigned to Company A as their original placement, those who were still with the regiment on June 21, 1865 were transferred from Company C into Company A that day.

Company C

Seymour Lucius Kneeland, Ziba H. McAllister, John W. Palmer,[4] **Jerome W. Parker** and **John K. Sterling** were mustered into Company C late in December 1863. Another Waitsfield man, **Bertrand Delos Campbell**, joined them in August 1864.

Company E

Alonzo James Cady enlisted from Granville, Vermont.[5] He was mustered into the regiment on November 19, 1861, and was assigned to Company E. Private Cady appears to have participated in all his company's actions for almost two years until he was transferred to the Veterans Reserve Corps (VRC) on September 1, 1863. Cady was discharged from service one month later.[6]

Organizational placements of the First Vermont Cavalry Regiment

Vermont's first (and only) cavalry regiment left for the nation's capital December 14, 1861. On Christmas Day the regiment moved to Annapolis in the first of a rather extraordinary series of movements and changes of assignment. Originally attached to the Army of the Potomac (in the V Army Corps), Vermont's cavalry subsequently was assigned to the II Army Corps where it fought with Major General John Pope's Army of Virginia throughout the summer of 1862. Following a seven-months' stint in the defenses of Washington, D.C. with the XXII Army Corps, commanded by Joseph Hooker until replaced by George Meade, the regiment rejoined the Army of the Potomac, serving there from April 1863 to August 1864 until it was assigned to the Army of the Shenandoah, defending the Middle Military Division.[7]

The First Vermont Cavalry participated in 75 battles and skirmishes according to unit historian William L. Greenleaf, achieving a reputation as one of the best fighting regiments of the army.[8]

Important engagements in 1862

The regiment encountered Confederate forces for the first time on April 16, 1862 in Virginia's Shenandoah Valley. Greenleaf, who had risen through the ranks to become a First Lieutenant, gives this account:

> [Vermont's First Cavalry Regiment] charged through the little village of Mount Jackson and drove Ashby's cavalry for more than a mile to the North Fork of the Shenandoah, where the enemy set fire to the bridge hoping to cut off further pursuit. Finding the stream unfordable, part of the regiment dashed over the burning bridge after the flying Confederates, while the remainder brought water from the river in their feed-bags and extinguished the flames.[9]

In support of Union General N. B. Banks' retreat down the Valley that

May and June, "[T]he regiment had its full share of fighting," according to Greenleaf. He cites engagements at McGaheysville, Middletown and Winchester, Virginia.[10]

Later that year the First Vermont Cavalry fought under John Pope in the latter's Northern Virginia Campaign (August 16–September 2, 1862), participating at Luray Court House, Culpeper Court House, Orange Court House, Kelly's Ford and Waterloo Bridge.

In the Second Battle of Bull Run (Second Manassas to the Confederates), the First Vermont—with Alonzo Cady still present—was stationed behind the First Michigan, Fourth New York and First West Virginia cavalries in column near the Francis Lewis farm, Portici. Their brigade commander, John Buford, was preparing them to receive a charge he anticipated after having learned of the presence of Confederate cavalry just to the west of the ridge behind which he'd placed his troopers.

A first, almost accidental, encounter occurred between a detachment of Thomas Munford's Second Virginia Cavalry and a squadron of Buford's men. Those Confederates charged and "crashed into the small [Union] band," dispersing them easily, according to John Hennessey, a park historian at the Bull Run battlefield. But when "[the] Virginians pursued to the crest of the next ridge," they saw Buford's men drawn up "ready to fight". The detachment's leader immediately requested reinforcements and was answered by the entire Second Virginia Regiment being ordered in, quickly followed by the rest of its brigade.

Unfortunately, General Buford failed to deploy his entire brigade in countering the subsequent Confederate charge. He brought forward his 1st Michigan and 4th New York regiments but left the 1st West Virginia and the 1st Vermont behind the ridge's crest. "[W]hy he elected to meet them with only half of his command is a mystery," Hennessy remarks.

The 7th and the 12th Virginia regiments rode into the front and right flank of Buford's two deployed regiments. Hennessy's account of this August 30, 1862 battle continues:

> During the first charge the Yankees had enjoyed the advantage of surprise. Now they had no such benefit, and the sight of veteran Confederate cavalry charging on them proved daunting... By the time the rebels closed to within pistol range, the Union line began to disintegrate...The 1st Michigan retreated immediately. 'From that time on there was no order or organization' wrote a Michigander whom Hennessy quotes.
>
> The retreat of the 1st Michigan and the 4th New York also carried away the 1st Vermont and 1st West Virginia. Despite the best efforts of Buford...,

within five minutes all four Federal regiments were in rapid retreat across Bull Run at Lewis Ford.

Buford's cavalry helped guard the Union retreat across Bull Run to its camps at Centreville, Virginia.[11]

A rest and recovery period for the First Vermont Cavalry

"Being reduced in numbers by its arduous service," Greenleaf writes, "the regiment was assigned to duty in the defenses of Washington." [12]

On March 27, 1863 *The Caledonian* reported positions of all Vermont regiments then in the field.[13]

> The First Vermont Brigade [the state's volunteer infantry regiments 2 through 6] is at White Oak Church, Virginia; the 7th Regiment is at Pensacola, Florida; the 8th is at Brasher City, La.; the 9th is at Chicago; the 10th is at White's Ford, near Poolesville, Md.; the 11th is at Washington; the 12th and 13th are at Wolf Run Shoals, Va.; and the 14th, 15th and 16th are at Fairfax Station. The 1st, 2d and 3d companies of Sharp Shooters are near Falmouth, Va. The 1st Battery is at New Orleans. The 2nd Vermont Battery was at Baton Rouge, La. on the 2d of Mar. and was expecting to be ordered forward immediately, with a strong force, to attack Port Hudson. The Headquarters of the 1st Vermont Cavalry is near Fort Scott, Va., but the regiment is doing picket duty in some places. Some are at Drainsville, some at Annandale, some at Lewinsville, and some at Vienna.

During the winter of 1862/63 detachments from the cavalry regiment frequently had engaged in conflicts with Confederate guerrilla forces, including those of John Mosby. When one such detachment sought to capture Mosby near Broad Run (April 1, 1863), it was repulsed with heavy losses. There was another meeting with General Mosby's force at Catlett's Station on May 30th. On that occasion—the last time the regiment faced Mosby's men—the guerrillas were routed.[14]

At Chancellorsville, Virginia, a major engagement in early May 1863 that generally is considered General Robert E. Lee's greatest victory of the war, the 1st Vermont Cavalry was not involved. Cavalry could not have been of use in the dense, dark woods. (For the same reason, Union artillery was of little aid.) Instead, the Cavalry Corps of the Army of the Potomac was sent to raid Lee's supply lines. The Corps damaged two railroads and captured a number of supply wagons.[15]

Meanwhile, the First Vermont Cavalry—which was not yet part of that

Cavalry Corps—remained in their various detachments. Presumably Private Cady was with one of those detachment, although I have no information as to whether that was at Dranesville or another part of Virginia where the First Vermont was picketing.

Contemporary historian Jeffrey Wert describes casualties from the Chancellorsville battle as exceeded only by those of the Battle of Gettysburg and the series of battles at Spotsylvania.[16]

The Vermont Cavalry heads to Gettysburg

Greenleaf gives the following account of the First Vermont Cavalry's incorporation into the Cavalry Corps and inclusion in the Army of the Potomac as that army moved to block Lee's Army of Northern Virginia which was making a second major incursion into the North:

> Early in June, 1863, the scattered detachments of the regiment assembled at Fairfax Court House, preparatory to joining the Army of the Potomac then on the march to Gettysburg. On the 28th of June it was attached to the Cavalry Corps of that army and was afterward associated with it until the close of the war. During the campaign of 1863 the regiment bore a conspicuous part in the brilliant operations which first brought the cavalry into notice as a valuable arm of the service, . . .[17]

As a member of Co. E of the First Vermont Cavalry, Private **Alonzo Cady** may have participated in its actions during the Gettysburg Campaign.[18]

Throughout the Gettysburg Campaign Union cavalry performed its many functions admirably, engaging the Army of Northern Virginia from the onset of the ANV incursion into Maryland and Pennsylvania through its retreat back into Virginia after being defeated in the three-day Battle of Gettysburg. But on at least one occasion the cavalry was employed recklessly, causing Vermont men to fall or be taken captive needlessly.

On Day 3 of the Battle of Gettysburg an unsound decision by General Judson Kilpatrick, commanding the Third Division, led to many casualties. Kilpatrick ordered Elon Farnsworth to lead his brigade (consisting of four regiments including the First Vermont Cavalry) in a charge over totally unsuitable ground. Among those sacrificed was Farnsworth himself, the only Union general officer killed within enemy lines during the war.

An after-action report by the First Vermont Cavalry's Lieutenant Colonel A. W. Preston describes that fatal charge:

> July 3d, in the attack made by Gen. Kilpatrick on the right flank of the

enemy at Gettysburg, this cavalry led the advance. Companies "A," "D," "E," and "I," dismounted, were deployed as skirmishers, and soon drove the enemy's skirmishers back to their main lines.[19] The contest was continued by the opposing batteries and dismounted carbineers until five o'clock, P.M. when Gen. Farnsworth, commanding the Brigade, was ordered to charge the enemy, strongly posted behind stone walls, and in the woods, . . . Gen. Farnsworth dashed forward closely followed by his men.

Leaping one stone wall under a severe fire, our forces drove the enemy in all directions, over still another stone wall, and through a field swept by the rebel batteries, and succeeded in piercing the enemy's second line, where nearly all of our dead were found. . . .

On the hill between the two forces, we encountered a fresh regiment of the enemy, sent in from the right to intercept the retreat of our first column and to re-establish their lines. The struggle for this hill became most desperate, but was at length carried by our boys, with severe loss, the greater part of the enemy being captured. Our loss this day, killed, wounded and missing, 75 men.[20]

In the aftermath of the Battle of Gettysburg

In the early days of General George Meade's pursuit of Lee's retreating army, Kilpatrick's division, including the First Vermont Cavalry, suffered intensely. Recollections follow of two such instances. Private Cady may have been present on those occasions.

Kilpatrick's division fought at Monterey Gap during the night of July 4/5. That action was fought in two states across both sides of the Mason-Dixon Line. It was fought at night "during a severe thunderstorm" when only "bright flashes of lightening" illuminated the intense darkness.[21]

On the night of July 7/8 Kilpatrick kept most of his division awake all night, for fear that J. E. B. Stuart's Confederate cavalry might attack in the dark. "The bivouacs outside Boonsboro [sic] became scenes of utter misery," historian Edward Longacre writes. Longacre cites a chaplain's memory of the men standing for hours "dismounted in a ploughed field in line of battle, in a heavy storm of rain, without fires and with clothes thoroughly saturated… standing in mud to our knees, every horse remaining saddled and in position, and every man at his horse's head. . . This was one of the most wretched nights of all our experience in the cavalry service." [22]

During the Gettysburg Campaign, the First Vermont Cavalry participated in engagements at Boonesboro, Hagerstown, Leitersville, Smithsburg and Falling Waters (all in Maryland), and at Hanover, Hunterstown and Monterey Gap in Pennsylvania as well as on the Gettysburg battlefield itself.[23]

The First Vermont Cavalry after the Gettysburg Campaign

After Gettysburg, three major cavalry battles were fought in a seven-week period in and around Culpeper County, Virginia. (Both armies had returned to their earlier positions on the Upper Rappahannock River.) That period, states Jeffrey Hunt, represents "the critical connective tissue between Gettysburg and the upcoming Bristoe Station and Mine Run campaigns." [24]

Cavalry skirmishes occurred in August and September 1863. The First Vermont Cavalry fought at King George Court House and at Lamb's Creek Church near Port Conway, Virginia. Between September 1-3 the Vermont regiment joined cavalry units from Michigan, New York, Pennsylvania and West Virginia (supported by a United States artillery battalion) in an expedition to Port Conway that destroyed two Confederate gunboats, *Satellite* and *Release*.

The first day of the Port Conway expedition coincided with Private Cady's transfer to the Veteran's Reserve Corps, so he was not present for that expedition or any subsequent activities of the regiment. The next time the First Vermont Cavalry would include any Waitsfield recruit was December.

Five Waitsfield men enter the First Vermont Cavalry Regiment

During the winter of 1863/64 while the First Vermont Cavalry Regiment was engaged in picketing along the Rapidan River from its Virginia base at Stevensburg, five Waitsfield men joined Company A of the regiment: **Seymour Lucius Kneeland, Ziba H. McAllister,**[25] **John W. Palmer, Jerome W. Parker** and **John K. Sterling.**[26]

Like their townsman Alonzo Cady before them, these Waitsfield recruits had to learn quickly the particular requirements of cavalry service, including care and feeding of their mounts and the handling of equipment and arms they had not previously encountered. By this time in the war, Union cavalry forces were supplied with Spencer repeating rifles. Each First Vermont cavalry soldier also carried a scabbard; one or two revolvers; a "McClellan" saddle and a saddle cushion (often doubling as a sleeping blanket); forage for his horse and rations for himself; ammunition; and a canteen. This equipment's total weight was kept under 60 pounds so as not to overburden the mounts.[27]

Winter camp gave these men ample opportunity to learn the unit's history, as well. While Private McCallister had seen the horrific deaths and mutilations of the Gettysburg Campaign from his perspective as an infantry soldier, it is likely he also was aware of the contributions made by fellow Vermonters in cavalry engagements during that campaign. Whether or not these Waitsfield men knew of the First Vermont Cavalry's exploits and losses before they joined up, they surely would have heard about them from their new companions.

General Kilpatrick's raids around Richmond; the Dahlgren affair

Cavalry raids were important components of both Southern and Northern forces during the American Civil War. Raids served both political and military strategic aims of each side.[28]

In the section above on the Gettysburg Campaign, attention was paid to certain actions by General Judson Kirkpatrick's cavalry division that included a brigade to which the First Vermont Cavalry belonged. That brigade (commanded by Nathaniel P. Richmond after the death of Vermonter Elon Farnsworth) was left behind to picket the Rapidan River near the Stevensburg camp when Kilpatrick conducted a series of raids around Richmond, Virginia late in the winter of 1863/64.[29]

Those raids involved some 4000 troopers and had multiple objects: Primary was the liberation of Union prisoners held in Richmond; then destruction of enemy stores in and near that city, capture of Confederate reserve artillery nearby, capture of the Virginia RR, and distribution throughout the region of the Emancipation Proclamation promulgated by President Abraham Lincoln the previous year. The purpose of the latter was to inform enslaved persons that they would be deemed free if they made their way to any of the advancing Union forces in the greater Richmond area.

An undeclared, infamous (and officially denied) additional and highly secret mission was undertaken by Kilpatrick's second in command, 21-year-old Colonel Ulric Dahlgren: the assassination of Confederate President Jefferson Davis.[30]

About 460 picked horsemen rode out with Dahlgren. They included detachments from a number of states' cavalry regiments, including veteran troopers from Vermont's First Cavalry. (All new recruits were left behind, along with the regiment's sick.) The picked men started off with Dahlgren on February 28.

A veteran of the Dahlgren action, S. M. Dufur from Fairfield, Vermont, was among the raiders from Company B, First Vermont Cavalry who were captured on March first. Thirty-seven years to the day later Dufur commenced writing a memoir based on a diary he had kept while interned in Confederate prisoner-of-war camps. Dufur's memoir, published the following year (1902), begins when he opens his "worn and faded memorandum" on the anniversary of his 1864 capture.

> As I pause for a moment to peruse the dim lines that time has nearly erased, I ask myself, "Is this real? Did I write these lines in such a terrible place, and while surrounded by scenes that almost baffle description?"
>
> Yes. Each page, grim with age, bears undisputable evidence of sickness, starvation and death. I am looking upon the same lines that thirty-seven years ago I wrote while the pangs of hunger, the ravages of disease, and the burning rays of a southern sun were doing their awful work.
>
> I carefully lift the first tender leaf. My now impaired vision rests upon the nearly obliterated words:
>
> March 2nd. Taken prisoner last night. I am badly wounded, and in Libby prison. What misery I behold!
>
> March 3rd. Dick Turner, the commanding officer [of Libby Prison], told six of us who were with Dahlgren's command, that we would be shot. We are not guilty. Have not yet had my wounds dressed. God help us, in this our suffering condition.
>
> 4th. They accuse us of murdering women and children. The Richmond papers call us murderers. The guard told us to-day that there is no hope for us.
>
> 5th. I asked Dick Turner for some crutches; he replied, "No, you will be in h—l with your commanding officer before you have a chance to use them." We are more afraid of being lynched, than of being shot.
>
> 6th. O how I suffer. If I am murdered or die, and this book is saved, never let it be seen by my father or mother. God knows that I am not guilty of any crime. I only did a soldier's duty.

Ambushed on March 1st, Dahlgren had been slain with 16 shots to the head and body. Dufur himself had suffered a saber cut that nearly severed the heel from his right foot and a lesser wound to his left arm.[31]

Dufur's diary was maintained through the spring and summer, during which time he was imprisoned at various sites including Charleston and Florence, South Carolina and Andersonville, Georgia. He made the following entries at Andersonville, the first on July 24, 1864.

> Another soldier has been taken from our family—Frank B. Jocelyn, of our company.[32] How poor Frank wanted to live. He gave me a message to carry to his widowed mother, should I live to go out.
>
> July 26th. The members of our family, who are gradually growing fewer in number, today mourns the loss of another—Milo Farnsworth. I found him dead at my side, at three o'clock this morning. He died between the hours of twelve and three.
>
> July 27th. One hundred and sixty-three deaths during the past twenty-four hours. Report says that cholera is in camp. God help us if this is true.
>
> 28th. Two men were shot near the south gate, for stepping beyond the

Dead Line. Capt. Wirz said to-day that we would soon be paroled.

August 2nd. The heat is suffocating. I counted 177 dead bodies at the gate, awaiting the last act of the drama—to be drawn away, and like dead dumb beasts, thrown into a trench. The stench arising from the dead bodies at the gate, and the excremental matter in the swamp, and other parts of the prison, make the air almost stifling.[33]

No other original diary entries appear in Dufur's memoir but he does record his life in several P. O. W. camps, including harrowing instances of escape and recapture. Despite Captain Wirz's pledge in July 1864, Dufur was not paroled for another six months.

The First Vermont Cavalry during the Overland Campaign

The First Vermont Cavalry Regiment took part in the huge Union initiative that commenced with a crossing of the Rapidan River on May 4, 1864 and eventually involved a prolonged siege of Petersburg, Virginia.

Besides the First Vermont Cavalry, many other Vermont units that included Waitsfield men were engaged in the Overland Campaign: The Old Vermont Brigade (consisting of the 2nd through the 6th Vermont Volunteer Infantry Regiments); two other Vermont infantry regiments, the 10th and the 17th; the Third Vermont Light Artillery Battery; and the First Vermont Heavy Artillery Battery (formerly the 11th Vermont Infantry). Additionally, there were Waitsfield men in the Second United States Sharpshooters Regiment in that campaign.[34]

Large and very deadly battles of the Overland Campaign included The Wilderness, Spotsylvania, Cold Harbor and North Anna River.

Late in the summer of 1864 Ulysses Grant separated certain forces from the Army of the Potomac for a special operation. Grant ordered his Cavalry Corps commander, Major General Philip ("Phil") Sheridan, to the Shenandoah Valley region of Virginia. Sheridan's detached command included Vermont's First Cavalry Regiment, assigned to the cavalry arm that accompanied George Crook's Eighth Army Corps.[35]

Sheridan's mission was to destroy foodstuffs and forage being raised and stored throughout the Valley in support of Lee's Army of Northern Virginia. In a three-month succession of battles and burnings of farms, mills and warehouses, Sheridan's destruction became the stuff of legend (and infamy, in Southern memory).

First Vermont Cavalry with Sheridan in the Shenandoah Valley

Moving into the Valley, the First Vermont Cavalry Regiment was brigaded with two companies of the 3rd Indiana Infantry and with the 1st New Hampshire and the 8th and 22nd New York cavalry regiments. The brigade was led by Colonel William Wells from Waterbury, Vermont.

Among the notable movements and engagements of Colonel Wells' men as they moved toward the Shenandoah Valley region of Virginia in July 1864 were these, described by H. K. Ide, a member of Company K of the First Vermont Cavalry:

July 11   Arrived at Martinsburg, Maryland with the VI Corps.

July 15   Returned to Boonsboro, Maryland.

July 16   Proceeded to Harper's Ferry. Ide notes the regiment crossed the Potomac on a pontoon bridge and slept in the burnt-out armory buildings. [Sometime in the period between July 11–17, the regiment skirmished with Jubal Early's men at Rutherford's Farm (*aka* Carter's Farm) and at Stephenson's Depot as Early's army retreated toward Winchester, Virginia where the Confederates had both a hospital and a supply base.]

July 17   Crossed the Shenandoah River in the morning, "riding down the river at the foot of Loudon Heights." The regiment took a position to cover the infantry which was crossing on pontoons at Berlin (near Point of Rocks), after which it forded the Potomac.

July 17/18   Fought in the Battle of Snicker's Gap, *aka* the Battle of Cool Spring.

July 18   Camped near Purcellville. "Forges were brought up and the horses shod."

July 19   Moved to a post between Upperville and Ashby's Gap, Virginia.

July 20   Drove Early's men from Ashby's Gap. Camped that night near Upperville.

July 21   Was ordered to Snicker's Gap, "which [the regiment] held till the 23rd."

July 22   Camped near Salem.

July 23   Went to Warrenton, "where we found [Union] General Newton with the First Corps in possession." Camped at Upperville that night.

July 24   Went to Warrenton Junction; camped near Amissville.

July 25   Returned to Warrenton where the regiment rejoined their brigade and "turned over our horses…Major Wells collected together the dismounted men of the whole division and took them into Washington on the cars for remounting."

July 26   "We drew our horses from a corral at the upper end of the city and crossing the Aqueduct Bridge, camped about one mile from it."

July 27   Camped just beyond Centerville. "From there to the Rappahannock [we] guarded a train of army and sutlers' wagons."[36]

Those entries by Horace Ide give just the smallest idea of the almost-constant movements by the First Vermont Cavalry.[37]

It may be useful to review the organizational placement of the First Vermont, which had been re-assigned many times. Shortly after the period just described, Judson Kilpatrick, who'd been on a leave of absence, returned to head the Third Division of cavalry in the Army of the Shenandoah. The First Vermont Regiment of Cavalry belonged to the Second Brigade of that division.

A most complete narrative of Vermonters in the Shenandoah Valley in the summer and fall of 1864 can be found in an Honors Thesis submitted in April 2003 by James Michael LaMonda to the Honors Board of Norwich University. From that thesis I've chosen to reference material that addresses a period beginning September 30, 1864 when General Philip Sheridan's men had returned to Harrisonburg, Virginia far up the Valley, that is, at the Valley's southern end. In that situation, Sheridan was far from his base of supplies at Harper's Ferry. He was facing a dilemma, whether to return to Harper's Ferry or join Ulysses Grant (who finally allowed Sheridan to exercise his own judgment) before he decided to head down the Valley (northward).

Sheridan's army began the move on October 5 and 6. "As they did so, Sheridan's men continued destroying all supplies in the upper valley, putting the torch to the area between Harrisonburg and Strasburg," LaMonda writes.[38]

The infantry reached Woodstock, Virginia on October 7th in time to camp there for the night. The cavalry, including the First Vermont troopers, served as rearguard to the army. Confederate General Jubal Early was very aware of the Union movement and he ordered his own cavalry to pursue, harassing Sheridan's cavalry as much as possible.

"On at least one occasion a group of the Vermont men were actually flanked and cut off," LaMonda records: They got away only by scaling a wooded mountain. Later that day, with the men preparing to be attacked, their commander had them dismount. Confederates drove the dismounted men into the First Brigade (retreating ahead of them), a distance of almost two miles.

The delegated holders of the horses of the dismounted men had departed, and only an order by the regiment's Adjutant caused them to return so that the Vermont troopers could regain their mounts and escape. Writing to Grant that evening, Sheridan reported his intention to destroy all the valley in the direction of Fisher's Hill.

LaMonda writes of the Vermont regiment's part in the Battle of Tom's Brook: Sheridan had summoned his cavalry commander Alfred Torbert and had ordered him to attack the rebel cavalry the next day, October 9. After a hard-fought 30 minutes' cavalry engagement, the Confederates fled. The Vermonters divided up to pursue two groups of fleeing Confederates, pushing them off Mount Olive and driving them some 25 miles before abandoning the chase and returning to their Strasburg camp. "The Union cavalry had come away from Tom's Brook with eleven Confederate artillery pieces, as well as numerous ambulances, wagons, and prisoners," LaMonda writes. Unfortunately, Sheridan's pleasure with the performance of his men led him to believe that Early's force was broken and would present no further problems.[39]

An additional account of the Tom's Brook engagement is offered by Elliott Hoffman in his 2000 editing of Horace Ide's 1872 manuscript.

Early on the morning of October 9, Hoffman writes, Torbert's cavalry forces "deployed along Tom's Brook, just south of the entrenchments at Fisher's Hill." General George Armstrong Custer's division (some 2,500 men) formed on the right flank along the Back Road, facing 3,000 Confederates under General Thomas L. Rosser. General Wesley Merritt with another 2,500 troopers faced 2,000 Confederates under Lunsford Lomax to the east of the Valley Turnpike. "The fight took place in the open, the fences having long ago disappeared."[40]

Hoffman writes that Colonel Wells had ordered First Lieutenant John Bennett to move his command to the right of the Back Road to support the division's artillery, "where the Vermonters remained under fire for almost an hour" before the men were ordered to the left of the artillery and "straight uphill towards the enemy."[41]

Three battalions fought the Confederates at the top of a hill for a half hour, sometimes hand to hand. The southerners were badly whipped, all agreed. The Vermont regiment then divided: One part followed fleeing Confederates for ten miles to Columbia Furnace; the other chased Confederates who were headed towards New Market. The regiment reunited that night near Strasburg, having captured two guns.

During the week that followed, Hoffman notes, Sheridan's army retired behind Cedar Creek north of Strasburg, with Custer's division taking up a position on October 11 picketing the extreme right of the line along the Back

Road. Sheridan discounted the threat of attack posed by Jubal Early's force even after "a bloody skirmish" occurred at Hupp's Hill near Strasburg (October 13) and a squadron of Connecticut cavalry was captured (October 16).[42]

Hoffman cites Edward J. Stackpole's 1961 history, *Sheridan in the Shenandoah: Jubal Early's Nemesis*, in describing what came next: The Battle of Cedar Creek.

> Jubal Early conducted one of the most successful surprise attacks in American history, launching his outnumbered army on the unsuspecting Federals before dawn on October 19th, thus routing the Eighth Corps from its camps, defeating and forcing the Nineteenth Corps to retreat, and driving the Sixth Corps from its camps. The Confederate infantry and Jubal Early drove the Union forces until they expended their momentum. The Sixth Corps effectively traded space for time, anchored by the hard-fighting Vermont Brigade of Getty's Second Division. In one of its most notable combats, they blunted Early's infantry, giving the army of the Shenandoah time to organize a defense four miles from where the fighting had begun. Likewise, this action gave Sheridan, just back from a conference in Washington, the opportunity to loosen a counterattack that swept Early's forces from the battlefield. In the course of the day's fighting, Wells's Brigade, protecting the right flank, was the only Federal unit that did not retreat in the face of Confederate attacks. However, the cavalry on the right had only to face the inept attacks of Rosser's demoralized troopers, not the desperate assaults of Confederate infantry. Well's men did have to move back from time to time to maintain their alignment on the right flank of the Sixth Corps.

After Sheridan's assignment concluded with the virtual elimination of the CSA Army of the Valley, a third of Sheridan's cavalry and infantry force returned to George Meade's army at Petersburg and took part there in the closing stage of the siege that choked off supplies into Richmond such that Robert E. Lee evacuated his Army of Northern Virginia (ANV) from its defensive trenches and fled westward, finally surrendering at Appomattox Court House.

The First Vermont Cavalry participated in the "Battle of Appomattox," actually a week of daily battles that produced more than forty thousand casualties. Union losses are estimated as 10,000–13,000; Confederate losses, as approximately 30,000. Confederate casualties included not only the usual categories of "killed" and "wounded" but enormous numbers who were surrendered and others who, without waiting for the formal surrender ceremony, had just up and left for home, especially after Sailor's Creek.[43]

Battlefield casualties among Waitsfield men in the First Vermont Cavalry Regiment

Waitsfield's **Bertrand Delos Campbell** entered Company C of the First Vermont Cavalry on August 11, 1864, at age 20, following previous service in Vermont's 6th Volunteer Infantry Regiment.[44] He accompanied the First Vermont Cavalry when it was detailed to Sheridan's operation in the Shenandoah Valley. Private Campbell was part of the cavalry only long enough to be killed in action on September 19 at the Third Battle of Winchester (*aka* the Battle of Opequon, Virginia). Campbell was felled by a gunshot wound to the abdomen.

Fig. 19. CSA General Jubal Early, Phil Sheridan's opponent throughout the Valley Campaign.

Photo courtesy Library of Congress

Of the five Waitsfield privates remaining,[45] three more became casualties during Sheridan's campaign. **Ziba McAllister** was wounded on October 7, 1864 at Columbia Furnace, a tiny village devoted to the production of iron ore. **Seymour Kneeland** was captured by men from the 12th Virginia Cavalry while he was on picket duty near Woodstock, Virginia on December 19, 1864 and, according to Jones' 1909 history, was confined in Richmond's Libby Prison until he was paroled on March 10, 1865.[46] **Jerome Parker** incurred an unspecified abdominal injury serious enough to entitle him to a pension.

Kneeland, McAllister, Palmer, Parker and Sterling were transferred to Company A on June 21, 1865. They likely all took part on the first day (May 23, 1865) of a two-day Grand Review of the Army of the Potomac in the nation's capital. Between late May and early August, the regiment was shuttled from Washington, D.C. to Burlington and St. Albans, Vermont and then to postings in northern New York State until the men's term of service expired. All five were mustered out on August 9, 1865.

Notes

1. *The Caledonian*, St. Johnsbury, Vermont (September 20, 1861).
2. William L. Greenleaf, in Peck 1, 214.
3. *Ibid.*
4. John W. Palmer is named J. Wells Palmer in some records.
5. Private Cady qualifies as a Waitsfield soldier in this work because of his 1883 burial in Waitsfield's Common Cemetery. A photograph of Cady's stone in that cemetery appears on the Ledoux & Associates website: https://www.vermontinthecivilwar.org.
6. Although I did not find information ascribing Cady's transfer to either a debilitating wound or the effects of severe illness, he must have suffered one or the other to have been moved to the Veterans Reserve Corps (VRC). He may have been hospitalized even before his transfer. Cady was mustered out of the VRC on October 1, 1863 and lived twenty more years.
7. Dyer, III, 1647–1648.
8. Greenleaf, in Peck, *loc. cit.*
9. Greenleaf, in Peck, 1, 215. Greenleaf's account doesn't mention that General Thomas Jonathan ("Stonewall") Jackson came very close to being captured on that occasion.
10. *Ibid.*
11. Material cited in the paragraphs above appears in Hennessy's *Return to Bull Run*, 430–435.
12. Greenleaf, *op. cit.*, 215.
13. It may interest readers to learn how widely scattered Vermont soldiers were across the United States. (*The Caledonian* article describes land units only; that is, the United States Navy is not mentioned.) Two locations are misspelled: Brasher City should be "Brashear City" and Drainsville should be "Dranesville". This article was cited in *The Camp Griffin Gazette* (XX, 3), March 2013, 5.
14. *Ibid.*
15. Jeffrey D. Wert (2005), 235-236.
16. Wert, *op.cit.* (252) cites "a recent tabulation" that places Union losses in Chancellorsville at 1,694 killed and mortally wounded; 9,672 wounded; 5,938 missing or captured, for a total of 17,304; and Confederate losses at 1,724 killed and mortally wounded; 9,223 wounded; 2,593 missing or captured, for a total of 13,460. In a council of war that General Hooker called at midnight May 4/5 the

chief polled his five available corps commanders (Sedgwick had withdrawn his VI corps by then) about staying *vs.* withdrawing, but then he overruled their 3–2 vote to remain on the field. He ordered the artillery reserves to start for U.S. Ford while the infantry was held in position throughout May 5 before they, too, commenced retreating toward the ford at 7 p.m., preparatory to re-crossing the Rappahannock.

17. Greenleaf, cited in Peck, *op. cit.*

18. Cady was not transferred to the Veterans Reserve Corps (VRC) until September 1863. I have not found in the primary sources a reason for his transfer but it is possible he was wounded and hospitalized during the Gettysburg Campaign. (A severe wound or a protracted illness would be the reason a disabled soldier would be assigned to the VRC.)

19. In Preston's description of the action, E Company (presumably including Private Cady at the time) was among the dismounted skirmishers denoted here as *carbineers* during this early stage of the action.

20. Preston's report to P. T. Washburn (then Vermont's Adjutant and Inspector General), sent from Boonsboro', Maryland on July 10, 1863, appears in Péladeau's *Burnished Rows of Steel*, 190–191.

21. YouTube presentation by the Adams County (PA) Museum, April 2, 2021.

22. Gracey (1886), 186, *Annals of the Sixth Pennsylvania Cavalry* (PA: E. H. Butler & Co.), cited in Longacre, 280.

23. Most historians date the Gettysburg Campaign as running from June 9-July 14, 1863, although a case can be made that the campaign lasted until July 23. Note, for example, an account of the period between July 14 and July 23, 1863 at https://en.wikipedia.org/wiki/Gettysburg_Campaign (retrieved May 2, 2017).

24. Jeffrey William Hunt, in "Meade & Lee: The Road to Bristoe" (zoom lecture, April 20, 2022). Hunt notes that the Official Records consider Bristoe Station to be the last battle of the Gettysburg Campaign.

25. McAllister had served previously with the 13th Vermont Volunteer Infantry Regiment, a 9-month regiment that fought at Gettysburg. Throughout his time with the 13th Vermont McAllister was detailed to the regiment's headquarters where he served as an orderly to Colonel Francis Randall. He was mustered out of the 13th Vermont on July 21, 1863 and now, six months later, he joined the cavalry.

26. Kneeland was mustered in December 15, 1863; the four other men, on Christmas Day.

27. Longacre (1986), 59–60.

28. Note the analysis by Archer Jones in *Civil War Command & Strategy*, Chapter 11 (138–155).

29. Thus, it seems certain that the new Waitsfield men were not part of those raids. Dyer (1959, II, 931) shows Kilpatrick's raids as covering a period from February 28–March 4, 1864.

30. One eminent contemporary historian, Stephen Sears, believes that Dahlgren was acting under orders from Secretary of War Edwin Stanton. (No one ever has suggested that Lincoln was aware of any such plan.) Dispute continues, however, whether the alleged plot actually was a fabrication by the Davis cabinet to stir up already-outraged southerners.

31. Dufur (1902), 21.

32. Frank B. Jocelyn from Georgia, Vermont did indeed die on July 24, 1864 in the Andersonville prisoner-of-war camp. His body lies in that camp's cemetery.

33. The italicized diary material appears in Dufur, 6–8.

34. Most of the Union land forces engaged in Grant's initiative (the Overland Campaign) belonged to the Army of the Potomac, Major General George G. Meade commanding. That army was supplemented by Ambrose Burnside's Ninth Army Corps which operated separately from Meade's command and reported directly to Grant. The Army of the James [River], commanded by Benjamin Butler, also had a role. There were no Waitsfield men in Burnside's or Butler's forces.

35. By July of 1864 George Crook had succeeded David Hunter as commander of the Union's Army of West Virginia. While pursuing CSA General Jubal Early's forces in the Valley, Crook reported to VI Corps commander Major General Horatio G. Wright.

36. This material, from a manuscript by Horace K. Ide, appears in Hoffman's *History of the First Vermont Cavalry* (2000), 126–129.

37. For a list of the First Vermont Cavalry's military actions, see Dyer (1959), III, 1647–1648.

38. LaMonda (2003), 117.

39. LaMonda's account of Sheridan's march down the valley appears at 106–119.

40. Hoffman, 216.

41. *Op. cit.*, 216–217.

42. *Op. cit.*, 219.

43. In a talk delivered to the Green Mountain Civil War Round Table on February 11, 2017, Patrick Schroeder stated that 28,231 Confederates received paroles as part of the surrender of Lee's Army of Northern Virginia.

44. Campbell had enlisted at age 17 in Co. H of the 3rd Vermont, but he never was mustered in. (Presumably, he was found to be underage and was rejected.) Two months later, while still 17, he enlisted as a Corporal in Co. G of the 6th Vermont; he was discharged by a surgeon from a Philadelphia hospital for illness one year plus a week later. Trying once more almost two years later, Campbell (now 20) enlisted from Barton, Vermont. Campbell's name appears on a family gravestone in Waitsfield's Wait Cemetery, although that is a cenotaph for him. The L&A website carries a photo of Private Campbell from the John Gibson Collection.

45. Kneeland, McAllister, Palmer, Parker and Sterling were still fighting with the regiment.

46. Despite Jones' 1909 history declaring that Seymour Kneeland was confined to Libby Prison, I believe it more likely the Private Kneeland was confined at Belle Island prison (also in Richmond). Belle Island housed enlisted men; Libby Prison was used for Union prisoners of war who were officers. While Libby did serve as a receiving depot for all prisoners taken in the Richmond area, enlisted men soon were moved over to Belle Island in the James River.

2nd Vermont Battery, Light Artillery

Benjamin Henry Adams, Walter F. Adams, Joseph P. Davis and **Franklin Stoddard** served in the Second Vermont Battery, Light Artillery though not all at the same time. That battery was organized in Brandon, Vermont on December 13, 1861 for a three-year term of service.

Joseph Davis was mustered into the Second Battery, Light Artillery (L.A.) early in January of 1864, intending to serve three years, but on June 21st of that year he was honorably discharged because of an unspecified disability. (The term "for disability" often signified a serious illness but he may have been wounded.)

Walter Adams and **Franklin Stoddard** were one-year enlistees who joined the Second Battery, L.A. in August 1864. Stoddard served there until March 1, 1865 when he was transferred to the First Vermont Company, Heavy Artillery. Walter Adams completed his enlistment with the Second Battery, L.A. and was mustered out at Burlington, Vermont on July 31, 1865.

Benjamin Adams had fulfilled an earlier nine-month enlistment with the 12th Vermont Volunteer Infantry Regiment, being mustered out of that regiment in mid-July 1863 following service at Gettysburg. The next year he enlisted for one-year in the Second Battery, L.A. and was mustered in the very day of his enlistment, August 5, 1864. Along with Franklin Stoddard, Benjamin Adams was transferred to the First Vermont Company, Heavy Artillery on March 1, 1865. (That unit's history is referenced in sections of this work titled "11th Vermont Volunteer Infantry Regiment" and "1st Vermont Company, Heavy Artillery".)

Service by the Second Vermont Battery, Light Artillery prior to the arrival of anyone from Waitsfield

The Battery had traveled from Vermont to Boston and on by sea transport to Ship Island, Mississippi. There it was attached to a brigade commanded by General John W. Phelps and was assigned to the Department of the Gulf.[1]

Following the Union capture of Forts Jackson and Saint Philip near the mouth of the Mississippi River, the battery started up the Mississippi to New Orleans, landing there May 2, 1862. The Second Vermont Battery, L.A. was "the first Union battery in the city," according to Battery Captain John W. Chase.[2]

In New Orleans, sections of the battery were quartered at the U.S. Mint, others at the St. Charles Hotel which was serving as headquarters for General Benjamin Butler's military administration, until they all moved to Camp Parapet, some seven miles upriver. The Second Vermont Battery, L.A. saw 16 men dead and 22 others disabled from disease in the five months it was based there.

On October 31, the battery returned to New Orleans where it was quartered at Annunciation Square and Factor's Cotton Press. There, for the first time, the battery was fully mounted. On December 29 it departed by the steamer *Cumbria* for Galveston, Texas. The battery participated in action at Galveston on January 1, 1863 before returning once more to New Orleans.[3]

Other expeditions the Vermont Second Battery, L.A. had made prior to any Waitsfield man joining it included to Donaldsville, Baton Rouge,[4] Port Hudson and Plain's Store, all in Louisiana. Between May 24 and July 9, 1863, the battery participated in the Siege of Port Hudson. Captain Chase's history notes that from July fourth until the surrender of Port Hudson on July ninth, "the battery was under fire most of the time."[5] Chase writes:

> The Second Vermont Battery, being the most exposed of any light battery during the siege, had the honor of being the first battery inside.[6]

On August 2, 1863 a section of the Vermont Second Battery was ordered to Jackson, Louisiana. It was attacked there the next day by a cavalry force under CS General Nathan Bedford Forrest. The expedition's commander was captured with his 15 men. Although the commander was paroled, the men were sent to the Andersonville, Georgia prisoner of war camp, where five of them died.

Waitsfield enlistees' service in the Second Vermont Battery, Light Artillery

The battery was performing garrison duty at Port Hudson when the first

Waitsfield enlistee arrived in January 1864.[7] Six months into Joseph Davis' enlistment term he was discharged for disability, as noted above. Thus, Davis' service period and those of the other men from the Town did not overlap, as they arrived two months after Davis' discharge.

Walter Adams was the only townsman still with the Second Battery when it left Port Hudson on July 7, 1865, marched to Baton Rouge, took a steamer upriver to Cairo, Illinois and presumably traveled by train to Burlington, Vermont, where it arrived on July 20. The Battery spent eleven days in Burlington before being mustered out.

Notes

1. The assignment changed in December 1862 when that brigade became part of the Nineteenth Corps, Army of the Department of the Gulf. By the time the first Waitsfield man joined the battery, it was part of the Garrison Artillery at Port Hudson.

2. Chase, in Peck (1892), II, 633.

3. Dyer, III, 1649.

4. At Baton Rouge the Second Vermont Battery, Light Artillery was attached to a division led by Major General Christopher C. Augur.

5. Chase, *op. cit.*, 634.

6. *Ibid.*

7. A reminder: The term "Waitsfield men" as used in this work includes not just residents of the Town but also any who had been born there but were living elsewhere when they enlisted, and also any who died or were buried in Waitsfield. All four men serving with the Second Battery, L.A. were born in Waitsfield. Both Adams boys—presumably brothers—enlisted from Chelsea (each at age 19, one year apart). Franklin Stoddard enlisted from Warren. Davis was the only one of the four whose enlistment was credited to the Town.

3rd Vermont Battery, Light Artillery

Five Waitsfield men served in the Third Vermont Battery, Light Artillery, **Hiland G. Campbell, George Burton Hall, William Wordsworth McAllister, Edward M. Savage** and **Ira C. Williams**.

Waitsfield connections of these men

Savage and Campbell were born in Waitsfield. Hall and Williams were born elsewhere but it seems they resided in town when they enlisted, as their enlistments were credited to Waitsfield.[1] McAllister, born in Northfield, was credited to Barre upon his enlistment, but he died in Waitsfield.[2]

George Burton Hall

Hall had served with two other units prior to enlisting in the Third Vermont Battery, Light Artillery (L.A.). His original service was with the 9th Vermont Volunteer Regiment, followed by six months with the 17th United States Infantry Regiment. After his discharge from the latter, Hall mustered into Vermont's Third Battery, L.A. alongside Savage and Williams on New Years Day, 1864. Three weeks later Hall was promoted to Corporal, although he was reduced in rank to Private at the end of the year.

Edward M. Savage

Savage had served with Co. E of the 4th Vermont Volunteer Infantry Regiment until discharged "for disabilities". Eleven months later Savage signed up for the Third Vermont Battery, Light Artillery. At that enlistment (December 31, 1863), Savage likely was back home (Rochester, Vermont). He was promoted to Corporal upon enlistment and just one day later (January 1, 1864) he was mustered into the Third Battery, L.A.

Ira C. Williams

Williams was mustered in with George Hall and Edward Savage on New Year's Day, 1864. Hall, Savage and Williams would have been together in winter camp until U.S. Grant's Overland Campaign commenced in the spring. Presumably these three men took part in all the Battery's subsequent engagements until the fall of Petersburg, after which the Battery moved to City Point, Virginia. On March 3, 1865 it began its march back to Washington.

Hiland G. Campbell

Campbell was mustered in on November 2, 1864, the same day he enlisted for a one-year term of service. The Ledoux & Associates website states that Campbell was kicked by a horse and lay in hospital for eight months.[3] That suggests Campbell was still hospitalized up to the time members of the battery were discharged the following June.

William Wordsworth McAllister

McAllister was another one-year enlistee. A 19-year-old presumably named for English poet William Wordsworth,[4] McAllister (like Campbell one week earlier) was mustered into service the very day he enlisted, November 9, 1864, in Barre.

McAllister joined the Third Battery, L.A. during the Siege of Petersburg and would have participated with the Battery at the fall of Petersburg and the evacuation of Richmond which preceded Meade and Grant's pursuit of Lee's Army of Northern Virginia that ended with the surrender of Lee's army on April 9, 1865. However, as noted above, the Third Battery, L.A. did not join in that pursuit. Instead, it was sent to City Point, Virginia (recently General Grant's headquarters) to await the end of war in the Eastern Theater. From there it moved in May to a camp outside Washington, D. C. while a Grand Review and the disbandment of Union armies were being planned.

Instruction period of the Vermont Third Battery, Light Artillery; its first assignments

Two weeks after the Third Battery was mustered in, it left Burlington for Washington, D.C. There it was quartered at Camp Barry, an artillery instruction camp lying just northeast of the Capitol. By February 20, 1864 it was fully armed and equipped as a mounted artillery battery, reports Captain Romeo Start, who had recruited all its original members and acted as Battery historian.[5]

Immediately upon completing its instruction in camp (April 2, 1864), the Battery joined the IX Corps in crossing the Potomac River into Alexandria, but it remained there only a week before it was ordered to Manassas Junction, Virginia to protect the Army of the Potomac's line of communication.

Corporals Hall and Savage and Private Williams would have been among the artillerists of the Vermont Third Battery, L.A. who were ordered forward upon the opening of the Overland Campaign (May 4, 1864). Their battery crossed the Rappahannock River on the afternoon of May fifth and the Rapidan River the next morning, entering the Virginia Wilderness. From then until it crossed the James River on June 17, the Third Battery (complemented by a Pennsylvania artillery battery and a mixed division of cavalry and infantry) provided protection to the Army of the Potomac's ammunition and provision trains.

"While it took no part in the great battles of Spottsylvania [sic], North Anna or Cold Harbor," Battery Captain Start writes, "it was almost within cannon shot of all those engagements; and while it escaped many of the trying scenes of battle, its hardships and exposures were none the less severe, ..."[6]

Between June 18 and October 25, the Battery served in six forts.[7] Briefly, it supported the II Corps as Reserve Artillery when that Corps attempted to cut the railroad at Ream's Station.

The Third Battery with its three earliest Waitsfield volunteers surely was present at the July 30 explosion of the Petersburg Mine, *aka* the incident of the Crater.

On October 25 the Battery was sent to City Point, Virginia to defend that major federal supply base. It remained there until mid-January 1865, both defending City Point and occupying Fort McKean. It's likely that Privates McAllister and Campbell reached the Battery before the close of that period, although it is not known how long Campbell served before his disabling accident.

The five Waitsfield men (with the possible exception of Private Campbell, depending on when his accident occurred) are assumed to have been with the Battery during its occupation of Fort Fisher, at Petersburg. "One section of the battery was ordered out upon the skirmish line to assist an advance on March 25, 1865," Captain Start's history records.

> As this section moved out to take position it met with a severe artillery fire from the enemy's batteries on the left of Fort Fisher, and from a battery in front. It took up its position within some six or seven hundred yards of the enemy's batteries in front, and at once opened fire, which was vigorously replied to by the enemy.[8]

Role of the Third Vermont Battery, Light Artillery in bringing about fall of Petersburg

The battery had orders to fire a signal gun from Fort Fisher at 4 A.M. on April 2, 1865. "At the appointed time the signal gun was fired, but owing to some misunderstanding on the part of the division commanders, the infantry failed to advance," Start writes. Another gun was fired at 4:15 A.M. and the Union assault began.

> At eight o'clock of that day the battery left Fort Fisher and moved out to the front on the line occupied by the infantry under Major-General Gibbon, to assist in the attack on the first line of the enemy's works defending the approaches to Petersburg on the West, and it accordingly moved and took up a position some three hundred yards in front of the Confederate batteries, Owen and Gregg. Owen was occupied by the enemy's sharpshooters, and Gregg the artillery and infantry. [T]he battery at once opened fire on Fort Gregg, which was returned by the enemy with great spirit. After an hour's severe and well directed firing, the Rebel guns were silenced, and the works were carried by assault.
>
> The battery was then moved forward and took up a new position some two hundred yards in front and on the right of its first position, in order to attack the enemy's second line of works, and from which he opened a severe artillery fire on our infantry in the captured works. After half an hour's heavy firing from this position it again moved forward and occupied a position immediately in front of batteries Owen and Gregg, which protected it partially from the enfilading fire of the enemy's guns on our left, and again opened fire on the works commanding the heights, their second and last line of works.

That last move was made about 11:30 A.M., Start continues, with the battery keeping up a vigorous fire all day, until nightfall put an end to the artillery duel.

> It remained in this position ready to renew the conflict at day-break on the following morning, but the dawn of April 3 found no enemy in the formidable works along our front, they having retired during the night, and at daylight we pushed forward and entered Petersburg without opposition.[9]

Disbanding of the Third Vermont Battery, Light Artillery

All five Waitsfield men were released from service on June 15, 1865 when the Vermont Third Battery, Light Artillery was disbanded.

Notes

1. George Burton Hall was born in Rutland, Vermont; Ira Williams, in Franklin, New York.

2. McAllister is buried in Irasville Cemetery, Waitsfield.

3. The *Vermont in the Civil War* website: https://www.vermontinthecivilwar does not give a date for that accident.

4. William Wordsworth was an English lyrical poet widely admired in the United States at the time McAllister was born.

5. Dyer, III, 1649; Peck, 2, 643.

6. Start, in Peck (1892), II, 645.

7. *Op. cit.*, 643 and 645. Those six forts are given by Start as Fort Morton, opposite to the site of the Mine explosion (also called "the Crater"); Fort Hell (where the opposing federal and Confederate lines were closest together}; Fort Michael; Battery 27; Battery 16; and Fort Phillips.

8. Start, *op. cit.*, 645.

9. *Ibid.*

1st Vermont Company, Heavy Artillery

In the final months of war in the Eastern theater, a new Vermont military unit was formed in the Western theater. Two Waitsfield "boys" served in that unit: **Benjamin Henry Adams** and **Franklin Stoddard**. On March 1, 1865 those two, already serving in the Second Vermont Battery, Light Artillery (L.A.), were recruited into the new unit, a 118-man 1st Vermont Company, Heavy Artillery.[1]

This new company of Heavy Artillery was formed entirely from Vermonters then enrolled with the Second Vermont Battery, L. A., many of whom had served in that L.A. unit since May 1862. Privates Adams and Stoddard, who had not joined that Light Artillery unit until 1864, brought much less artillery experience to the new unit than most of the other Vermonters who were transferred with them.[2]

The 1st Vermont Company of Heavy Artillery served in the Army of the Department of the Gulf, as did the Second Vermont Light Artillery Battery from which it was recruited. That Army originally was commanded by Benjamin Butler, the somewhat-infamous Massachusetts "political general." Later, when Butler headed the Army of the James [River] in Virginia, Stephen Hurlbut and Nathaniel Banks headed the Gulf army for short periods at the direction of the Department's commander, Edward R. S. Canby.

History of the 1st Vermont Company, H.A.

Our foremost source for information about Vermont units, Peck's 1892 *Revised Roster*, does not contain a military history for this Heavy Artillery unit comparable to its histories of other Vermont units. It does note the 1st Vermont Company of Heavy Artillery began with 3 officers and 115 men, of whom 13 men were lost (none in battle). The three officers and 102 men were mustered out of service at Burlington, Vermont on July 28, 1865.[3]

Fig. 20. Crew of a Union heavy artillery piece, c. 1864. The 100-pounder Parrott rifle in the Southwest Bastion was the largest gun at Fort Ward and could fire a distance of about 5 Miles.

Fort Ward Museum & Historic Site, Alexandria, Virginia and Library of Congress

Wikipedia offers some information about the 1st Vermont Company, H.A. at this site: https://www.familysearch.org/wiki/en/1st_Company,_Vermont_Heavy_Artillery. Readers are cautioned not to confuse the 1st Company, H.A. with another older and much larger military unit known as the 1st Vermont Volunteer Heavy Artillery Regiment, a name conferred when the 11th Vermont Volunteer Infantry Regiment in the Army of the Potomac was converted to an artillery unit in December 1862. (In May 1864 that unit reverted to infantry service.) See the 11th Vermont Volunteer Infantry section of this work.

Light vs. Heavy Artillery units

"Light Artillery" in the American Civil War denoted mobile army units that used horses to move their cannon and caissons on a battlefield. About six animals were required per gun, and six or eight for the gun's carriage which transported ammunition and powder.

"Heavy Artillery" units remained inside a fort or other defensive position, for the most part, although they sometimes were hauled by train, as to a siege site, for offensive purposes. Each "heavy" piece weighed far more than the light, or field, pieces which themselves weighed more than a thousand pounds. Heavy Artillery pieces were used by both Union army and naval forces.[4]

Franklin Stoddard and Benjamin Henry Adams served in the 1st Vermont Heavy Artillery Company during the last months of their army service (March first until July 28, 1865). It's likely, however, that they did so as infantrymen rather than as artillerists. There was precedent for such a switching of mission and it's doubtful there was any need for heavy artillery while the 1st Company was performing garrison duty at Port Hudson, Louisiana after that place had surrendered.

Contemporary Port Hudson battlefield

Unlike most Civil War battlefields open to the public which are administered by the National Park Service, the Port Hudson battlefield in Jackson, Louisiana is a state historical site. Re-enactments are held annually, and the park is open year-round for other Civil War educational opportunities as well as for recreation.

Notes

1. Peck, 2, 652. (However Dyer, III, 1649 states that the new unit was created in April 1865.)

2. Adams had more army experience overall than Stoddard did, as he had joined the Second Battery, L.A. about 13 months after he completed a nine-month enlistment with the 12th Vermont Volunteer Infantry Regiment.

3. Peck, *op. cit.*, 652–654. (Again, Dyer's account is slightly different than Peck's, stating the company was mustered out July 25, 1865.)

4. Source: "10 Facts: Civil War Artillery," American Battlefield Trust website (retrieved February 17, 2023).

Waitsfield Men Who Served in Other States' Units

Beyond the 87 men cited in Matt Bushnell Jones' history as having enlisted in Vermont regiments from the Town of Waitsfield,[1] Jones named separately another 18 who enlisted elsewhere. Typically, those men were born in Waitsfield but had moved elsewhere in the state before the war. In the present volume their stories are included with those of other Waitsfield men who served in Vermont state volunteer units or United States units.

This section includes information for Waitsfield men whom Jones associated with regiments raised by other states. A few of those men traveled across a Vermont state line to enlist, while others enlisted much farther afield. It's likely the latter men had left Waitsfield years earlier, some perhaps having moved with their families as children, others having struck off later on their own. Federal policy may have encouraged some to leave the state.[2]

To the men Jones named I have been able to add others, gleaned from primary sources and walks in local cemeteries.

In this section the service of all Waitsfield men known to have enlisted with non-Vermont state regiments is organized by states, alphabetically. Each man's unit is cited, with any other information I've found with respect to his military service.

Illinois

Alonzo Henderson
Co. D, 89th Illinois Infantry Regiment

Charles D. Tewksbury
Co. B, 52nd Illinois Volunteers. Enlisted 1861. Mustered in October 25, 1861 as Corporal. Wounded at the Battle of Shiloh, 1862. Promoted April 1864 to Sergeant. Mustered out July 6, 1865.

Kansas

Lucius S. Shaw
2nd Kansas Infantry Regiment

Massachusetts

Theron Lucius Bailey
1st Massachusetts Heavy Artillery Battery

John D. Crane
Co. H, 56th Massachusetts Infantry Regiment. Buried in Waitsfield's Common Cemetery.

Michigan

Isaac N. Tewksbury
[unspecified Michigan regiment]. Killed at the battle of Pittsburg Landing (date not given). Pittsburg Landing is the same 1862 battle as Shiloh, although some writers use "Pittsburg Landing" to denote that part of the Shiloh battlefield closest to the Tennessee River.

Missouri

Oliver Shaw
Co. A, 11th Missouri Infantry. Believed to be buried in Farmington (Arkansas) Cemetery, but there's a stone in Waitsfield's Common Cemetery (a cenotaph?). The latter shows a death date of 12/22/1899 at age 92. The Ledoux & Associates website confirms this soldier's company and regiment, while noting that his enlistment was credited to Vermont.

New Hampshire

Gurley A. Phelps
14th New Hampshire Infantry Regiment

James N. Shepard
18th New Hampshire Infantry Regiment

New York State

Charles H. Clay
Co. H, 96th New York Volunteers. Buried in Waitsfield's Village Cemetery.

John McLaren
Co. B, 77th New York Volunteers

Harlan Gaius Newcomb
Co. K, 145th New York Volunteers. Enlisted 1862. Mustered in September 1862. Transferred March 1864 to Co. I, 107th New York Volunteers. Detailed September 1864 to Division Headquarters. Rejoined his company May 23, 1865. Mustered out June 19, 1865.

George E. Spaulding
Co. G, 10th New York Volunteers. Enlisted 1862 from Albany, NY. Served from April 1862 to August 1865.

George Aaron Walker
Co. F, 26th New York Cavalry (the Frontier Cavalry). Born 1846, Waitsfield. Enlisted December 30, 1864 in one of two Vermont companies of this New York State unit that was created after the St. Albans, Vermont raid, to patrol the border. Organized in Burlington and quartered initially in barracks on the old fair ground there, the company was moved in mid-winter to newly-constructed barracks in St. Albans (Dyer, 2, 656). Walker was mustered in as a Private January 10, 1865; credited to Springfield. Mustered out June 27, 1865. Died May 22, 1929. Buried at Mattapan, Massachusetts.

Wisconsin

Matthias Joslin Bushnell
Co. B, First Wisconsin Cavalry. Enlisted 1861. Mustered in as Corporal August 24, 1861. Killed near Madison, Arkansas, August 3, 1862 at age 27, while guarding a wagon train. Buried in Waitsfield's Common Cemetery.

Israel Childs
30th Wisconsin Infantry Regiment. Performed some three years of service, per Jones.

Langdon S. Hadley
Co. C, 32nd Wisconsin Infantry Regiment. Died 12(?)/30/63 at age 23, per a headstone in Waitsfield's Irasville Cemetery.

Solon Poland
14th Wisconsin Infantry (company not given) and Company K, 19th Wisconsin Infantry Regiment. Died in service 9/3/1863 at Fortress Monroe, VA. Buried at Hampton, VA but has a stone (cenotaph) in Waitsfield's Common Cemetery.

James C. Russ
Co. A, 42nd Wisconsin Infantry Regiment. Mustered out June 28, 1865.

Notes

1. Jones (1909), 84–93.

2. The Homestead Act of 1862 granted 140 acres of public land to citizens willing to settle on such free parcels; most who did farmed their new property and eventually became owners of that land.

12th United States Infantry Regiment

One local soldier is known to have served in the 12th U.S. Infantry Regiment, *i.e.*, a federal infantry unit, not one of Vermont's volunteer units. **George Julius Ainsworth**, born in Waitsfield about 1842, enlisted from Warren at age 19 as a Private with the Second Vermont Volunteers. Ainsworth served with the army from June 1861 until June 1864, including a transfer from an army hospital to the Veterans Reserve Corps (VRC) six months after he was wounded on Marye's Heights (Fredericksburg, Virginia) on May 3, 1863. Ainsworth's wound was severe enough that he required hospitalization from May until November before being judged sufficiently recovered to finish out his term of service in the VRC, a corps created for convalescents deemed able to perform light duties but not well enough to return to their regiments.

One month after his June 1864 discharge from the Veterans Reserve Corps, Ainsworth traveled to Burlington to enlist in the Twelfth U.S. Infantry Regiment. The 1892 *Revised Roster* shows Ainsworth as residing in Arlington, Vermont when he joined the Twelfth. During the time Ainsworth belonged to the 12th U.S. Infantry, it was associated with the V Corps, Army of the Potomac.[1]

He served a full enlistment term with the federals before being mustered out at Fort Hamilton, NYS on July 23, 1867, three years to the day from when he had joined.

Following his death at age 47 George Julius Ainsworth was buried in Providence, Rhode Island. There is a cenotaph for him in Waitsfield's Village Cemetery where other members of the Ainsworth family are buried.[2]

Military service of the Twelfth U.S. Infantry Regiment before Julius Ainsworth joined that regiment

When Ainsworth joined "the regulars" a month after his discharge from the VRC, the 12th U.S. Infantry already had been in existence three years and had participated in many Civil War campaigns: In 1862, the Peninsula Campaign, Pope's campaign in Northern Virginia (including the Second Battle of Bull Run), and the Maryland Campaign (including the Battle of Antietam), as well as the Battle of Fredericksburg, Virginia that December. In 1863 the Twelfth U.S. had participated in the Chancellorsville Campaign, then the Gettysburg and Mine Run Campaigns.[3]

The 1864 Overland Campaign's terrible battles in the Virginia Wilderness and at Spotsylvania had come and gone before Julius Ainsworth joined the regiment in July 1864.

Action Julius Ainsworth would have seen with the 12th U.S. Regulars

Ainsworth's service with the 12th United States Infantry Regiment commenced while that unit was engaged in the Richmond-Petersburg Campaign. It is possible Julius Ainsworth observed the Mine explosion at Petersburg July 30, 1864. (The 12th was held in reserve that day.) His subsequent engagements with the 12th U.S. Infantry likely included all these 1864 confrontations: Weldon Rail Road, Poplar Springs Church, Peeble's Farm, Boydton Plank Road and Hatcher's Run.

In the first week of November 1864 the regiment was moved to New York State. It was divided into two battalions, one stationed at Elmira and the other at Fort Hamilton in New York Harbor, where Ainsworth served. Presumably Ainsworth completed his three-year federal enlistment at Fort Hamilton despite the Twelfth's disbandment on June 28, 1865. His own military career did not conclude until 1867, as noted earlier.

Notes

1. That covered the period from June through November 1864, when it was assigned to the Department of the East until its disbandment in July 1865.

2. Luther Ainsworth, Captain of Co. B, 13th Vermont Volunteer Infantry Regiment, is buried in the Village Cemetery.

3. The 12th U.S. Infantry seems always to have been joined with the 8th U.S. Infantry, whether serving in the Defenses of Washington (its first station), in its transfer to the Department of the Shenandoah and then to Major General John Pope's Army of Virginia, or at V Corps Headquarters, the Army of the Potomac. The merged units separated when the 12th was transferred organizationally to the Department of the East in November 1864. The Twelfth's final commander (April through June of 1865) was Brigadier General Joseph Hayes.

17th United States Infantry Regiment

One Waitsfield soldier served in the 17th United States Infantry Regiment. **George Burton Hall** had begun his Civil War service at age 18.[1] He was serving in **Co. I** ("eye") of the 9th Vermont Infantry when he was discharged from that regiment on January 15, 1863 to enter the 17th U.S. Infantry that very day.[2] Private Hall was assigned to **Company B, Second Battalion** where he served six months until he was ordered discharged on June 15, 1863.[3]

Hall was not finished with the war, however. Three months later he enlisted with the Third Vermont Battery, Light Artillery.[4] Hall was promoted to Corporal three weeks after he joined that Vermont unit. He was reduced in rank in December, and was mustered out as a Private on June 15, 1865.

Although neither Peck's *Revised Roster* nor the Ledoux & Associates website (which includes a lengthy obituary) cite any wound or severe illness in their accounts of Hall's service, he was granted a military pension.

George B. Hall's six months in the 17th United States Infantry Regiment

The little we know of Hall's service with the 17th U.S. "regulars" (between January 15–June 15, 1863) is that he presumably shared all the experiences that unit had during that period, as documented in Dyer's *A Compendium of the War of the Rebellion*.[5] Hall entered the federal unit while it was in its 1862–63 winter camp. Between January 20–24, 1863 the regiment participated in Ambrose Burnside's ill-conceived troop movement afterwards derisively dubbed the "Mud March". The regiment subsequently participated in the Chancellorsville Campaign, including fighting at the Battle of Chancellorsville, a major Union defeat.[6] Hall was gone before the regiment began its preparations for the Gettysburg Campaign.

The Ledoux & Associates website, https://www.vermontinthecivilwar, includes a full-length studio portrait (undated) of Hall in uniform.[7]

Notes

1. Hall, born in Richmond, was credited to Waitsfield upon his enlistment.

2. Hall's service with the 9th Vermont Volunteer Infantry Regiment had begun on July 9, 1862. See the 9th Vermont Volunteer Infantry Regiment section of this book for a history of that unit, including its capture at Harpers Ferry.

3. That June 1863 discharge may have reflected a medical problem.

4. Although Hall enlisted with the Third Vermont Battery, Light Artillery on September 24, 1863, his mustering-in was delayed until January 1, 1864.

5. Frederick H. Dyer (1959 reprint of his 1909 *Compendium*), III, 1715. During Hall's service, the 17th belonged to Sykes' V Corps of the Army of the Potomac, Ambrose Burnside commanding.

6. The Chancellorsville Campaign is dated April 27–May 6, 1863, with the Battle of Chancellorsville, May 1–5.

7. This photograph is part of the private John Gibson collection.

2nd Regiment, U.S. Sharpshooters

United States Sharpshooters were elite federal regiments. To be accepted into a U.S. Sharpshooters regiment, a prospective recruit had to meet rigorous criteria in a display of shooting prowess.

There were Vermonters, though no Waitsfield men, in the First Regiment of United States Sharpshooters that was raised in September 1861. But then another opportunity to become a U.S. Sharpshooter was presented that fall. In response, two Vermont companies were created: Those became **Companies E** and **H** of the Second Regiment, United States Sharpshooters.[1]

Still, it was a year before a Waitsfield man entered one of those companies. **James A. Foster** was mustered into **Company E** of the Second U.S. Sharpshooters (USSS) in September 1862.

Then, the week before Christmas one year later (1863), eight local men joined **Company H** of the Second USSS. Those men were **Leonard C. Berry, George M. Jones, Holland Jones, Eugene E. Joslyn**[2], **James L. Maynard, Thomas Theodore Prentis, John N. Richardson** and **Loren S. Richardson**. Three of those men (Berry, Joslyn and John Richardson) were transferred in from the Fourth Vermont Volunteer Infantry Regiment, while the other five men were new recruits.[3]

Company E

James A. Foster, born in Waitsfield, qualified at age 37 and joined E company in its camp near Sharpsburg, Maryland two weeks after the Battle of Antietam, where company losses had been heavy. The company's historian, William H. Humphrey, records that at Antietam his company "helped to fill the bloody lane," after which only the captain and four men were left fit for duty.[4]

Thirty recruits entered E Company before the month was out. Private James Foster and the other new men likely heard from the regiment's survivors of those experiences as they got settled in the camp.[5]

Fig. 21. Drawing of the Model 1859 rifle and bayonet used by U.S. Sharpshooters provided by Dr. Timothy Orr to attendees at the 2022 Civil War Institute of Gettysburg College

Afterwards, Private Foster would have been present with E company when the 2nd Regiment, United States Sharpshooters crossed the Potomac River at Harpers Ferry on November first, 1862. Preparatory to a move on Fredericksburg, Virginia the Union army established camps around Falmouth, Virginia, opposite Fredericksburg on the Rappahannock River. Company E settled into one such camp near Stoneman's Switch, Virginia. On December 12 Company E crossed the Rappahannock, taking up a position on the field at Fredericksburg. Following the Union's ghastly losses at the Battle of Fredericksburg the next day, the surviving sharpshooters returned to their Falmouth camp.[6]

While E company's post-war history does not cite the company's losses at the Battle of Fredericksburg, it does state that 1862 was a hard year for that company.[7]

Private Foster also would have participated in the futile movement of January 20–24, 1863, the so-called "Mud March" that ended General Ambrose Burnside's command of the Army of the Potomac.

Before the next major military campaign occurred, Foster was discharged "for disability" on April 16, 1863.

Company H

Company H was organized in Vermont at the very end of 1861. It was the eighth and final company to be organized in the Second Regiment, United States Sharpshooters. Other states represented by companies in that regiment were Maine, Michigan, New Hampshire and Pennsylvania.[8]

There were no men from Waitsfield present with the regiment during the eight months between James Foster's discharge and the mustering-in on December 18, 1863 of the eight Waitsfield men already named. For that reason, actions by the Second Regiment, USSS in 1863 are referenced below only from the time the eight Waitsfield men joined. Therefore, the regiment's important contributions at Gettysburg are not cited here.

Company H actions with Waitsfield soldiers present

Those original Co. H soldiers who elected to re-enlist (their three-year term of service having expired) had left camp on January 7, 1864 for an earned furlough. When they returned from leave, it was to a new camp at Culpeper, Virginia. New recruits, including the Waitsfield men, brought the Co. H roll up to full strength.

When the eight Waitsfield men entered the Second USSS., that regiment was part of the III Corps of the Army of the Potomac, commanded by Major General W. H. French. However, shortly before the 1864 spring campaign began, the remains of the III Corps were incorporated into the II Corps, under Major General Winfield Scott Hancock.

The following account of the Second USSS Regiment in the Wilderness of Virginia (written after the war by a First Lieutenant of that regiment, Curtis Abbott) appears in the 1892 *Revised Roster.*

> On May 5 [1864] Company H, having crossed the Rapidan the morning of the day previous, was brought under fire as flankers on the Brock road, just south of its intersection with the Orange Plank, and, resting there through the night on their arms, they advanced in solid ranks to the latter road, at the opening of the battle in the morning and the contest is bloody, with varying success, till at the burning log breast work in the evening, the enemy was repulsed.
>
> . . . .
>
> May 7 they skirmished to the front of the same field. May 8, leaving this bloody field in their rear, inspired by the tactics of their new commander-in-chief [Ulysses Grant] not to wait for the verdict, they marched to Todd's Tavern, . . .[9]

Abbott gives the Wilderness losses of Company H: Eight killed, including the company's Captain; 16 wounded; two missing. (Three of those casualties were Waitsfield men. Details appear below.)

Abbott's account continues with this description of Company H's fighting at Spotsylvania and beyond:

> [After Company H skirmished at Todd's Tavern, it] again crossed the Po River. Returning, they next join Warren's assaulting column. Finally at daylight on the 12th, at the capture of the angle,[10] the company gathered in several times its own numbers in prisoners. In this battle and their skirmish of the succeeding day, Company H lost 4 wounded. After several days more of alternate skirmish and rest at this field, they marched to the North Anna, there led the charge which captured the Telegraph road bridge, with the loss to Company H of one killed and two wounded, and in their next charge of Totopotomoy Creek, with their regiment, captured a number of prisoners

and the enemy's intrenched skirmish line.

>From June 2 to 13, during the operations and disastrous charge of the army at Cold Harbor, the loss of Company H...was one man killed and three wounded.[11]

Skirmisher duty by Company H "was almost incessant," Abbott writes, as the regiment crossed the James River and attempted to take Petersburg, Virginia by direct assault. The regiment led its division in a move against the Weldon Railroad on June 21, where Co. H took losses and the regiment's Colonel, Homer Stoughton, was captured. The Second Sharpshooters slogged on through an engagement at Deep Bottom and the disastrous Petersburg episode of the Mine (*aka* the Crater).

> September 10, under De Trobriand now their brigade commander, they share in the capture of the [Confederate] rifle pits on the Jerusalem Plank Road, in front of Forts Hell and Sedgwick.[12]

Abbott writes that the men's service over the next two months in the captured rifle pits was "irksome and dangerous," but was varied by marches to the left and two more battles:

> October 1, on the ground where Fort Fisher afterwards rose and became familiar to the [First] Vermont Brigade, and on October 27, beyond Burgess' Hill in a movement against the Southside railroad.[13]

The regiment celebrated Thanksgiving 1864 in the Petersburg trenches with roasted turkeys from home (and likely with preserves, cakes and pies, too). In early December the regiment crossed the Nottoway River and assisted the V Corps in destroying the Weldon Railroad.

The Second USSS was augmented when seventeen soldiers from the newly-disbanded First USSS arrived during the winter of 1864–65. The last skirmish of the Second Regiment, according to Abbott, occurred February 5, 1865 at the Vaughn Road crossing of Hatcher's Run. The men captured Confederate works there in the face of enemy fire.

On February 22, 1865 the Second Regiment, USSS was discontinued, with its men dispersed to infantry units of their respective states. Three Waitsfield men were still in Company H at that time.[14] They were sent to Vermont's Fourth Volunteer Infantry Regiment where they participated in the capture of Confederate lines entrenched before Fort Fisher, as well as the April 2nd breakthrough that led to the evacuation of Lee's soldiers from their Petersburg trenches, the fall of Richmond and the surrender of the Army of Northern Virginia one week later.

Casualties among Waitsfield men in Company H of the Second United States Sharpshooters

The eight Waitsfield men in Co. H had been mustered in December 18, 1863. Because they entered as part of recruiting to fill up the ranks while the regiment was in its winter camp, they did not engage in battle until the opening of spring campaigning, 1864 (Grant's Overland Campaign). In their very first battle, three Waitsfield men became casualties.

James L. Maynard was killed in action at the Battle of the Wilderness on May 6, 1864, by a gunshot wound to the head. Maynard was buried in an unknown Virginia grave.

George M. Jones also was killed in action that day, shot in the head while helping a wounded fellow soldier from the field, according to another Waitsfield private in the company who wrote to Jones' father about George's death.[15]

Eugene Joslyn was wounded in the shoulder that same day. At some time (perhaps just after the war), Joslyn provided the Jones family a map on which he noted the spot where George Jones had fallen. Many years after the war, Matt and Charles Jones, two nephews of Private Jones, traveled to the Wilderness battlefield and located the place where Jones had died, "just south of Orange Plank Road & at the top of a little hill."[16]

The two Jones brothers then traveled to the Fredericksburg, Virginia National Cemetery, burial site at that time (1911) of 15,000 Union soldiers, 12,000 of them unknown. Writing from Virginia to his father back in Waitsfield, Matt Jones confided, "[W]e feel that the probabilities are that Uncle Georges body lies here."[17]

As Grant's campaign continued through Spotsylvania and on to Cold Harbor, more casualties were incurred by Waitsfield men.

Loren S. Richardson was wounded at Cold Harbor on June 11.[18] Richardson was transferred to the Veterans Reserve Corps (VRC) on February 22, 1865.[19] He was mustered out from the VRC on July 20, 1865.

Leonard C. Berry was wounded in the arm June 16, 1864 and spent three months in a Washington, D.C. hospital.

Holland Jones was transferred to the Veterans Reserve Corps on Aug. 21, 1864 and "discharged on account of sickness" soon afterwards.[20]

Thomas Theodore Prentis was discharged "for disability" on September 8, 1864.[21]

Private Leonard C. Berry, Sergeant Eugene E. Joslyn and Corporal John N. Richardson were mustered out of service on July 13, 1865.

Notes

1. Humphrey, cited in Peck (1892), 2, 608. The Second Regiment, USSS. was brigaded with the Fourteenth Brooklyn Zouaves and three other New York infantry regiments, plus two cavalry regiments and a battery from the Fourth United States Artillery.

2. Dascomb's Waitsfield history (1867) spells Joslyn's surname as Joslin.

3. This suggests that a federal recruiting officer had come to town some time earlier to set up a marksmanship test for potential recruits, even as the three Waitsfield men already serving in the 4th Vermont Infantry arranged to have their required tests conducted within the First Vermont Brigade, perhaps because they wanted to join Waitsfield boys they knew from back home. Another possibility is that a USSS. marksmanship competition was being held elsewhere in the state and the would-be enlistees traveled to that location to try out for a place in the USSS.

4. Humphrey, *ibid.*

5. Antietam, fought September 17, 1862, remains the worst single day of combat in American history.

6. At that time the Second USSS was part of the I Army Corps, Army of the Potomac. From its inception at the beginning of April 1862, the unit had undergone multiple changes in its organizational placement. Additional changes continued during the time Waitsfield men were present, as noted in the text. Readers interested in the entire history of this Sharpshooters regiment should consult Dyer (1959), III, 1716-1717.

7. Humphrey, *op. cit.*, 609. A year-end tally reported by First Lieutenant Humphrey, the company's historian, shows only 84 remained of the 145 Company E officers and men. Of the company's 61 losses, seven men had been killed in battle or had died of disease, 43 had been discharged for wounds or disabilities and three had been transferred to the Invalid Corps. Six men had deserted. One had been promoted away from the company. (One man is not accounted for in Humphrey's summary.)

8. On a per capita basis, Vermont sent more sharpshooters to Union armies than any other state. Source: Vermont historian Howard Coffin in a lecture delivered at the Kellogg-Hubbard Library, Montpelier, Vermont on March 28, 2018.

9. Abbott in Peck, 2, 618. The Army of the Potomac still was led by George Meade. (U.S. Grant traveled with Meade's army, but he did not issue day-to-day orders for that army; instead, Grant functioned as commander of all Union armies in the field.)

10. Abbott's reference here is to the "Bloody Angle" at the Spotsylvania, Virginia battlefield.

11. Abbott, *loc. cit.*

12. *Ibid.*

13. *Ibid.*

14. Those three were Private Berry, Corporal Joslyn and Corporal John Richardson. (The latter two men had been promoted to Corporal in November 1864.) Joslyn received another promotion, to Sergeant, on June 24, 1865.

15. Coffin (2002) cites Leonard C. Berry's letter to Hiram Jones (May 20, 1864), 325.

16. Letter from Matt Jones to his father, cited in Coffin (2002), 370. It appears that George M. Jones was one of the ten grandsons of Waitsfield's Dr. Simeon Stoddard who served in the war, as noted by Coffin (2013), 399.

17. Coffin, *op. cit.*, 371. I think it likely that James Maynard's body may lie among the unknowns in the Frederickson National Cemetery, given that the federal government removed bodies from the Wilderness battlefield to the newly-created cemetery in 1866.

18. Jones (1909) gives slightly different dates for Loren Richardson's wounding and his later mustering-out than does the Ledoux & Associates website. As usual, I chose to use here the dates shown on the website. I have not found information about the nature of Richardson's Cold Harbor wound or whether he was hospitalized due to that wound.

19. The VRC, aka the Invalid Corps, had been created as a way to retain disabled soldiers deemed still capable of performing some service, rather than discharging them.

20. The Jones history gives the date of Holland Jones' discharge as September 14, 1864, but the L&A website gives it as September third.

21. Prentis had a post-war career as a diplomat, serving as U.S. Consul in the Seychelles (off the eastern coast of Africa), and at Port Louis, Mauritius and Saint-Pierre, Martinique. He perished at the latter place in the volcanic eruption of Mount Pelée, an explosion that killed 30,000 persons on May 8, 1902. (Source: Tom Ledoux & Associates website, ©2020.) Prentis' body was buried at Fort-de-France, Martinique's capital.

Captain Edwin C. Lewis
13th Regiment, U.S. Colored Heavy Artillery

Fig. 22. Portrait of Edwin C. Lewis, made while he was a 2nd Lt in Co. G of the Sixth Vermont Volunteers

13th Regiment, U.S. Colored Heavy Artillery

Edwin C. Lewis, who had served in the 1st Vermont and then the 6th Vermont Volunteer Infantry Regiments, was selected to officer a company in the 13th United States Colored Heavy Artillery (CHARTY) Battalion, becoming the only Waitsfield soldier to lead an army unit of Black soldiers during the Civil War. His selection came following a wound he suffered at Cold Harbor, Virginia on June 1, 1864 while fighting with Company G of the Sixth Regiment. Lewis might still have been recovering from that wound when he was discharged from the Sixth Regiment (August third) in order to be transferred to the 13th United States CHARTY. He was promoted to Captain at the same time.

The company of which Lewis became Captain was comprised of two previous units, the D and K companies of an existing 13th U.S. Heavy Artillery Battalion, United States Colored Troops.[1] Lewis' unit was based at Camp Nelson, a site about 20 miles south of Lexington at Nicholasville, Kentucky. Both free Blacks and formerly enslaved men were accepted into the 13th artillery, the last unit raised at Camp Nelson. (Enslaved persons emancipated themselves by appearing at the base.) Enlistees in the 13th Heavy Artillery Battalion were trained to operate siege artillery. The men performed garrison duty at Camp Nelson and at Smithfield, Lexington and other points within Kentucky until November 18, 1865 when they were mustered out. Captain Lewis had resigned a month earlier.

Political and military history of United States Colored Troops

Another Vermonter, Ira Hobart Evans from Barre (who himself officered two USCT regiments), has written an account of the Union's use of Black soldiers even before their recruitment was authorized by Lincoln's *Emancipation Proclamation*. Evans' account describes how "military necessity" supported Lincoln's policy against opposition even among some Unionists, and how that policy was judged correct on the battlefield. Evans quotes Hay and Nicolay, Lincoln's principal biographers:

> One point of doubt about employing negroes as soldiers was happily removed, almost imperceptibly, by the actual experiment. It had been a serious question with many thoughtful men whether the negro would fight.... Practical trial in skirmish and battle gave an immediate and successful refutation to this fear, and proved the gallantry and trustworthiness of the black soldier in the severest trials of devotion and heroism.

Evans' essay describes several battles in which Black units fought under General Benjamin Butler and later, in the XXV Army Corps, under General Godfrey Weitzel. The essay concludes by listing USCT engagements from Island Mound, Missouri to Appomattox, Virginia: 45 in all.[2]

Camp Nelson now a National Monument

First designated as a National Historic Landmark (2013), Camp Nelson became a National Monument in October 2018, one of the two most-recently named national monuments at the time this book was written. It is administered by the National Park Service. A park brochure describes its history as both a military training site and a contraband camp.[3]

Fig. 23. Whitney Maxfield of Barre, Vermont is a contemporary Civil War re-enactor. Here he wears a reproduction of the uniform worn by his maternal great-grandfather, Albert Francis Dodge, who led Co. F of the 39th USCT. Maxfield bears the Staff Officer's sword and scabbard that were presented to Dodge by his men. Dodge was brevetted a Major in March 1865 after leading his troops at the Crater and Fort Fisher, and then marching them to Raleigh, NC to play a role in Reconstruction.

Photo by Gail Blake, 2022

NOTES

1. That unit appears in a United States Colored Troops (USCT) section of Dyer (1959), III, 1722.

2. Evans, in Peck (1892), 2, 711–716. The Hay & Nicolay quotation appears on page 713.

3. https://www.nps.gov/cane/united-states-colored-troops.htm

United States Army Signal Corps

Waitsfield's lone member of the United States Army Signal Corps was **Henry Albee Dewey.** Born in Montpelier, Dewey had attended public schools in Waitsfield and was credited to the Town upon his enlistment at age 30 in Company B of the Thirteenth Vermont Volunteer Infantry Regiment, a company he had helped organize. Dewey was married with a young son at the time he enlisted. He served as First Sergeant in the company.[1]

An 1862 civilian portrait of H. Albee Dewey appears in the 13th Vermont Volunteer Infantry section.

Just three months after the Thirteenth Regiment was mustered out, Dewey joined the U.S. Army Signal Corps (October 28, 1863).[2] At that time the Signal Corps was a rather new organization. It relied on red and white flags and torches to communicate messages. Dewey was placed in command of the Signal Station at Fort Gaston, North Carolina, located on the south bank of the Trent River.[3] Eleven months into his service there (September 29, 1864) Dewey died from yellow fever after a three-day illness. He was buried in the New Berne Soldiers' Cemetery (now the New Bern National Cemetery).

Notes

1. Jones (1909) reverses Dewey's first name, listing him as "Albee Henry Dewey" and gives Dewey's date of death as September 28, 1864. As is usual, Dewey's name and death date as shown on the Ledoux & Associates website is what I use here.

2. He enlisted in the Signal Corps from Pennsylvania, where his family was located at that time. Source: Sturtevant & Marsh, 452, as cited on the Ledoux & Associates website.

3. One of a series of Union forts constructed in 1862–63 to protect the occupied New Berne, NC area. It seems likely that Dewey had earned one or more promotions, to have become an officer in charge of that signal station.

United States Christian Commission

While not military units, the United States Christian Commission and the United States Sanitary Commission ("NGOs" of their era) contributed mightily to the Union war effort, raising money for hospitals and medical supplies, and providing services directly to men in camps and hospitals.

Given that a man born and raised in Waitsfield served with one of these charitable organizations, it seems appropriate to acknowledge his service here.

Perrin Batchelder Fisk[1] served with the United States Christian Commission (USCC), presumably as a Chaplain.

The Christian Commission had been created in the fall of 1861 by civilian volunteers who brought experience with the operation of the Young Men's Christian Association (YMCA). It distributed religious literature and encouraged army leaders to supply regiments with chaplains for the conduct of (Protestant) religious services. The Commission also provided personal counseling and social services such as writing letters home for disabled soldiers. No doubt Fisk did that and more; and as an ordained minister, he also led church services in camp.

Fisk had been accepted as a delegate[2] of the Christian Commission soon after his 1863 graduation at age 26 from the Bangor (Maine) Theological Seminary. An 1894 account of Fisk's life that appears on the Ledoux & Associates website relates that Fisk's first appointment in the USCC was to the headquarters at that time of Meade's Army of the Potomac. There he discovered an abandoned coffee wagon and made it operational. "It proved a great success and is remembered with gratitude by many a veteran."[3]

Beyond counseling and coffee: the Christian Commission commences a cultural revolution

With the massive casualty lists that were emerging from the war's expansion, early Commission efforts such as Fisk's, with delegates supplying hot beverages in camps and assisting sick and wounded soldiers by writing letters on their behalf, evolved into an institutional commitment to a far more profound service. While never forsaking the personal services aspect of their mission, the 5,000 appointed delegates laboring in Union camps and hospitals began to accept as a fundamental responsibility "to give immediate and accurate information of the wounded and dead" to [Union] families and communities awaiting news of their missing soldiers. Faust estimates that Christian Commission volunteers wrote 92,000 such letters by the end of the war.[4]

Fig. 24. A USCC coffee wagon of the type operated by Perrin Fisk at City Point, Virginia
Source: Library of Congress

Moreover, even before war's end the Commission was expanding its self-imposed obligation:

> In the closing year of the war, Christian Commission representatives became increasingly involved not just in providing information to families but in working to ensure the preservation of the identities of the dead.[5]

In effect, the Commission had become "a graves registration service," Faust writes, that began the very day after the Battle of Nashville concluded (December 16, 1864). A few months later, following Appomattox, Christian Commission representatives searched the many battle areas around Richmond and Petersburg—locating, recording, and arranging protection for Union soldiers' graves. The Commission ultimately published the names of eight thousand dead with the locations of their bodies.[6]

Through Congressional actions, the Union army then was given that task. In December 1865 Edmund Burke Whitman, an army quartermaster, was appointed to direct the work and was provided with a small staff as the scope of the mission became more evident. Whitman's team set out from Tennessee, venturing into Kentucky as well as traveling throughout the states of the Deep South, devoting years to obtaining information about soldiers' burial places. Much too often, Union dead had not been buried at all, just left on the ground to be plowed over, or rot, or be eaten by hogs. The information Whitman gathered was used by the federal government as it considered whether to establish a system of national cemeteries.[7]

The work by Edmund Whitman and his contemporary Clara Barton was prompting a new view among the American public of the relationship between the state and its citizens, Faust writes.[8] We might characterize that newer view as a codicil added to the existing social contract.

Christian Commission Women's Auxiliary in Waitsfield

In *Something Abides* Howard Coffin notes that the red brick house situated as the second house on the left side of Waitsfield's Bridge Street (just off Main Street/state route 100) served as a tavern during the Civil War years. A women's auxiliary to the Christian Commission met there to organize supplies for their "boys" at the front.[9]

There also is a story to the effect that local women met regularly to make needed items. Initially they may have sewn *havelocks,* intended to help prevent sunstroke while soldiers were on the march. (Most soldiers gave those up early in the war.) They knit stockings and sewed cotton and linen shirts and flannel undergarments throughout the conflict. That Waitsfield group was dubbed *Mountain Maids,* suggesting they met at one or more of the uphill farms of the village, perhaps in the Floodwoods section of town. They certainly preceded and may have instigated the organization of the local Christian Commission women's auxiliary.[10]

Notes

1. Fisk's name is spelled "Fiske" in Fletcher B. Joslin's essay *Waitsfield, Vermont 1782 to 1979* which appeared originally in the 1979 *Waitsfield-Fayston Telephone Company Directory* and was reprinted in the 2019 *Waitsfield Champlain Valley Telecom Directory*.

2. "Delegates" were the unpaid volunteers upon whom the work of the Christian Commission rested, according to historian Drew Gilpin Faust in *This Republic of Suffering: Death and the American Civil War* (2008), 107.

3. Ledoux & Associates website, ©2002. The website's source for this quotation is given as Jacob G. Ullery, compiler, *Men of Vermont: An illustrated biographical history of Vermonters and sons of Vermont* Brattleboro, VT: Transcript Publishing Company, 1894, II, 138.

4. Faust, *loc. cit.*

5. Faust, *op. cit.*, 110.

6. *Ibid.*

7. Faust, *op. cit*, 219 ff.

8. Faust, *op. cit.*, 229–230.

I offer this personal reflection: A decade ago I traveled to the national cemetery in Schuylerville, New York to be present at the interment with military honors of an unknown Civil War soldier from a NYS regiment. His remains had been discovered two years earlier on the Antietam battlefield by a resident walking his dog. Thus, the work of 19th century Christian Commission volunteers and the efforts of Whitman's team and those of Clara Barton, are direct causal links to the current cultural expectation that a U.S. veteran's remains will receive a respectful burial by the government that citizen served, even after the passage of 150 years in this instance.

9. Coffin (2013), 399. For a photograph of Campbell's Tavern, see page 36 of the 2019 telephone directory cited in footnote #1 above. It shows a house built for Dan Richardson, constructed of bricks made at a nearby brickyard. The directory states that house/tavern was known (much later) as the Farr-Haskin house.

10. Howard Coffin shared this information about the Mountain Maids in a telephone conversation in 2020. Speculation that the Maids may have led to the formation of the local USCC women's auxiliary is my own.

United States Navy

Two Waitsfield residents served as officers in the United States Navy during the war: **Charles O. Carpenter** and **Roderick Julius Richardson**. Richardson's name is recorded sometimes as "R. Julius" or "R. J." Richardson.

Charles O. Carpenter

Charles Carpenter was credited to Waitsfield despite his birth (August 1838) in Windsor, Vermont. That suggests he may have resided in the Town when he was accepted as an Assistant Surgeon in the Navy as early as July 30, 1861.[1] Carpenter was appointed in 1862 as Assistant Surgeon on the Unadilla Class steam gunboat *Ottawa*, part of the South Atlantic Blockading Squadron. He may have been present when the *Ottawa* captured Fernandina, Florida and the Georgia barrier islands of Jekyll and St. Simons in March 1862; also, when the *Ottawa* participated in operations a month later on St. John's River, Florida.

Carpenter resigned his position in March 1863. He lived until March 7, 1902 and was buried in Elmwood Cemetery, Holyoke, Massachusetts, where a headstone gives Carpenter's military rank as "Lieutenant".[2]

Roderick Julius Richardson

Roderick Richardson was born in Waitsfield on May 30, 1840. He entered a locally prominent family as a grandson of a very early settler.[3]

Richardson graduated Norwich University, Class of 1861 and joined the United States Navy that September as an Assistant Paymaster. His assignment: the *Harriet Lane*, a vessel in the West Gulf Squadron.[4]

The *Harriet Lane* was a two-masted, side-wheeler, steam-driven brigantine commissioned in 1858 for the U.S. Revenue Cutter Service. ("Revenue cutters" were a class of ships belonging to the Treasury Department, stationed in U.S. harbors to collect federal taxes as ships entered.) With war threatening in March 1861, the U.S. Navy began acquiring revenue cutters along with tugs and ferry boats. Former revenue

Fig. 25. USS *Harriet Lane* being captured by Confederate forces, January 1, 1863, at Galveston, TX

Image credit: NH 57514, Naval History and Heritage Command.

cutters took on Navy duties that included blockading ports. The *Harriet Lane* was transferred from the Treasury to the Navy in March, and won distinction as the vessel that fired the first shot in Charleston Harbor during the Navy's attempt to relieve Fort Sumter.

Having been assigned to the *Harriet Lane* in September 1861, Richardson no doubt was aboard when that ship engaged Confederate batteries at Freestone Point, Virginia in December. Subsequently, Richardson's ship became part of a mortar flotilla that joined in a bombardment of Forts Jackson and St. Philip below New Orleans (April 18–28, 1862) that led to the subsequent capture of that famed city, the largest in the South and the sixth largest city in the United States at the time.

The *Harriet Lane* supported the occupation of forts at Pensacola, Florida the next month and covered operations at Vicksburg, Mississippi in June and July, 1862. It was engaged in the capture of Galveston, Texas in October 1862 but was itself captured when Confederates later re-took Galveston City.[5]

Richardson had been promoted to Paymaster after one year's service, so he must have been functioning in that capacity both at the time the *Harriet Lane* was victorious at Galveston and later, when Confederate forces reoccupied the city.

Richardson becomes a Confederate prisoner

During the night of December 31, 1862 (New Year's Eve) Confederate Brigadier General William Scurry led volunteers from three Texas infantry regiments, with militia and some artillery, across a two-mile-long railroad bridge that extended from the mainland across to Galveston Island. At 5:00 A.M. on New Year's Day Scurry's superior, General John Magruder (nicknamed "Prince John"), personally fired the first artillery round against a barricaded federal position on the wharf. That position was manned by Massachusetts men. Their defense was so fierce that Magruder almost was convinced to pull his men back.

But then, "in the early-morning light," Magruder saw two Confederate vessels, formerly little channel steamboats that he had arranged to have fitted out with sharpened iron bowsprits and cotton bales lining their decks, coming into view. The CS *Neptune* and the CS *Bayou City*, together, held 300 volunteers armed with cutlasses, bowie knives, and rifles. The commander of those so-called "Horse Marines" was Colonel Tom Green of Valverde fame, and just now he was directing both ships towards the *Harriet Lane*, one of the federal blockaders in Galveston Bay.

The *Neptune* quickly was put out of commission by a shot from another federal vessel; it sank in the Bay's shallow water. However, the barbed bowsprit of the *Bayou City* hooked onto the *Harriet Lane* as it rammed her, allowing men from the *Bayou City* to board and seize her, killing her commander, Jonathan M. Wainwright, and his executive officer, Lieutenant Edward Lea, and capturing its 100-man crew.[6]

Richardson and the other prisoners were paroled months later.

Richardson's subsequent service was aboard the steam frigate *Wabash* in the "brown water navy" of Admiral David Farragut on the Mississippi River. Later, Richardson served in the South Atlantic Blockading Squadron before he resigned October 17, 1864.[7]

Richardson died November 15, 1909 in Los Angeles, California.[8] He was buried in that city.

Notes

1. That date appears on the *Vermont in the Civil War* website, Ledoux & Associates, ©2023. Perhaps Carpenter was not given an onboard assignment until 1862, another date associated with his service on that website.

2. A photograph of Carpenter's headstone appears on the L&A website.

3. Richardson's grandfather, the Honorable Roderick Richardson, Sr., came to Waitsfield from Tolland, Connecticut as a young man in 1779. He owned the town's principal store and served as its Postmaster. Both he and his son (Roderick Julius' father) served as assistant judges in Washington County courts, accounting for their honorifics "the Honorable." Richardson's father also served as a state representative and a state senator. Source: Abby Maria Hemenway's *Vermont Historical Gazetteer*, vol. IV (1882).

4. That ship was named for a niece of James Buchanan, who preceded Lincoln as President. Buchanan was a bachelor and his niece served as hostess in the Executive Mansion.

5. Silverstone, Paul H. (1989), 82.

6. Josephy, Alvin M., Jr. (1991), 156–157.

7. The L&A website follows Peck's *Revised Roster*, 2, 694 with respect to Richardson's resignation date. I have chosen to use that source, knowing that it contradicts certain details of Richardson's service as given by Abby Maria Hemenway in her 1882 chronicle, *Vermont Historical Gazetteer*, IV, 786. (Hemenway states that Richardson served with the North Atlantic squadron and remained in the Navy until 1865.)

8. A link on the website to a Norwich University alumni book (page 658) gives Richardson's date of death as November 25th.

Epilogue

Documentary filmmaker Kevin Thornton presents evidence that Union soldiers from Vermont were nearly unanimous in after-war years in their assessment of "what the war was about." In a 2016 film titled *Death in the Wilderness: A Love Story* Thornton cites several veteran officers speaking at post-war reunions in their contention that the American Civil War was fought to preserve the idea of democracy. Mr. Thornton graciously has permitted me to employ passages from his narrative.[1]

Wheelock Veazey, addressing the Vermont Officers' Reunion Society in 1867, noted that belief was accepted by Union soldiers as early as 1864. Colonel Veazey explained the idea of democracy as encompassing security, freedom of speech, diffusion of knowledge, recognition of merit, property distribution, religious toleration and nationality of spirit. "What was saved by the war was nothing short of liberty itself."

When the Reunion Society met a few years later in Brandon, Colonel John R. Lewis continued the theme of the then-aging veterans' understanding of what the Civil War had been about. "They never forgot that the war had been fought for a reason, suppression of rebellion and treason. They never believed the sentimental argument that the Northern and Southern causes had been equally valid. They knew differently."

Sentiment is meaningless without moral purpose, Thornton declares. "The generation of the war needed to believe that the war had brought about a just and democratic society."

The Brandon tradition of young children strewing flowers on the graves of Brandon's fallen persists, I believe, not just because it is quaintly sweet to observe. These littlest citizens are being taught that marvelously brave and sad actions when undertaken for such a high purpose demand to be recalled and honored.

Notes

1. This film documents the 100+ year history of a practice of First Grade school girls in the small town of Brandon, Vermont placing flowers on the graves of that town's Civil War dead each Memorial Day. Some time after the film was produced, it seems, that flower-laying ceremony was moved from the local cemetery to Brandon's Civil War monument in a traffic island on Main Street. Thornton's film is available as a DVD in the Brandon bookstore. It also can be borrowed through Vermont's interlibrary loan program.

Acknowledgments

My thanks to the several librarians past and present of the Joslin Memorial Library, Waitsfield, Vermont who have been extremely helpful in obtaining materials for this work through the state's Interlibrary Loan (ILL) service. Also, I am grateful for the assistance of library staff at the following institutions who provided access to materials in restricted reference collections: Brownell Library, Essex; St. Albans Free Public Library, St. Albans; Helen Day Memorial Library, Stowe, and the Vermont Historical Society, Barre.

I appreciate the Waitsfield Town Clerk's office that assisted me on multiple occasions by confirming birth and death records for some men whose names I had encountered through walks in the town cemeteries, thus adding to the number of "Waitsfield" men who could be included in this work. Additionally, the Town Clerk in Sutton, Vermont assisted my search for information about a Waitsfield man who substituted for a Sutton resident.

Thanks also are due the Waitsfield Historical Society. An officer of that society contributed a photograph from its archive that was taken the day the Waitsfield Civil War Monument was erected.

A huge debt is owed by me and all Vermonters to a contemporary website created and maintained by Tom Ledoux & Associates, ©2020. The *Find a Soldier* section in particular presents military records for Vermont men known to have served in the American Civil War.

Of course, this work would not even have begun without the records compiled by 20th century Waitsfield authors Jones and Bisbee and 19th century Vermont historians Peck and Benedict, all cited in full in the Bibliography.

I am enormously grateful to the many authors and artists who graciously have granted permission to employ excerpts from their books and photographs from their private collections.

Continuing encouragement over the years of researching and writing has come from my friends in town and in Vermont organizations both in and apart from the Civil War community. You know who you are, and I thank you all.

Most especially I must name here Jim Dodds and Kitty Werner who edited my manuscript and moved this book toward publication. Rick Rayfield and Margaret Sombric offered guidance about publishing options while Jane Kendall and Anne Bordonaro provided many meaningful editorial suggestions.

Fig. 26. Mules pulling the Civil War memorial monument through Waitsfield.
Photo courtesy of the Waitsfield Historical Society.

About the Author

Alice Evans, an Ohio native, lived in ten communities in five states both south and north of the Mason-Dixon line before she settled in Vermont. For almost 30 years she has considered Waitsfield, Vermont as her adopted hometown.

Evans holds a master's degree in teaching and a Ph.D. Her career spanned classroom teaching, school district administration, consultant to school boards and positions in two state agencies of education, culminating with service as Vermont's first director of the National Assessment of Educational Progress (NAEP) program.

Evans raised four children, all born in different states. She has seven grandchildren and three great-grandchildren. While living in Connecticut she was elected to a term on a nonpartisan Representative Town Meeting. She participates in state and national-level organizations that seek appropriate disposal for nuclear waste and oppose any expansion of nuclear power plants. In 2017 she was convicted of trespassing on a Vermont site where a natural gas pipeline was being laid for the sole benefit of Canadian corporate consumers. She is active in CodePink, Indivisibles and several international anti-war groups.

Other interests include gardening and classical music, especially Grand Opera.

Bibliography

General Reference Works

Dyer, Frederick H., ed., *A Compendium of the War of the Rebellion*, 3 vols. New York: Sagamore Press, Inc., 1909. Reprinted as facsimile ed., New York: Thomas Yoseloff, 1959.

Johnson, Robert U. & Clarence C. Buell, eds., *Battles and Leaders of the Civil War*, 4 vols. New York: Thomas Yoseloff, 1884–1888.

Silverstone, Paul H., *Warships of the Civil War Navies*. Annapolis: Naval Institute Press, 1989.

Government Reports

Peck, Theodore S., Adjutant General. *Revised Roster of Vermont Volunteers and Lists of Vermonters Who Served in the Army and Navy of the United States During the War of the Rebellion.* Montpelier, VT: Watchman Publishing Co., 1892. Reprinted as Field Edition with index, 2 vols. Newport, VT: Vermont Civil War Enterprises, n.d.

Report of the Adjutant & Inspector General of the State of Vermont, From October 1, 1863, to October 1, 1864. Montpelier, VT: Walton's Steam Press, 1864.

Report of the Adjutant & Inspector General of the State of Vermont, From Oct. 1, 1864, to Oct. 1, 1865. Montpelier, VT: Walton's Steam Printing Establishment, 1865.

Articles

American Battlefield Trust, *10 Facts, Civil War Artillery* (retrieved February 17, 2023).

Eds., "Gettysburg!" A special issue of *Civil War Times Illustrated*, Gettysburg, PA: Historical Times, Inc., 2, 4, July 1963.

Hunt, Jeffrey William. *"Meade & Lee: The road to Bristol,"* online presentation, April 20, 2022.

Rickard, J. (5 July 2006), *Battle of Lee's Mill, 16 April 1862* http://www.historyofwar.org/articles/battles_lees_mills.html (retrieved May 2, 2017).

Tunnell, Ted. "With Banner, Gun, and Sword: Marshall Harvey Twitchell and the 4th Vermont Regiment Go to War", in *Vermont History* (59, 2), Spring 1991, 69–84.

Manuscripts

Dana family papers in the possession of Rick Swanson, Waitsfield, Vermont.

fitting and proper, a brochure distributed at the dedication of a monument to the Third Vermont Volunteer Infantry Regiment for its role in the Battle of Dam No. 1 in Newport News Park, Newport News, Virginia.

LaMonda, James Michael. *Closing the Backdoor to Washington: Vermont Civil War Soldiers in the Shenandoah Valley, 1864.* Honors Thesis, Norwich University, April 2003.

Newspapers and newsletters

(All but the Troy, New York paper are Vermont publications.)

The Caledonian, St. Johnsbury
The Camp Griffin Gazette, White River Junction
Daily Free Press, Burlington
The Green Mountain Freeman, Montpelier
St. Albans Daily Messenger, St. Albans
Troy Daily Union, Troy, New York
The Valley Reporter, Waitsfield
The Vermont Phoenix, Brattleboro

DVD

Death in the Wilderness: A love story (2016). Documentary history by Kevin Thornton tells a story of Brandon, Vermont's losses in the Civil War and its determination to commemorate the significance of that suffering through a Memorial Day practice that continues to this day.

Books

Abbott, Lemuel Abijah. *Personal Recollections and Civil War Diary, 1864.* Burlington, VT: Free Press Printing Co., 1908.

Achorn, Edward. *Every Drop of Blood: The momentous second inauguration of Abraham Lincoln.* New York: Atlantic Monthly Press, 2020.

Bastian, David F. *Grant's Canal: The Union's attempt to bypass Vicksburg.* Shippensburg, PA: Burd Street Press, © 1995.

Benedict, G. G. *Vermont in the Civil War: A History of the Part Taken by the Vermont Soldier and Sailors in the War for the Union, 1861-5*, 4 vols. Burlington, VT: The Free Press Association, 1886.

Bisbee, Richard M. *History of the Town of Waitsfield, Vermont, 1789-2000*. Barre, VT: L. Brown and Sons, 2007.

Catton, Bruce. *Reflections on the Civil War*, John Leekley, ed. New York: Berkley Books, 1981.

Child, Hamilton. *Gazetteer and Business Directory of Washington County, VT, 1783–1889, Part First, edited by William Adams.* Syracuse, NY: The Syracuse Journal Company, April 1889.

Coffin, Howard. *Full Duty: Vermonters in the Civil War*. Woodstock, VT: The Countryman Press, 1993.

_____. *Nine Months to Gettysburg: Stannard's Vermonters and the repulse of Pickett's Charge.* Woodstock, VT: The Countryman Press, 1997.

_____. *The Battered Stars: One state's Civil War ordeal during Grant's Overland Campaign.* Woodstock, VT: The Countryman Press, 2002.

_____. *Something Abides: Discovering the Civil War in today's Vermont.* New York: The Countryman Press, 2013.

Cross, David Faris. *A Melancholy Affair at the Weldon Railroad: The Vermont Brigade, June 23, 1864.* Shippensburg, PA: White Mane Books, 2003.

Dascomb, A. B. *The Memorial Record of Waitsfield, Vermont.* Published by vote of the town, 1867.

Davis, Burke. *They Called Him Stonewall.* New York: Wings Books, 1954.

_____. *The Long Surrender.* New York: Random House, 1985.

Davis, Daniel T. and Phillip S. Greenwalt. *Bloody Autumn: The Shenandoah Valley Campaign of 1864.* El Dorado Hills, CA: Savas Beatie, LLC, 2013.

Donald, David Herbert. *Lincoln.* New York: Simon & Schuster, 1995.

Dufur, S.M. *Over the Dead Line, or Tracked by Blood-Hounds.* Richford, VT: 1902. Reprinted in Canada: Vermont Civil War Enterprises, n.d.

Egan, Timothy. *The Immortal Irishman.* New York: Houghton Mifflin Harcourt, 2016.

Eisenschiml, Otto and Ralph Newman. *The Civil War: An American Iliad.* New York: Mallard Press, 1956.

Faust, Drew Gilpin. *This Republic of Suffering: Death and the American Civil War.*

New York: Alfred A. Knopf, 2008.

Fiske, John. *The Mississippi Valley in the Civil War*. Boston: Houghton, Mifflin and Company, 1900.

Fleming, Thomas. *A Disease in the Public Mind: A new understanding of why we fought the Civil War*. New York: Da Capo Press, 2013.

Foote, Shelby. *The Civil War: A Narrative*, 3 vols. New York: Random House, 1958–1974.

Gallagher, Gary W., ed. *Chancellorsville: The battle and its aftermath*. Chapel Hill: The University of North Carolina Press, 1996.

Goldfield, David. *American Aflame: How the Civil War created a nation*. New York: Bloomsbury Press, 2011.

Grant, U.S. *Personal Memoirs*, 2 vols., 1869. Reprinted as one volume, New York: Charles L. Webster, 1885-86.

Grimsley, Mark. *And Keep Moving On: The Virginia Campaign, May-June 1864*. Lincoln, NE: University of Nebraska Press, 2002.

Gross, James A. and Andre B. Collins. *The Souvenir Guide to the GETTYSBURG National Military Park*. Gettysburg, PA: Tem inc., 1991.

Guelzo, Allen C. *Mr. Lincoln: The life of Abraham Lincoln*. Chantilly, VA: The Teaching Company, 2005.

Hemenway, Abby Maria, ed. *Vermont Historical Gazetteer*, Vol. IV. Montpelier, VT: Vermont Watchman and State Journal Press, 1882.

Hennessy, John J. *Return to Bull Run: The campaign and battle of Second Manassas*. New York: Simon & Schuster, 1993.

Hess, Earl J. *Storming Vicksburg: Grant, Pemberton, and the battles of May 19-22, 1863*. Chapel Hill: The University of North Carolina Press, 2020.

Hoffman, Elliott W., ed. *History of the First Vermont Cavalry Volunteers in the War of the Great Rebellion*. Baltimore, MD: Butternut & Blue, 2000.

Holbrook, William C. *History of the Seventh Regiment of Vermont Volunteers*. Burlington, VT: Free Press Association, 1891.

Jones, Archer. *Civil War Command and Strategy: The process of victory and defeat*. New York: The Free Press, 1992.

Jones, Jacqueline. *Saving Savannah: The city and the Civil War*. New York: Alfred A. Knopf, 2008.

Jones, John B. *A Rebel War Clerk's Diary*, 2 vols. Philadelphia: J. B. Lippincott &

Co., 1866.

Jones, Matt Bushnell. *History of the Town of Waitsfield, Vermont, 1782-1908, with Family Genealogies*. Boston: George E. Littlefield, 1909.

Jordan, Brian Matthew. *Marching Home: Union veterans and their unending Civil War*. New York: W. W. Norton & Co., 2014.

Josephy, Alvin M., Jr. *The Civil War in the American West*. New York: Alfred A. Knopf, 1991.

Kennedy, Frances H., ed. *The Civil War Battlefield Guide, second edition*. Created for The Conservation Fund. Boston: Houghton Mifflin Co., 1998.

Kidd, James H. *Personal Recollections of a Cavalryman with Custer's Michigan Cavalry Brigade in the Civil War*. Iona, MI: Sentinel Printing Company 1908.

Longacre, Edward G. *The Cavalry at Gettysburg: A tactical study of mounted operations during the Civil War's pivotal campaign, 9 June-14 July 1863*. Cranbury, NJ: Associated University Presses, 1986.

Lonn, Ella. *Desertion During the Civil War*. Gloucester, MA: American Historical Association, 1928. Reprinted as Bison Books edition with introduction by William Blair, Lincoln NE: University of Nebraska Press, 1998.

Maharay, George S. *Vermont Hero: Major General George J. Stannard*. Shippensburg, PA: White Mane Books, 2001.

_____. *Vermont Hero: Major General Lewis A. Grant*. Lincoln, NE: iUniverse, Inc., 2006.

Manning, Chandra. *What This Cruel War Was Over: Soldiers, slavery, and the Civil War*. New York: Vintage Civil War Library, division of Random House, Inc., 2007.

Marshall, Jeffrey D., ed. *A WAR of the People: Vermont Civil War Letters*. Hanover, NH: University Press of New England, 1999.

McKone, William L. *Vermont's Irish Rebel, Capt. John Lonergan*. Jeffersonville, VT: Brewster River Press, © 2010.

Mitchell, Reid. *Civil War Soldiers: Their expectations and their experiences*. New York: Viking Penguin Inc., 1988.

Mudgett, Timothy B. *Make the Fur Fly: A history of a Union volunteer division in the American Civil War*. Shippensburg, PA: Beidel Printing House, Inc., 1997.

Newton, Steven H. *Joseph E. Johnston and the Defenses of Richmond*. Lawrence, KS: University Press of Kansas, © 1998.

Noyalas, Jonathan A. *The Battle of Cedar Creek: Victory from the jaws of defeat*.

Charleston, SC: The History Press, 2009.

Palmer, E. F. *The Second Brigade; or Camp Life*. Published in VT, 1864. Reprinted in Canada by Vermont Civil War Enterprises, n.d.

Peck, Eli Nelson, compiler. *Supplement to the History of the Thirteenth Regiment Vermont Volunteers*. No place given: The Self-appointed Committee of Three, 1911.

Péladeau, Marius B. *"Willie Went to War."* Newport, VT: Vermont Civil War Enterprises, 2005.

_____, compiler and editor. *Burnished Rows of Steel: Vermont's Role in the Battle of Gettysburg, July 1-3, 1863*. Newport, VT: Vermont Civil War Enterprises, 2002.

Pfanz, Harry W. *Gettysburg: The second day*. Chapel Hill: The University of North Carolina Press, 1987.

Poirer, Robert G. *They Could Not Have Been Better: Thomas O. Seaver and the 3rd Vermont Infantry in the war for the Union*. Newport, VT: Vermont Civil War Enterprises, 2005.

Reardon, Carol. *Pickett's Charge in History & Memory*. Chapel Hill: The University of North Carolina Press, 1997.

_____. "The Other Grant: Lewis A. Grant and the Vermont Brigade in the Battle of the Wilderness," in *The Wilderness Campaign,* Gary Gallagher, ed. Chapel Hill: The University of North Carolina Press, 1997, 201-235.

Rhea, Gordon C. *The Battle of the Wilderness, May 5-6, 1864*. Baton Rouge: Louisiana State University Press, 1994.

Scott, Robert Garth. *Into the Wilderness with the Army of the Potomac*. Bloomington, IN: Indiana University Press, 1992.

Sodergren, Steven E. *The Army of the Potomac in the Overland & Petersburg Campaigns: Union soldiers and trench warfare, 1864-1865*. Baton Rouge: Louisiana State University Press, 2017.

Stackpole, Edward J. *Sheridan in the Shenandoah: Jubal Early's nemesis*. Harrisburg, PA: Stackpole Company, 1961.

Stevenson, Louise. *Lincoln in the Atlantic World*. New York: Cambridge University Press, 2015.

Sturtevant, Ralph Orson and Carmi Lathrop Marsh. *Pictorial History of the 13th Regiment Vermont Volunteers, War of 1861-1865*. No publisher or place given: 1910.

Taylor, Richard. *Destruction and Reconstruction*. New York: D. Appleton & Co., 1879.

Trudeau, Noah Andre. *Bloody Roads South: The Wilderness to Cold Harbor, May-June, 1864.* New York: Fawcett Columbine, 1989.

Tucker, Glen. *High Tide at Gettysburg.* Old Saybrook, CT: Konecky & Konecky, n.d.

Wait, Oscar E. *Three Years with the Tenth Vermont,* Don Wickham, ed. Newport, VT: Vermont Civil War Enterprises, 2006.

Walker, Aldace F. *The Vermont Brigade in the Shenandoah Valley, 1864.* Burlington, VT: The Free Press Association, 1869. Reprinted, Newport, VT: Vermont Civil War Enterprises, n.d.

Ward, Eric, ed. *Army Life in Virginia: The Civil War letters of George G. Benedict.* Mechanicsburg, PA: STACKPOLE BOOKS, 2002.

Webb, Alexander S. *The Peninsula: McClellan's Campaign of 1862.* New York: Charles Scribner's Sons, 1881.

Wert, Jeffry D. *The Sword of Lincoln: The Army of the Potomac.* New York: Simon & Schuster, 2005.

Wickham, Donald H., ed. *Letters to Vermont from Her Civil War Soldier Correspondents to the Home Press, vol. 2.* Bennington, VT: Images from the Past, Inc., 1998.

Williams, J. C. *Life in Camp.* Claremont, NH: The Claremont Manufacturing Company, 1864. Reprinted, Newport, VT: Vermont Civil War Enterprises, n.d..

Winters, John D. *The Civil War in Louisiana.* Baton Rouge: Louisiana State University Press, 1991.

Young, Carleton. *Voices from the Attic: The Williamstown Boys in the Civil War.* Syracuse, IN: William James Morris, Inc., 2015.

Index

The names of Waitsfield men appear in **bold** face.

A

Adams, Benjamin Henry 113, 114, 115, 191, 193
Adams, Walter F. 181
Ainsworth, George Julius 16
Ainsworth, Luther 57, 58
Allen, Edward L. 47, 49
Annis, Nathaniel Edwin 77
Appomattox Court House 11
Arlington House 23
Armies
    Army of Northeastern Virginia 6, 9, 151
    Army of Northern Virginia 9, 14, 49, 51, 73, 91, 97, 100, 109, 114, 125, 139, 154
    Army of Northern Virginia (CS) 165, 170, 174, 178, 186, 208
    Army of Observation 68, 74
    Army of the Department of the East 201
    Army of the Department of the Gulf 191
    Army of the District of West Florida 71
    Army of the Military Division 67
    Army of the Military Division of West Mississippi 67
    Army of the Peninsula (CS) 31
    Army of the Potomac 6, 9, 14, 18, 19, 21, 22, 29, 30, 31, 33, 34, 37, 47, 48, 49, 55, 57, 61, 62, 67, 68, 94, 95, 97, 104, 114, 124, 139, 140, 149, 151, 153, 162, 164, 165, 170, 175, 178, 187, 192, 199, 201, 204, 206, 207, 210, 219, 237, 238
    Army of the Shenandoah 6, 49, 80, 82, 162, 172
    Army of Virginia 22, 151, 162, 201
    Army of West Virginia 80, 178
Atherton, John B. 154, 157
Augur, Christopher C. 184

B

Babcock, Thomas 110
Bailey, Theron Lucius 196
Baird, Alexander 86
Baird, John 119, 130
Banks, Nathaniel B. 162, 191
Barnard, Albert D. 119, 130
Barton, Clara 221
Battles
    Battle of Antietam 16, 28, 34. *See also* Battle of Sharpsburg
    Battle of Appomattox 174
    Battle of Baton Rouge 70
    Battle of Big Bethel 5, 29, 240
    Battle of Bloody Angle 97, 98, 211
    Battle of Bull Run 6, 9, 14, 29, 163, 200
    Battle of Cedar Creek 38, 43
    Battle of Chancellorsville 22
    Battle of Cold Harbor 22, 54, 55
    Battle of Cool Spring 171
    Battle of Fair Oaks 9, 34
    Battle of Fisher's Hill 52, 54, 62
    Battle of Fredericksburg 28, 29, 35
    Battle of Gettysburg 23
    Battle of Lee's Mill 28, 31, 32, 33, 34,

38
Battle of Little Bethel 5, 243
Battle of Malvern Hill 34, 43
Battle of Manassas. *See* Battle of Bull Run
Battle of Marye's Heights 16, 22
Battle of Monocacy 48, 83, 100, 126, 140
Battle of Nashville 220
Battle of Opequon 52, 54, 62. *See* Battle of Third Winchester
Battle of Sabine Pass 79
Battle of Sailor's Creek 11
Battle of Savage's Station 14, 15
Battle of Second Bull Run 22
Battle of Seven Pines 9, 34
Battle of Sharpsburg 34. *See also* Battle of Antietam
Battle of Snicker's Gap 171
Battle of Spotsylvania 36
Battle of Spotsylvania Court House ix, 64, 97, 154, 156, 245
Battle of the Wilderness 16
Battle of Third Winchester 52, 54, 62. *See also* Battle of Opequon
Battle of Tom's Brook 173
Battle of Wilderness 16, 21, 48, 54, 55, 56, 58, 59, 61
Battle of Williamsburg 33, 42

Beauregard, P. G. T. 6, 155
Benedict, Charles M. 11
Benedict, G. G. 104
Bennett, John 173
Berry, Leonard C. 44, 205
Billings, Charles D. 119, 124
Biscorner, Mitchell 57, 58
Blake, Gail iv, 57, 215
Blunt, Asa 113
Booth, John Wilkes 81
Brooks, W. T. H. 43
Brown, Stephen F. 131
Brown, Thornsbury Bailey 7
Buchanan, James 226

Buford, John 163, 164
Burke, Thomas 103, 107
Burns, Edward A. 68
Burnside, Ambrose 57, 153, 178, 203, 204, 206
Bushnell, Fordis O. 119
Bushnell, Henry N. 57, 58
Bushnell, Matthias Joslin 197
Butler, Benjamin 76

C

Cady, Alonzo James 161, 162, 163, 165, 167

Campaigns
    Bristoe Campaign 19, 22
    Chancellorsville Campaign 22, 28
    Fredericksburg Campaign 16, 22, 28, 29, 35, 43, 54, 56, 57, 58, 59, 99, 104, 199, 200, 206, 209
    Gettysburg Campaign 17, 23, 35
    Mine Run Campaign 19, 35
    Mobile Campaign 72, 143
    Northern Virginia Campaign 163
    Overland Campaign 36, 43, 48, 56, 57, 59, 61, 64, 95, 101, 104, 110, 153, 170, 178, 186, 187, 200, 209, 234
    Peninsular Campaign of 1862 vii, 14, 16, 31, 33, 34, 48, 200, 243
    Seven Days Campaign/Retreat from Richmond 22, 34, 43
    Shenandoah Valley Campaign 43, 49, 54, 59, 62, 79, 80, 83, 100, 105, 107, 108, 162, 170, 171, 172, 175, 233, 234, 238
    Vicksburg Campaign 69, 70, 71, 76, 78, 79, 82, 224, 233, 235

Campbell, Bertrand Delos 28, 54, 161, 175
Campbell, Hiland G. 185, 186
Campbell, Oliver C. 86

Camps
    Camp Barry 186
    Camp Baxter 27

Camp Carusi 123, 124
Camp Chase 93, 138, 144
Camp Death 71
Camp Douglas 85, 86, 243
Camp Fairbanks 4, 4–5, 4–5
Camp Griffin 22, 30, 37
Camp Holbrook 77, 78
Camp Nelson 213, 214
Camp Parapet 182
Camp Phelps 68
Camp Seward 144
Camp Tyler 85
Camp Underwood 12
Camp Vermont 114, 123, 144, 147, 148
Camp Williams 71
Canby, E. R. S. 72, 142, 145, 150, 152, 191
Carpenter, Charles O. 223
Chase, John J. 54
Chase, Luther 57, 58
Chase, Mark C. 57, 59
Childs, Israel 197
Christian Commission Women's Auxiliary 221
Clay, Charles H. 196
Clough, Columbus T. 75
Coffin, Howard 50, 95, 97, 151, 155, 210, 221, 222
Crane, John D. 196
Crater. *See* Mine, The
Crook, George 170, 178
Cross, David Faris 105
Custer, George Armstrong 173, 236

D

Dahlgren, Ulric 24, 168, 169, 178
Daley, Vespucius 27, 28, 35, 36
Dana, Chester Stephen 93, 99
Dana, Edwin Harvey 93, 98
Dana, Henry Francis 28
Dana, Samuel Jackson 119, 130
Dana, Stillman Foster 28, 33, 36, 37
Dana, Wesley Emerson 155, 157, 158
Dano, Leonora 145
Davis, Jefferson 9, 155, 168
Davis, Joseph P. 181, 183
Davis, Myron M. 119
Dewey, Henry Albee 119, 217
Dike, Hiram F. 57, 58
Donahue, John D. 147, 150
Doubleday, Abner 117
Doying, Francis W. 110
Drum, Henry 145
Dumas, Julian J. 119
Dumas, Morris 77
Durkee, Alba B. 86
D'Utassy, Frederick 151

E

Early, Jubal 18
Elliott, Isaac H. 86
Emancipation Proclamation 65, 168, 213

F

Fairbanks, Erastus 4, 8, 26
Farnsworth, Elon 165
Farnsworth, Milo 169
Farragut, David 76, 225
Fisher, George W. 54, 57
Fisk, Edward Anson 119, 130
Fisk, Perrin Batchelder 219
Floodwoods militia 4, 8
Forrest, Nathan Bedford 182
Forts
  Battery 16 189
  Battery 27 189
  Battery Morris 89
  Fort Fisher 44
  Fort Gaston 217
  Fort Hamilton 199, 200
  Fort Harrison 90
  Fort Hell 189

Fort Lyon 114, 148
Fort McDermett 73
Fort McKean 187
Fort Michael 189
Fort Morton 189
Fort Phillips 189
Fort Saint Philip 69, 182
Fort Sedgwick 208
Fort Slocum 104
Fort Stevens 54, 62, 104
Fort Sumter 3, 8, 155, 224
Fort Totten 104
Fortress Monroe 5, 31, 34, 48, 79, 197
Foster, Daniel T. 93, 99
Foster, Henry Ephraim 77
Foster, James A. 205
French, Herman Ralph 86
Fuller, Ephraim H. 57, 58

G

Gage, Virginia 144
Garibaldi Guard 151
Garibaldi, Guiseppe 151
Getty, George W. 95, 110, 174
Gibbon, John 134
Gilson, Eli 54, 57
Gleason, David 119, 130
Gould, Charles 51
Grand Review 44, 62, 81, 159, 175, 186
Grandy, Daniel 119, 130
Granger, Gordon 72
Grant, Lewis A. 62, 104, 236, 237
Grant, Ulysses 49, 64, 78, 91, 95, 99, 102, 105, 170, 172, 207
Green Mountain Boys 12
Green, Tom 225
Greenslit, William H. H. 86
Griffin, Charles 156
Grout, William W. 147, 148, 149, 151, 152

H

Hadley, Charles L. 47, 49

Hadley, Langdon S. 197
Halleck, Henry 159
Hall, George Burton 86, 185
Hancock, Winfield Scott 134
Harriman, James 54, 56
Hastings, Edgar A. 119
Haynes, Reverend Dr. Edwin M. 94
Heath, Eaton A. 119
Henderson, Alonzo 195
Hill, A. P. 14, 15
Hines, John 119
Hoffman, Philip 86
Holbrook, Frederick 93
Homestead Act of 1862 198
Hooker, Joseph 57, 162
Howard, Oliver O. 14
Hoyt, Manley N. 54, 55
Hunter, David 178
Hurlbut, Stephen 191
Hyde, Breed 33

I

Invalid Corps 23

J

Jackson, Thomas Jonathon 69, 87, 99, 119, 130, 133, 134, 149, 162, 176, 182, 193, 224
Janes, Dr. Henry 102
Jocelyn, Frank B. 169
Johnston, Joseph E. 6, 9, 236
Jones, George M. 205, 211
Jones, Holland 205, 211
Jones, John B. 107, 110
Jones, John F. 54, 55
Joslyn, Daniel 54. *See* **Stoddard, Daniel**
Joslyn, Eugene Edwin 41, 44, 205
Joslyn, Rollin O. 147, 150

K

Kelley, Daniel 107

Keyes, Erasmus 37
Kilpatrick-Dahlgren Raid 24
Kilpatrick, Judson 20
Kneeland, George S. 57, 58
Kneeland, Seymour Lucius 161, 167, 175, 179

L

Lathrop, Zimri 67, 142
Lea, Edward 225
Lee, Mary Anna Custis 23
Lee, Robert E. 7, 14, 23, 34, 91, 114, 164, 174
Lewis, Edwin C. 4, 5, 5–10, 53, 54, 55, 213
Lewis, John G. 113, 114
Lewis, John R. 227
Lincoln, Abraham 3, 6, 8, 26, 31, 81, 93, 102, 113, 128, 137, 233, 168, 233, 234, 235, 235, 1, 235, 236, 237, 238
Lomax, Lunsford 173
Longstreet, James 14, 15
Luce, Hiram Andrew 93

M

Magruder, Jeb 15
Manum, Augustine E. 137
Martin, Francis (Frank) 17, 19
Martin, Henry 39
Maxfield, Whitney 215
Maynard, James L. 205
McAllister, William Wordsworth 185, 186
McAllister, Ziba H. 119, 131, 133, 161, 167, 175
McCarty, Daniel 68
McCarty, Eugene 67
McClellan, George B. 14, 15, 31
McDowell, Irvin 6
McLaren, John 196
Meade, George 18

Mehuron, Allen E. 54, 56
Mehuron, Mary Kathleen 65
Merritt, Wesley 173
Miles, O. G. 134
Mine, The 159
Miner, Henry A. 156, 157, 160
Mix, Victor B. 77
Morrill, Edwin J. 106
Mosby, John 18, 81, 117, 149, 164
Mountain Maids 221, 222
Mud March 28, 57, 203, 206
Munford, Thomas 163

N

Newcomb, Harlan Gaius 197
Newcomb, Ireneaus P. 57
Newton, John 117
Nichols, William T. 142
Nourse, Lucius W. 113, 114, 115

O

O'Connor, Anthony J. 144
Olds, Harmon 29
Ord, E. O. C. 89, 90
Orne, William Henry 27

P

Page, Alson D. 119
Palmer, Edwin Franklin 119
Palmer, John W. 161, 167, 176
Palmer, William 155
Parker, Dexter F. 119, 130
Parker, Edward B. 106
Parker, Jerome W. 161, 167, 175
Peabody, Levi C. 68, 70, 71, 75, 76
Peck, Theodore 119
Phelps, Gurley A. 196
Phelps, John W. 4, 182
Pickett, George 89
Pingree, Samuel 33

Platt, Lemuel B. 161
Poland, Benjamin 54, 57
Poland, Solon 197
Prentis, Thomas Theodore 205
Preston, A. W. 165
Prisoner of War Camps
   Andersonville 57, 59, 105, 106, 107, 110, 111, 169, 178, 182
   Belle Island 179
   Camp Douglas (US) 85, 86
   Camp Tyler (US) 85
   Charleston 105, 169, 224, 237
   Columbia 105, 106, 110, 113, 173, 175
   Florence 105, 110, 169
   Goldsboro 105
   Libby Prison 169, 175, 179
   Millen 105, 107
   Salisbury 105
Proctor, Redfield 147, 148, 149, 151, 152

Q
Quigley, John H. 86

R
Rains, Gabriel J. 4
Randall, Francis 131
Reed, Loren B. 119, 124
Reed, Oscar C. 119, 124
Reserve Army Corps 113
Revenue cutters 223
Reynolds, John F. 117
Richardson, Edwin R. 57, 59
Richardson, John N. 41, 44, 205
Richardson, John W. 119, 130
Richardson, Judson W. 57, 59
Richardson, Loren S. 205
Richardson, Roderick Julius 223, 226
Richmond, Nathaniel P. 168
Ripley, E. H. 90
Rosser, Thomas L. 173
Roulston, Charles 42

Ruggles, William F. 160
Russ, Daniel 86
Russ, James C. 197
Ryder, Charles H. 103, 105, 106

S
Sanders, Thomas 86
Savage, Edward M. 41, 42, 43, 185
Savage, Lucius D. 14, 15, 23
Savage's Station 14, 15
Schroeder, Patrick 178
Scott, Julian 33, 38
Scott, William 37
Scott, Winfield 5, 6, 14, 134, 207
Scurry, William 225
Seaver, Levi W. 119
Sedgwick, John 18
Selleck, Albert H. 14, 16
Sharpshooters 41
Shaw, Henry Charles, M.D. 47
Shaw, Lucius S. 196
Shaw, Oliver 196
Shepard, James N. 196
Shepherd, Daniel P. 57, 58
Shepherd, Mason C. 55, 57, 58
Sheridan, Philip 49, 50, 62, 79, 80, 82, 100, 111, 170, 171, 172, 173, 174, 175, 178, 237
Sherman, William Tecumseh 111
Ships
   Alabama 4, 6, 8, 67, 68, 72, 73, 74, 143
   Bayou City 225
   Ben de Ford 6
   Continental 137
   Cumbria 182
   Harriet Lane 223, 224, 225
   Iberville 69
   Morning Light 70
   Neptune 225
   Ottawa 223
   Premier 68

Release 167
Satellite 167
S.R. Spaulding 6
St. Mary 79
Tamerlane 68
Whitman 69, 220, 221, 222

Sieges
   Siege of Petersburg 110, 186
   Siege of Port Hudson 182
   Siege of Spanish Fort 143
   Siege of Vicksburg 76
   Siege of Yorktown 42

Sloan General Hospital 102
Smith, A. J. 72
Smith, Emery L. 54, 56
Smith, William Farrar 30, 31, 34, 38
Somerville, James H. 54, 57
Sons of Vermont 12, 13
Sons of Vermont in New York [City] 13
South Atlantic Blockading Squadron 223, 225
Spaulding, Franklin Edwin 60
Spaulding, George E. 197
Spaulding, Lewis M. 57, 59
Spaulding, Solon 59
Spotsylvania Court House 64, 97, 154, 156
Stannard, George J. 12, 83, 86, 117, 123, 139
Stanton, Edwin 178
Stearns, Oscar A. 119
Steinberg, George W. 47, 49
Sterling, John K. 161, 167
Stevens, Hazard 50
Stoddard, Daniel 53
Stoddard, Dorric Smith 119, 130
Stoddard, Franklin 181, 184, 191, 193
Stoddard, Harlan Page 14, 16
Stoddard, Horace B. 16, 19, 21, 24, 155, 159
Stoddard, Lathrop Thompson 119, 130, 131, 154
Stoddard, Lyman Brown 54, 56
Stoddard, Simeon 59, 155
Stoddard, William Henry 57, 59
Stoddard, William Tell 155
Stoughton, E. H. 113, 114, 123
Stuart, J. E. B. 114
Sykes, George 204

T

Taylor, Richard 74, 143
Terrill, John T. 29
Tewksbury, Charles D. 195
Tewksbury, Isaac N. 196
Thayer, Cyrus G. 119, 124
Thayer, James M. 119, 131
Thayer, Nathan 57, 59, 65
Thayer, Willard M. 93
Thoburn, Joseph 80
Thornton, Kevin 227
Tidball, John C. 133
Tucker, Julius E. 54, 56

U

Underwood, Benjamin 5
United States Sanitary Commission 219

V

Varney, Harrison W. 110
Veazey, Wheelock G. 33
Veterans Reserve Corps 16
VRC 16, 23. *See also* Veterans Reserve Corps

W

Wainwright, Jonathan M. 225
Waite, Oscar 98
Wait, Harvey M. 119
Walker, Almon 57, 60
Walker, George Aaron 197
Washburn, Peter T. 102

Weitzel, Godfrey 74
Welch, George P. 103, 107
Wells, William 171
West Gulf Squadron 223
Whitcomb, Edmund 119
Whiting, Henry 11
Whitman, Edmund Burke vi, 69, 220, 221, 222
Wilder, Orcas C. 119, 123, 131
Wilder, William F. 28, 35

Williams, Ira C. 185, 186
Williams, Thomas 76
Wilson, James H. 134
Wirz, Henry 106, 170
Wood, Hira 67
Woodard, Franklin 110
Wright, Horatio G. 178

Y

Young Men's Christian Association 219

www.ingramcontent.com/pod-product-compliance
Lightning Source LLC
Chambersburg PA
CBHW061252230426
43665CB00026B/2915